CW01468132

HDA-X

The Surreal Visions of
Hernán Díaz Alonso / HDA-X

Thames & Hudson

with over 500 illustrations

Contents

In Pursuit

John Hoke, III, Chief Design Officer, Nike, Inc.

Hernán Díaz Alonso and I met in 2017. At the time, Nike Design and SCI-Arc were engaged in dialogue to bring our creative communities together, and ponder the ever-blurring, intersectional boundaries of architecture and product design. We agreed to co-sponsor a mid-semester design sprint – a week-long charrette that would pair SCI-Arc students from Los Angeles with Nike designers in Portland. Teams were asked to re-imagine athlete data collection, augmented human anatomies via body appliance, and apparel systems that would act as mobile surrogates to architecture, and to question the limitations of human biology, rethinking the natural and manmade ecologies where future athletes will compete.

The output of this collaboration was an impressive show of radical design exploration. Creative freedom was unleashed, imaginations were uninhibited and ideas flowed unencumbered. The collective work gave a powerful glimpse forward. This was my introduction to the brilliance of Hernán, his provocative work, and his deep passion to shape-shift our future.

As designers, we are wired to grapple with the complexities and possibilities of our roles as citizen designers, driven to toil in the challenges and joy of searching for a future utility and an expanded vocabulary. Our shared pursuit is often one of distillation and synthesis – the act of balancing and blending multiple, often divergent, constraints. This unspoken contract with the future sparks an unending re-framing, re-contextualizing and re-imagining of design concepts. Our most important contribution is to make things better. We manifest ideas that push our culture forward. At our best, we capture the imaginations of those we serve and, perhaps, create goose bumps – a visceral response that signals an emotional connection between human and object. Hernán is a designer whose work does just that.

I believe Hernán to be an architect in pursuit of the future. His mind fascinates me. I imagine his inner creative world as a vast hothouse, where he diligently tends to germinating, grafting and pruning a new species of architecture.

Rooted in discovering a fresh connection between people, place and experience, his work invites our imaginations to wander, yet requires our full attention. It pushes on the traditional maker/trade crafts of formalism and fantasy, but with a boldly different point of departure. His work defies a common definition and encourages a longer gaze. It embodies a search for new meaning, new ritual, a new nature and a new creative process.

Hernán's dedication to this search lets him reset our expectations of architectural possibility. He forces a fundamental reappraisal of our orientation to the built environment, historical reference and the architectural pedagogy. He engages us in a new argument on traditional questions. As a result of these investigations, a new meaning in spatial experiences is discovered through the deliberate weaving of radical forms and restructured narratives. This approach shifts the work beyond the obvious predictable conclusions of inhabitable space, so that new experiences are offered and new stories are told.

As the narrative shifts, so do the inherent rituals between the architectural stage and the drama enacted upon them. Hernán draws from ancient themes here: sense of place, processions between spaces, new forms of inhabiting space. Much of his work shows a tendency to defiantly break from the status quo. In doing so, our understanding of a building diagram and the obvious markers of place-making and compositional wayfinding are re-framed and re-ritualized. These evolved rituals question how we see, feel and sense boundaries, hierarchies, structures and volumes. As the parameters of a fertile new architecture arise, so, too, can new behaviours. One can sense a new script unfolding, a new set of habits forming. This is a design ethos that stirs emotion with intent. This ritualistic shift is as much a part of his design prowess as the final, physical solution.

An obvious area of experimentation is the indirect connection to 'nature', or the push beyond a completely organic state of natural order. Hernán has a way of shifting from a designer simply deploying an appreciation of biomimicry to an inventor unleashing his biomastery. His work feels as if it was derived from an organic genesis. But its origin isn't from a nature within a known genus. It is, in effect, a new breed of natural intelligence. Forms appear as if sculpted from an unspecified, hybrid organic code. It is all part of his journey to bend design back to a new natural order, derived from a uniquely personal and accelerated evolutionary cycle. Hernán's work features all the hallmarks of an organic ecology that might well have been grown, rather than designed. Because of this mastery, we are left mesmerized by its subtle beauty and tranquil fragility.

Finally, one of the most dynamic endeavours displayed throughout Hernán's portfolio is his push into 'quantum craft', a pioneering stretch towards an advanced tectonic craftsmanship, multiplied by the intoxicating precision of computational calculus. Throughout his process, we see cutting-edge 3D technologies on display, mastered and exploited in ways that birth a new utility and an original beauty. We are shown designs that simply could not be drawn by hand, nor modelled in traditional media. They must be generated and modified in a dizzying, progressive sequence that hand tools alone simply could not summon. This is not your standard computer-aided design: it is Hernán's imagination and spatial wizardry on rocket fuel. The tools are not autonomously in control of the outcome. The creator is able to harness and hack their capabilities in a flurry of wonderfully abstracted compositions. Hernán acts as a poetic mediator, adjusting data inputs and outputs. The convergence of this data and his dreams is forged skilfully. The end state is a stunning assemblage of futuristic landscapes without peer.

Bold foresight and true originality are rare. The work presented here is both a prediction and a call to action. It lives in the bright light of a new artistic dawn. In this work, we are given clarity of vision, and a bold ambition, that pushes beyond the hazy limitations of constraints. This body of work represents an architect in pursuit of the future. It is a magnetic true north of innovative and imaginative design.

Fragments of a Conversation

Hernán Díaz Alonso and David Ruy, on a road trip to Las Vegas

It has always been uncomfortable for me to write about my work, or maybe I'm just lazy when it comes to words. But I've always believed that my way of working has been a form of conversation with multiple voices in my head – so here we go …

DR: What is this book for?

HDA: I'm not sure I know yet. Maybe it's a goodbye tour for the work I've done previously? I hope it marks the end of something and the start of something else.

DR: Well, a book is very good at capturing a moment in time.

HDA: Yes. I want to take a snapshot of where my head is at right now, so that it is not so much a traditional monograph, but a weird trip through the things that inspire me. The work is organized by categories of interest, rather than chronologically.

DR: So, a philosophical work?

HDA: Well, I wouldn't go that far. I have always been and always will be a visual person, so it is about how the work looks to me. I don't think about the meaning of a project before I do it. When I look back on it, it's like doing an autopsy. I speculate about what the work means after it's finished.

DR: After it's dead?

[laughter]

HDA: In a way, the book is an autopsy, a look back at a 'body of work', to figure out what the motivations were. So, of course, it is seen through the eyes of the present. In the future, I will likely see different things in it, as well. This book is not the final word on what the work means.

DR: So the book doesn't have a narrative ...

HDA: I don't think that my work ever has a clear narrative. It has a definite style, but style and meaning are different things. There are recurring aesthetic interests and obsessions, but no central concepts or meanings. The work is also deeply speculative in nature, so I think it proceeds with a degree of uncertainty at all times.

DR: I want to know more about a term you use a lot: 'agencies of contamination'. What do you mean by that?

HDA: Well, over the years the work has had different phases. This book represents projects since 2004. I would say that the early work, like much of what was happening during the transition to digital technologies, was preoccupied with tools and techniques. Like many of my colleagues, I was interested in the idea of a single-surface architecture. After that, I became more interested in how digital tools could absorb more of my interests. When the computer was first adopted as a means of architectural production, the interest in parametric modelling and algorithmic form generation tended to overemphasize the purity of mathematics. It created the desire to look for ways of disrupting it, to produce imperfections in the forms.

I began to think that form could be contaminated by science, history or culture. The first time I began introducing this idea of contamination was when I started thinking about the aesthetics of horror. I was fascinated by computer-rendered blood and flesh in horror movies like *Blade* (1998), and began to push my forms to look more horrific. During this period, I was looking a lot at things like blood cells, biological mutations and surgical techniques.

After this initial period of playing with a more contaminated formalism, I began looking at ornamentation. Though I was initially resistant to ornament because of my Modernist training, it was a breakthrough to contaminate pure digital forms with older architectural histories of ornament. This made the work stranger in an interesting way, and more difficult to read relative to the projects' historical affiliations.

Lately, I've become interested in rituals. Out of my studies into ornament, I began noticing the amazing ornamentation in Argentinian gaucho culture. I am Argentinian, of course, so I was looking at my own heritage. I became fascinated with the rituals and how the ornamentation of objects embodied the cultural aesthetics. There is an amazing combination of low- and high-end in gaucho culture. Something raw and primitive often coexists with something refined and sophisticated, which interested me a lot. The evolution was from the biological to ornamentation, to rituals. These represent the agencies of contamination, and what's being contaminated is architectural form. It disrupts the neat and tidy formalisms of architecture.

DR: OK, so the agencies of contamination are responses to late Modernism and digital architecture. When everyone was celebrating a new kind of perfect architectural form, you found that perfection dull and boring. Is 'boring' the right word?

HDA: 'Boring' would be one word, but more accurately, I didn't think it produced sufficient originality. Now, I know that pure originality is impossible to achieve in a creative process, but I think the search for it remains crucial in any creative endeavour. I remain committed to a principle of authorship. Perhaps this is a contrarian stance these days, but I am proud to be old-fashioned in that way.

DR: What do you think of the idea of beauty being connected to the true?

HDA: Well, I think beauty is a cultural construction like all aesthetics. Therefore, I don't think 'beauty' is a big general term that we can associate with truth. It's just one of many aesthetics in our culture. There are other aesthetic judgments like 'cute', 'horrifying', 'awkward', even 'ugly'. I would argue that any creative art is an act of fiction, and as such, there's no such thing as truth. This thing about the pursuit of truth in the arts reminds me of a scene in *Seinfeld*, where George Costanza says: 'It's not a lie if you believe it.'

[laughter]

DR: I also think of that meme I showed you the other day, with a person doing something odd with a chair, which said: 'You're not doing it wrong if no one knows what you're doing.'

[laughter]

HDA: Yes. If you believe that, you've picked the right option: it's right, because no one knows what you're doing anyway. Architecture is a genius solution to a nonexistent problem.

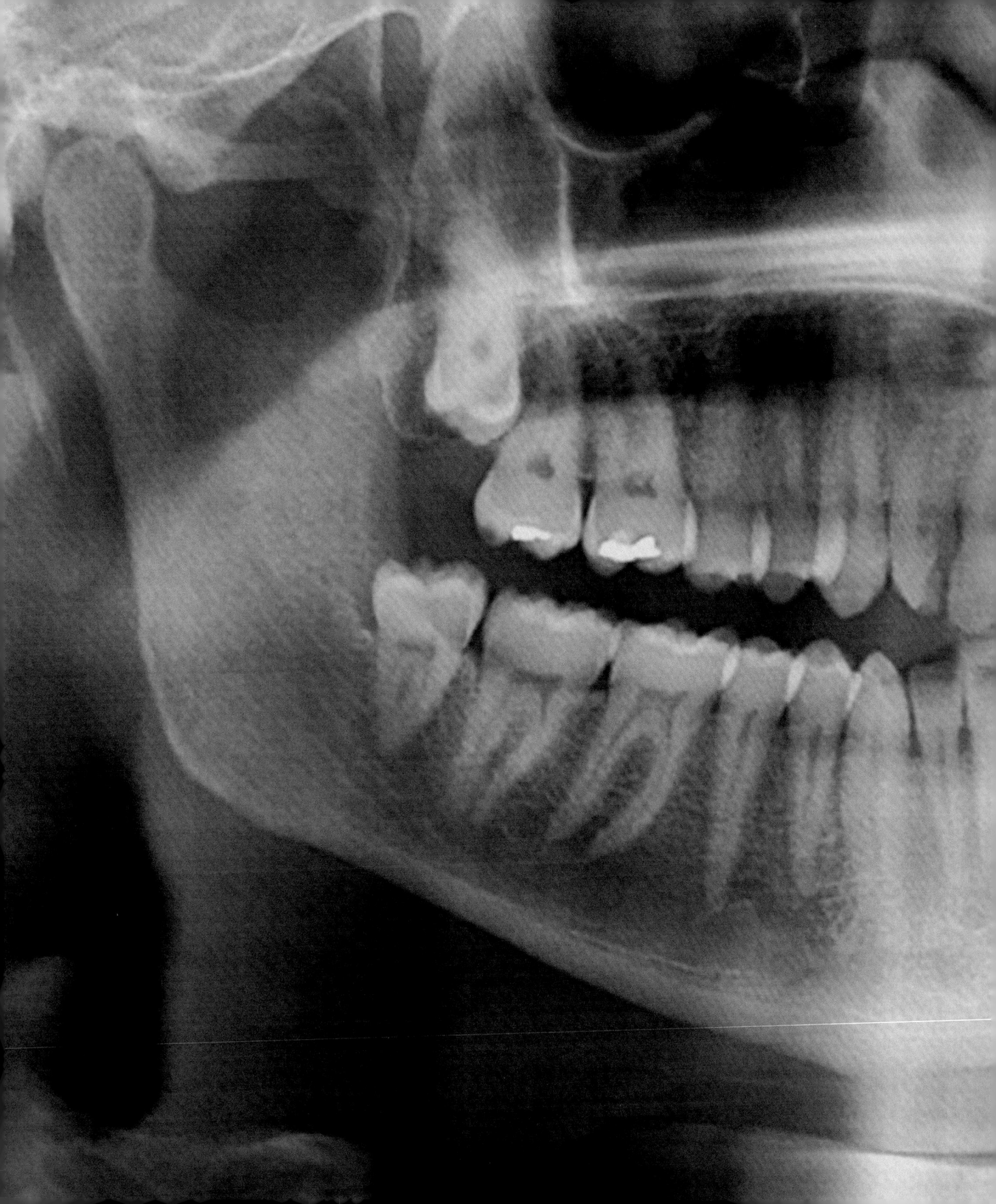

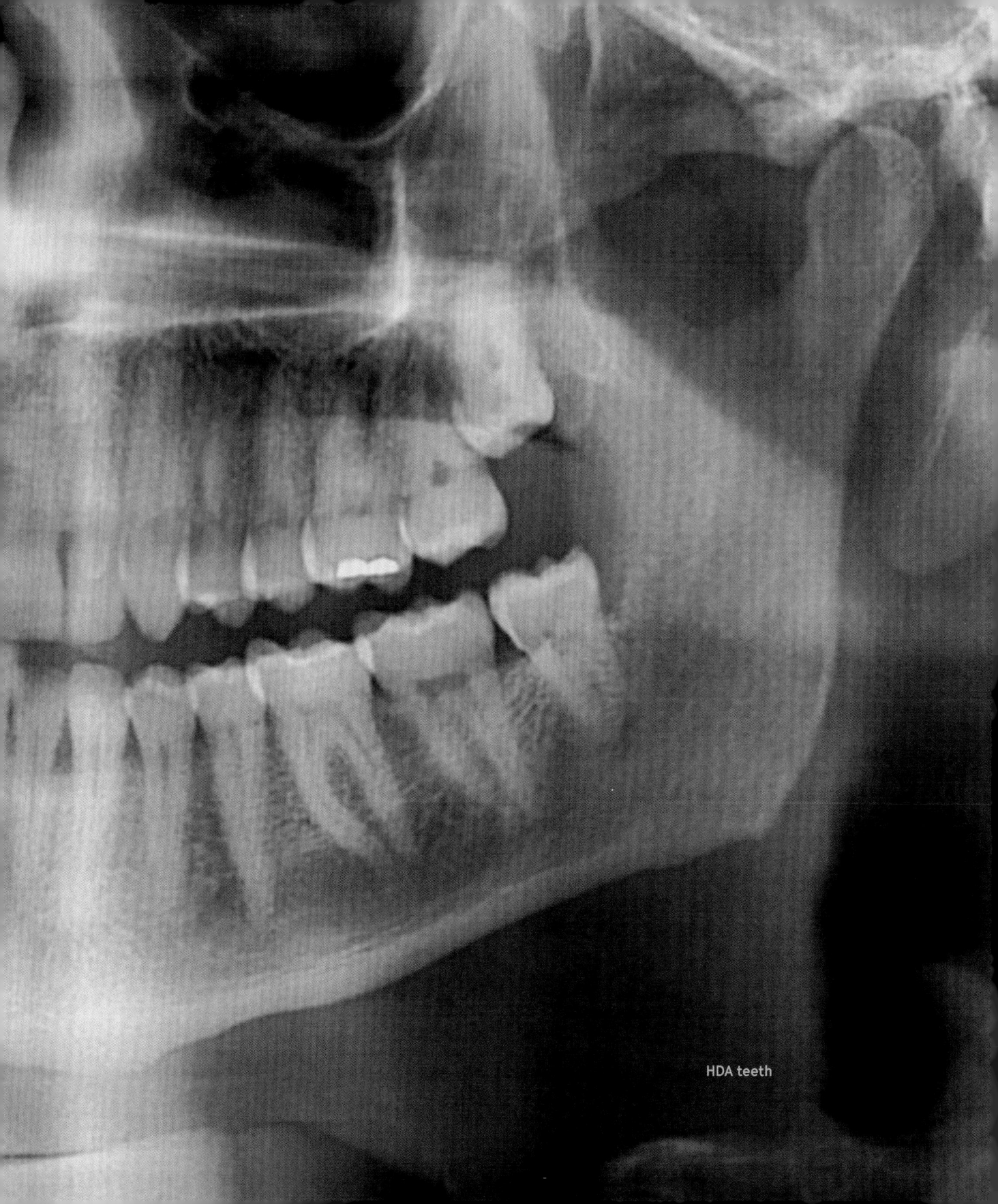
HDA teeth

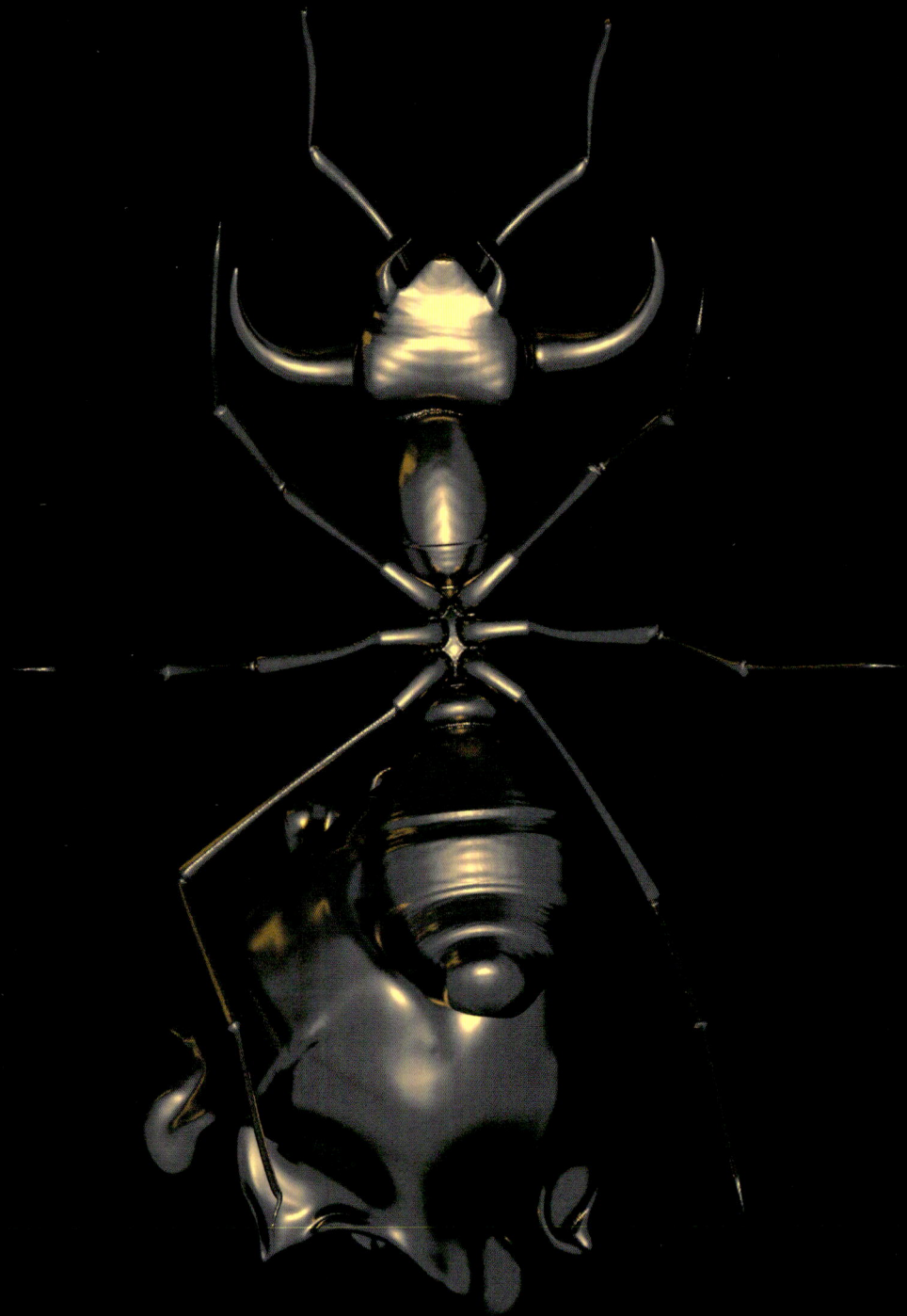

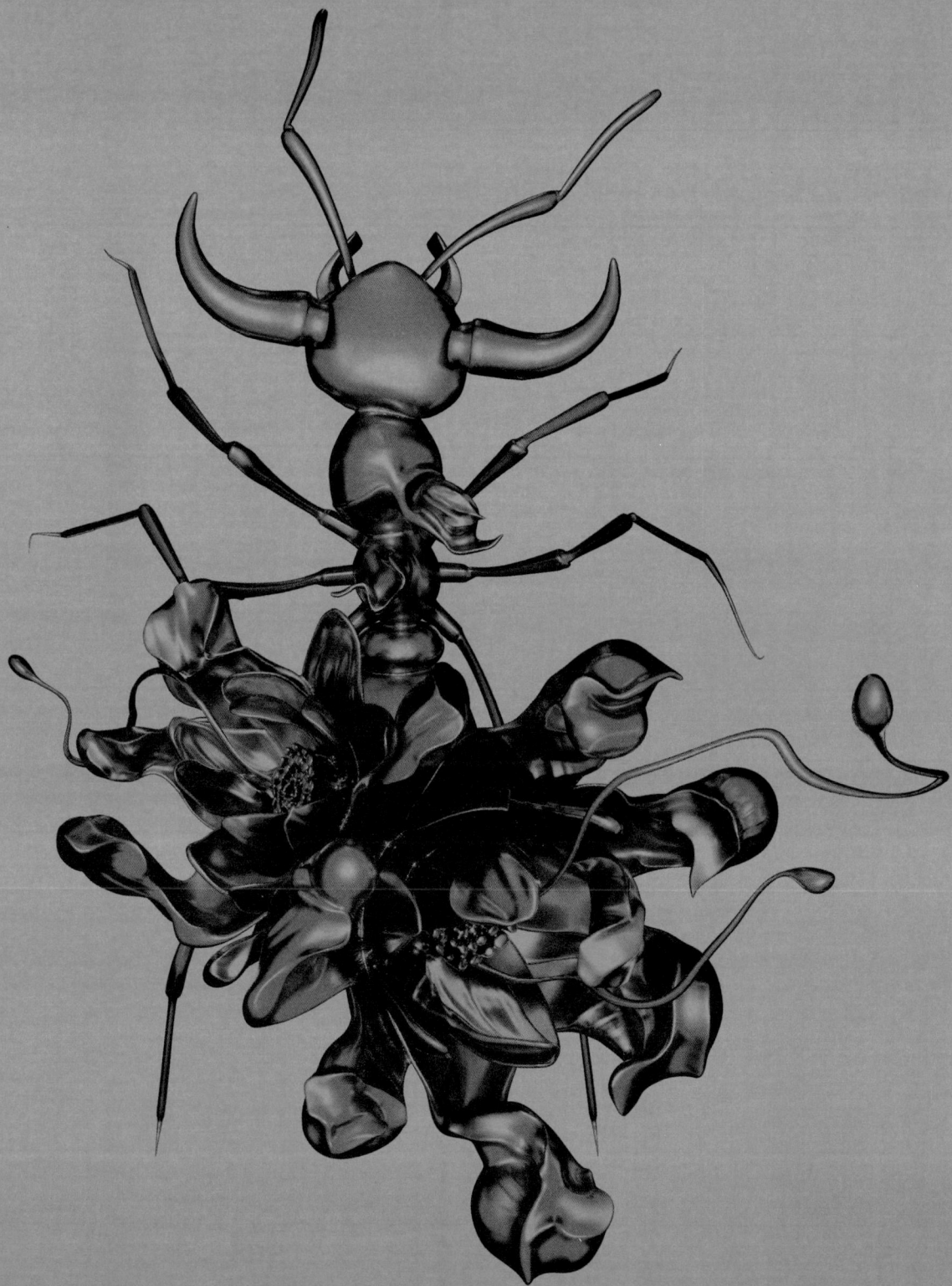

From Hero to Miró

Joe Day

Hernán Díaz Alonso is tender-footed. When travelling, he always wears the same Nike trainers, custom-ordered in black, lately with some red highlights. The same hues dominate his wardrobe more generally, and – along with ample jewelry and tattoos – contribute to the persona that he cultivates of a Postmodern pirate, a puckish, sturdy counterpoint to Johnny Depp's Captain Sparrow. Keith Richards clearly fathered both swashbucklers, though at very different ports of call. If Depp's mascara and eyeliner underscore the costume-play in his periodic, wildly lucrative ride through a Disney franchise, Hernán's custom Nikes are instead workaday prostheses, his proverbial wooden legs. He is a Method marauder – no slipping out of character.

Piracy has, of course, become a leitmotif of the new millennium, in both its ancient and new-fangled manifestations. Actual pirates ply the South China Sea and the Horn of Africa; virtual pirates abound online; Hollywood and Milan lament the digital and material piracy of their blockbusters and fashions. Today's pirates may be hyper-violent or stealthy in their approach, undetectable or heavy-handed in their methods. Never before has the term 'booty' been in such common and diversified parlance.

In his most recent collection of essays, art critic Dave Hickey divides the creative world into pirates and farmers – the risk-takers and the risk-averse – and begs for more gamblers. Díaz Alonso fits that bill, but from an unexpected quarter, as Hickey finds architecture and its schools disappointingly agrarian, a bunch of smallholders tilling parched fields of formalism and minimalism.[1] Díaz Alonso abides the first, but not the second. He may be the world's leading purveyor of bio-miasma, and thus no minimalist, but remains a High Church Formalist, denomination Eisenman. In crucial respects, the Nikes and the Rolling Stones allusions are feints, misdirections. Díaz Alonso imagines his architecture in a larger global sphere of popular culture, but he produces it within stringent disciplinary boundaries.

There's an argument to be made that all of Díaz Alonso's projects are, in fact, the same ongoing pursuit, and that, in a direct parallel with biological evolution, they actually share some common digital DNA. However, some schemes breathe and grow more than others. I prefer the realized to the virtual (not the case for most of HDA's contemporaries); the veiled, rather than the shiny; the corporeal more than the tendrilled (though most involve both). Consider three projects, escalating in scale: a gallery installation; a house, heavily indebted to a sculpture; and a museum.

Emotional Rescue

Emotional Rescue, Díaz Alonso's inaugural installation at SCI-Arc in 2002, delivered both. A loose sketch of copper tubing that spun through the gallery like a looping pen-line scrawl in three dimensions, the installation was a miracle of weightless delineation. The intermittent surfacing proved its architectonic potential, but more crucially provided an internal graphic field against which to read the larger pattern. Emotional Rescue rescued SCI-Arc from a decade of piecemeal collage and announced a new era, still in play 15 years later under Díaz Alonso's leadership. And it was emotional: the tension between advanced spline-curvature and its translation via the ancient art of radiused pipe-bending, built with an elegant frisson. Even the encapsulated rose petals, which seemed a bit much at the time, now make sense – they are, in fact, the sense in which I best recall the piece. There were a series of breakthroughs in that installation, and, for Díaz Alonso, a crucial coming to terms with his two major influences, Peter Eisenman and Enric Miralles. Eisenman's clarity and methodological rigour shape the project's overall logic and iterative resolution, but its fluid articulation and melding of digital and artisanal practices owes more to Miralles. It is an unusual dual pedigree, but a surprisingly robust point of departure.

In Still Flesh (2012; p. 304) and TBA 21_2.0 (2011; p. 240), a related sculptural event and dwelling proposal, Díaz expanded (on) his appetites.

Still Flesh is notoriously composed of meatballs, encased and connected by a loopy network of filigreed chrome fittings, much like the gleaming skullcap Merlin wears in the film *Excalibur* (1981). The sirloin spheres, and flayed cuts in between, are in fact integral to the structural integrity of the work, the ballast and tensile surfaces enabling the otherwise delicate, attenuated composition to stand. As unlikely a strategy as this was for an installation or for product design, Díaz Alonso upped his own ante by transposing and rescaling Still Flesh into the Argentinian countryside for a model home in TBA 21_2.0. There, steak becomes barbecue, the raw cooked, and the cultural and actual landscapes of Díaz Alonso's native pampas merge into a Pop tableau worthy of Archigram. Architecture must burn, to paraphrase Wolf D. Prix, but perhaps after the flames, we can look forward not just to ashes, but also to *asado*.

The competition to design the Guggenheim Helsinki (2014; p. 98) elicited over 1,000 proposals, few as contrarian as the version proposed by Xefirotarch (it was mocked by the real-estate website Curbed as one of the most absurd entries,[2] when in fact it was one of only a handful that had anything to do with the Guggenheim's architectonic legacy). Had the scheme been chosen, that staid Scandinavian city would have hosted its own devouring and digestion in a museum more convulsively alimentary than Frank Lloyd Wright's original Guggenheim, once dubbed a 'concrete stomach' by Robert Smithson. A series of spiralling vortices churn through gelatinous orthogonal masses scaled after the neighbouring waterfront blocks. From the harbour, the purple-veiled scheme presents a vast, undulating wall of sound; from above, a tightly reasoned cluster of galleries and atria, each with a circular oculus in counterpoint to the square courtyard rule of surrounding Helsinki. It was contextual in precisely the sense that a gargantuan boa constrictor might appear to echo its surroundings, once sated and now bulging with contents the size and shape of its more normative neighbours. If in Emotional Rescue Díaz Alonso repays his mentors Eisenman and Miralles, and in TBA 21_2.0 responds to the post-'68 visionary avant-garde, the Guggenheim

He may be the
world's leading
purveyor of
bio-miasma, and
thus no minimalist

Helsinki proposal is an embrace of Frank Gehry and Zaha Hadid, and their trajectory of fluid, often spiralling cultural spaces that reawaken dormant cities.

Though Díaz Alonso often invokes his limitations in spoken English (for rhetorical advantage, as his command is excellent), he knows to talk rock 'n' roll with his elders, movies with his peers and gaming with his students. This informal, constant, multi-field fluency is Díaz Alonso's true lingua franca, and a key to the specific language evolving in his architecture (as well as the broader pedagogical discourse of SCI-Arc).

Fredric Jameson offered an inaugural lesson in this kind of cultural hybridization when he framed the evolution of Postmodernism in the high/low terms of painting and footwear.[3] He used iconic pictures of shoes by Vincent van Gogh, Walker Evans, René Magritte and Andy Warhol to illustrate four attitudes towards commodity culture spanning the 20th century. In Jameson's quadratic diagram, Van Gogh's richly textured boots beget both the photographic modernism of Evans's dry, dusty ones and Magritte's Surrealist foot-boot amalgamation, all of which, in turn, yield, stage right, to Warhol's silver slippers – and the Postmodern, Q.E.D.

But Joan Miró, who shares Díaz Alonso's Spanish roots, painted a shoe in 1937 that doesn't fit comfortably in Jameson's matrix. Driven from Barcelona by the Spanish Civil War, Miró broke with his own more flat, graphic and upbeat habits to produce a work that he saw as his *Guernica* in microcosm. Predominantly black, *Still Life with Old Shoe* is a study in violation: a many-tined fork stabs a rotten apple; a bottle appears less wrapped in newsprint than engulfed in flames, its cork extending like a hangman's noose out of frame; in the more abstract upper corners, blurred surges of colour seize nebulous black eels and rays swimming through their murk. The old shoe of the title radiates with a red and gold heat signature of all its use and abuse, double-haloed in amorphous colour – its steam and stink? – and then, in more black, to a wavy tabletop horizon. It is a painting of mourning, but also of melodrama. In his book *Encounters and Reflections*, Arthur Danto described his encounter with it:

'But how could one tell, descending the coiled ramp of the Guggenheim Museum, that this is a piece of political art, an exile's meditation on war and loss, a dark poem in a dark time, a counter-thrust in the style wars of Paris? It looks like what its title says it is: a still life with a shoe. The shoe is luminous, parti-coloured, comical. But the image is otherwise realistic and recognizable, like a good cartoon ... *Still Life with Old Shoe* ought to have stood darkly against the ambient gaiety like the Ancient Mariner at the wedding feast. Instead, it looked like part of the carnival, as if the wedding guests had refused to accept the spell of the old loon's tale, had decked the mariner out with silk and ribbons and made him part of the dance.'[4]

For Danto, Miró's *Old Shoe* is a spectacular conundrum, at once ominous and hilarious (not unlike Díaz Alonso's favourite concluding scene of the film *Fight Club* (1999), in which all of Los Angeles collapses to the strain of the Pixies). The painting struggles – heroically, absurdly – both to capture a moment of global historical crisis, and to register the painter's tactical ambitions to eclipse his peers. The distance of Miró's *Old Shoe* from those in Jameson's four corners is akin to that of separating Díaz Alonso's worlds from those of his contemporaries. Of the generation just ahead of Díaz Alonso, he is perhaps closest to Greg Lynn and Andrew Zago. However, if those two are likely the last great Cartesian designers (see, for example, Lynn's early curvatures through egg crates, or Zago's grid-woven gestalt objects), Díaz Alonso is perhaps the first visionary designer without an X, Y, Z default for either the generation or the resolution of his projects. He is a captain without a map.

But the GPS and sonar seem to be working. I suspect Miró's *Still Life with Old Shoe* would make far more sense in the Guggenheim Helsinki by Xefirotarch than it did to Danto, hung in Wright's stark spiral. In Díaz Alonso's museum, the Miró would escape its conflicted origins and deliver something else, something better suited to this century than the last. In it, we would find a meal fit for a pirate.

[1] Dave Hickey, *Pirates and Farmers* (New York, 2013). See also Jacob Mikanowski's excellent review and profile of Hickey, 'Sunshine of Absolute Neglect', in *Los Angeles Review of Books*, 29 May 2015; https://lareviewofbooks.org/article/sunshine-of-absolute-neglect/#!.

[2] Spencer Peterson, 'The 36 Weirdest Proposals for the Guggenheim Helsinki', 24 October 2014. Accessed 11/26/16 at https://www.curbed.com/2014/10/24/10031636/guggenheim-helsinki-competition-designs.

[3] Fredric Jameson, *Postmodernism, or the Cultural Logic of Late Capitalism* (Raleigh, 1991), introduction and chapter 1. The connection here is Michael Speaks, who wrote his PhD under Jameson at Duke, and, as Graduate Chair at SCI-Arc, hired Díaz Alonso in 2000.

[4] Arthur Danto, *Encounters and Reflections* (Berkeley, 1990). Accessed 11/26/16 at http://www.artchive.com/artchive/M/miro.html.

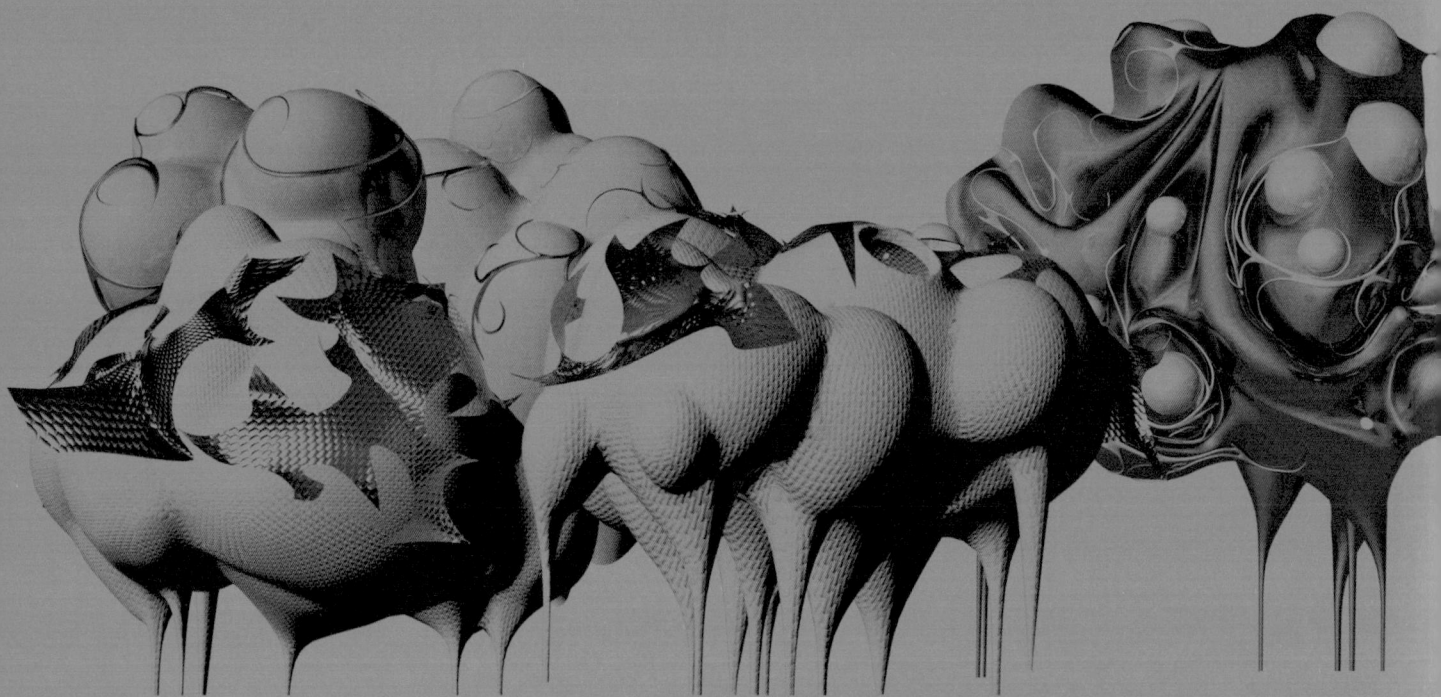

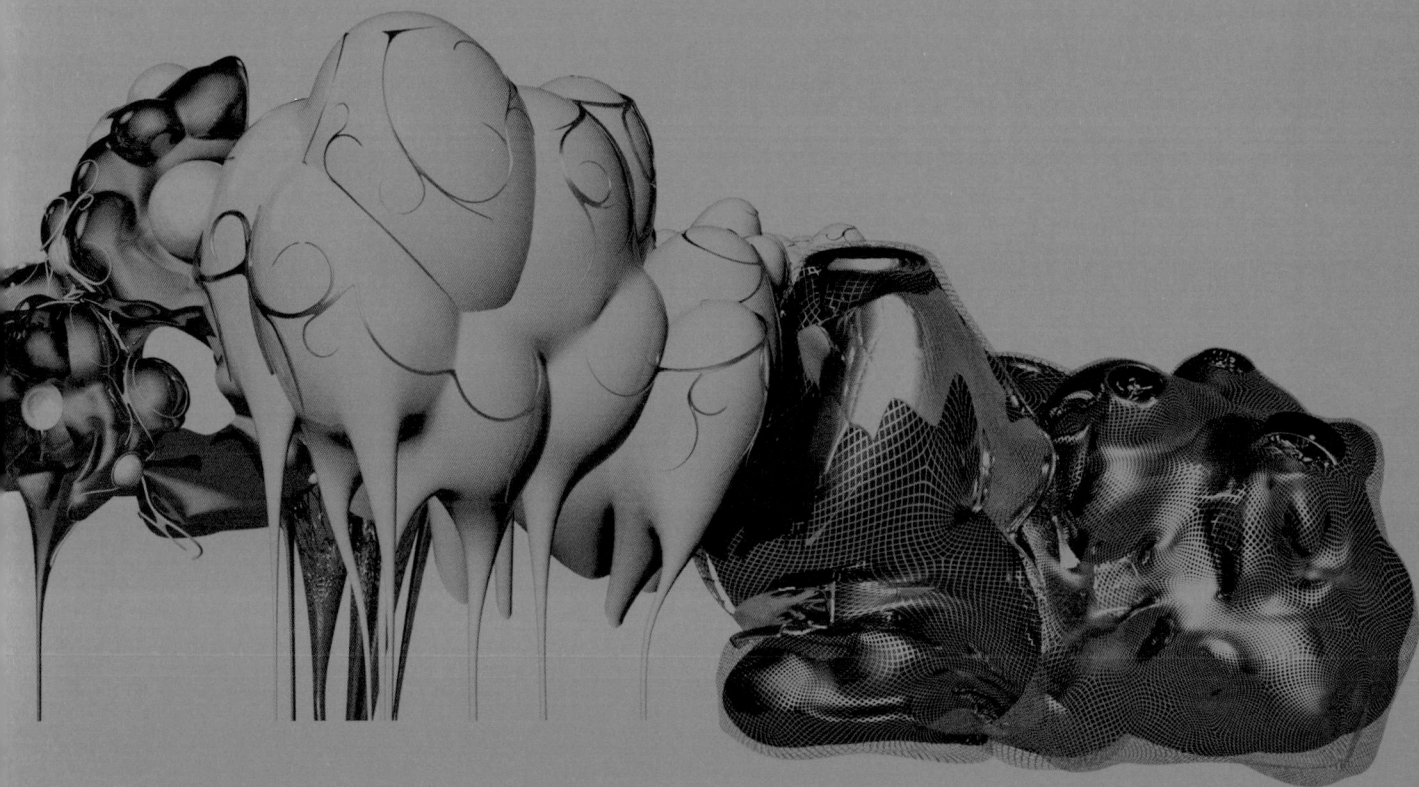

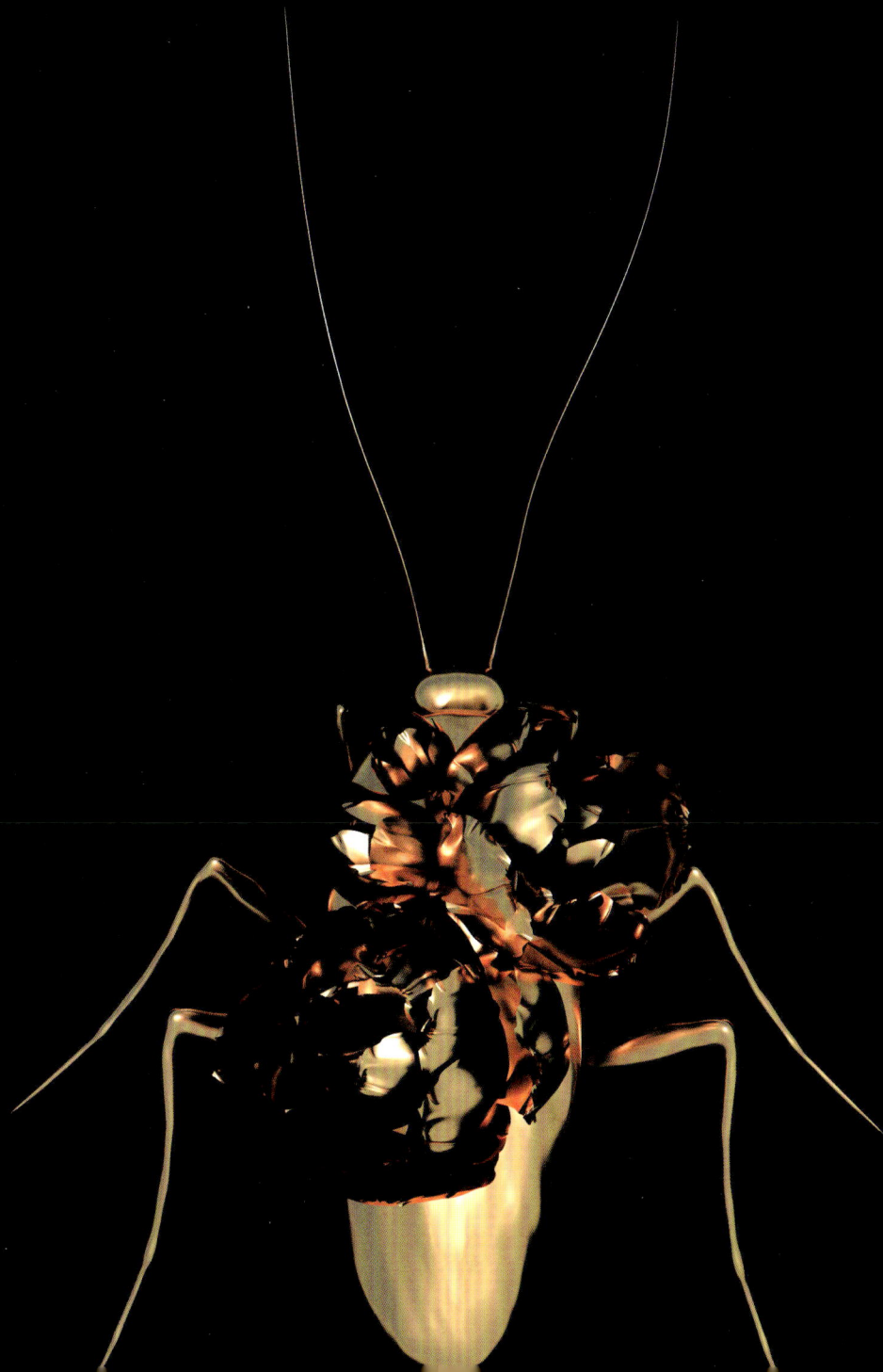

SINGLE SURFACE

PS1 MoMA

With the flair of a circus and the ambience of
a playground, this project activates effects
and sensations. A mode of playful distraction
and absorption is created, as familiar spatial
vibrations are stimulated through unfamiliar
figures and aesthetics emerge to define
a grotesque and horrific effect. As circus
flamboyance, the space is intensified in mood
and play through contortion and exuberance.
It is dense and textured, the light is filtered
but bright. It is not loud, but incisive and
disturbing. In this sense, time doesn't exist,
but becomes a kind of parallel situation.

Location: New York, New York
Date: 2005

Related projects
Tabakalera, 2008 (p. 140)
Sant Adrià de Besòs, 2014 (p. 154)
Rusuupuisto, 2015 (p. 246)

Sangre

This sculptural installation was the centrepiece of the exhibition *Xefirotarch/Design Series 4*, held at SFMoMA in 2006. Sangre (Spanish for 'blood'), which was finished with factory-issue paint in Ferrari Red and filled an entire gallery, suggested both the sleekness of a manufactured object and the biomorphic oddity of an alien creature. It incorporates architectural models and design maquettes from earlier projects, including Busan Metropolitan City (2004), U2 Tower (2002), Cell Phone Prototype Concepts (2006) and PS1 MoMA (2005; p. 28). The exhibition also featured six monitors that played animations, as well as a number of small-scale models.

Location: San Francisco, California
Date: 2006

Related projects
La Chaise Grotesque, 2012 (p. 42)
X-Plosion, 2008 (p. 60)
Miami Ritz Sculpture 1.0, 2011 (p. 66)
Pitch Black, 2008/2016 (p. 164)

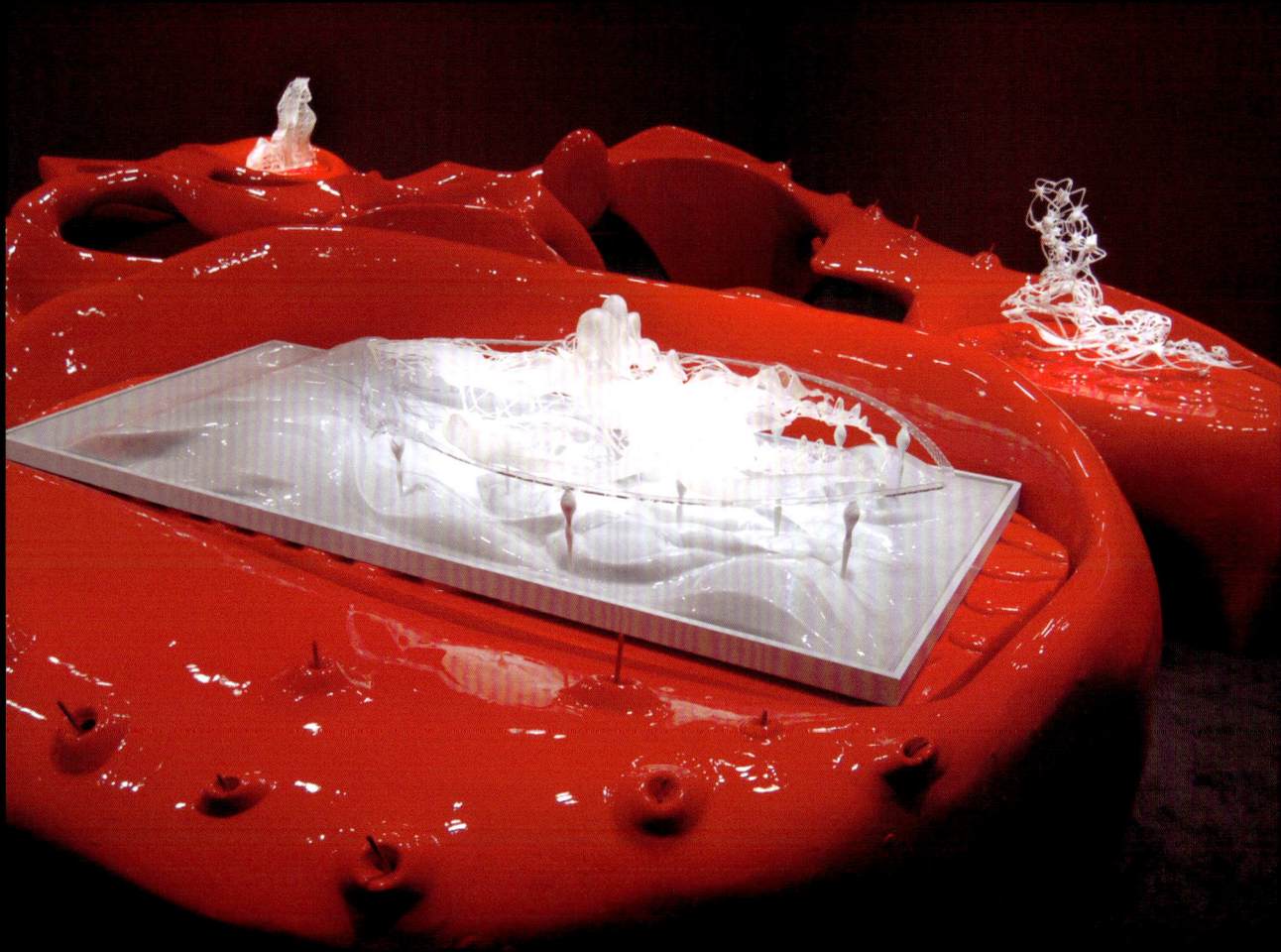

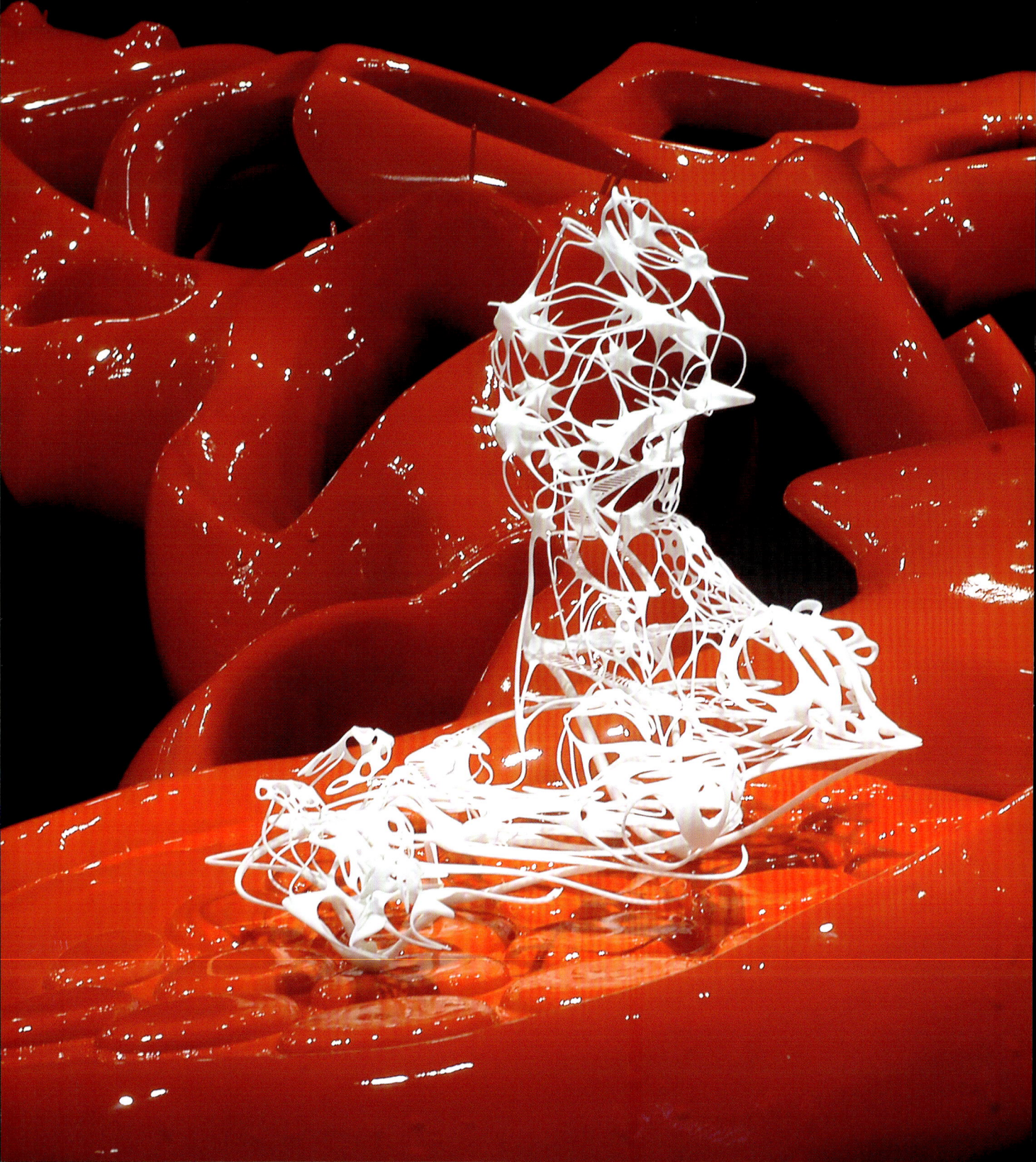

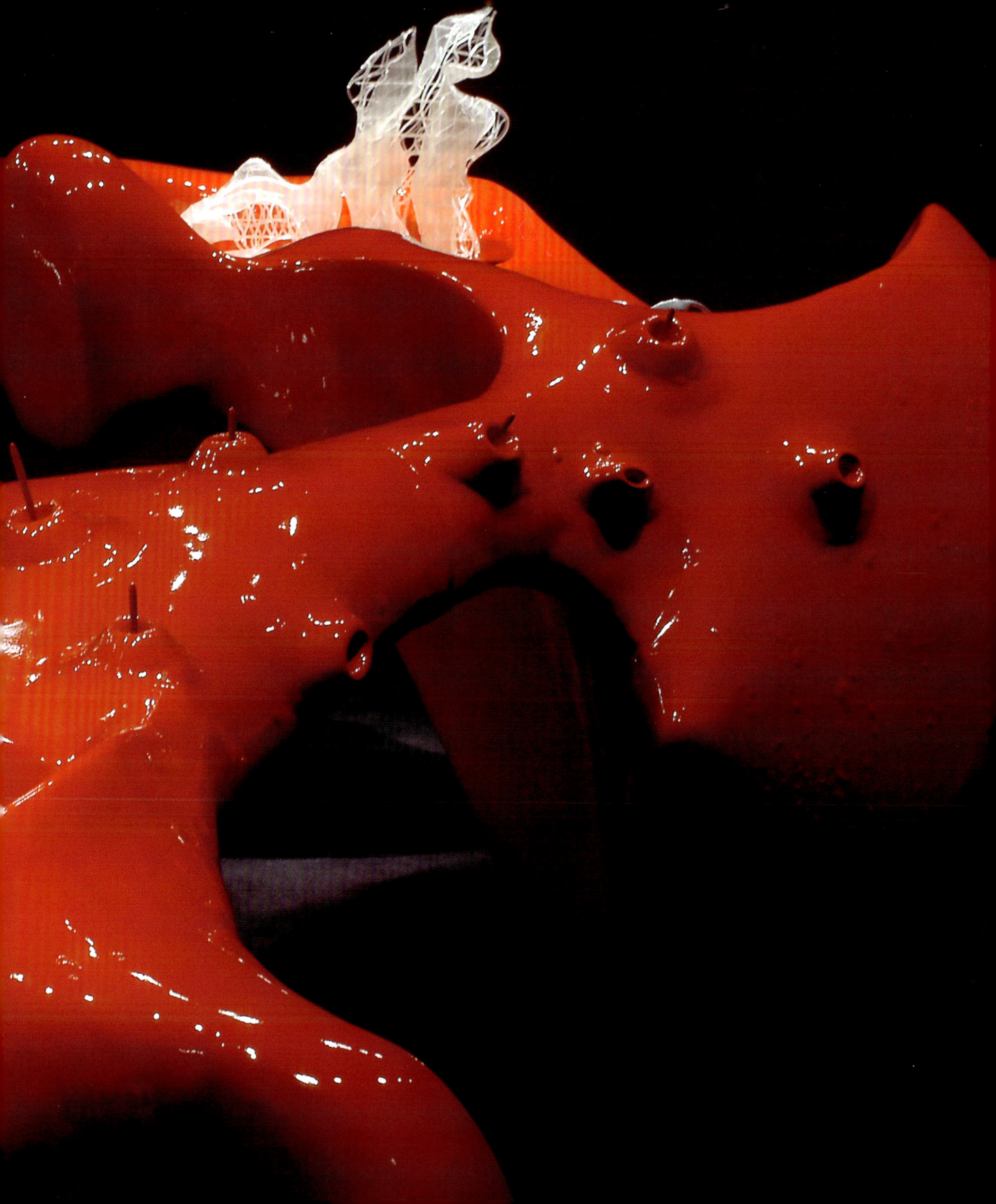

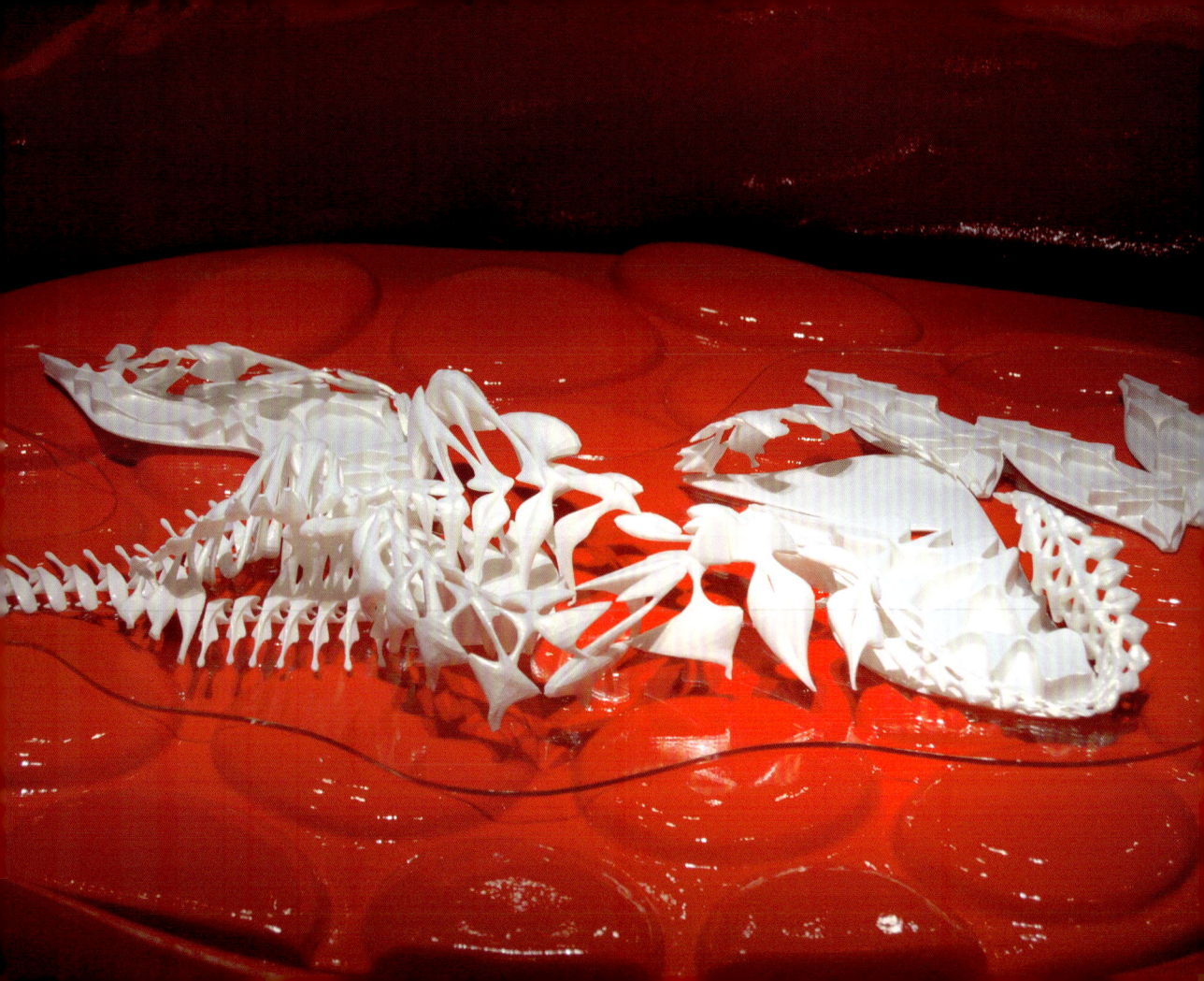

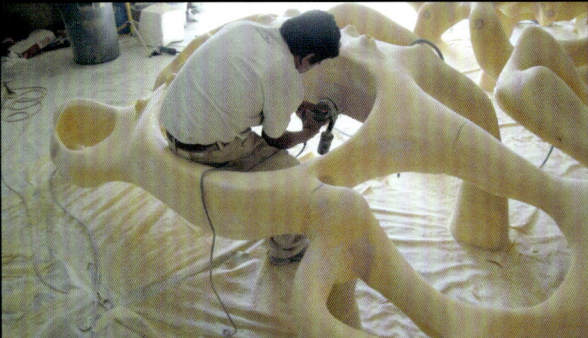
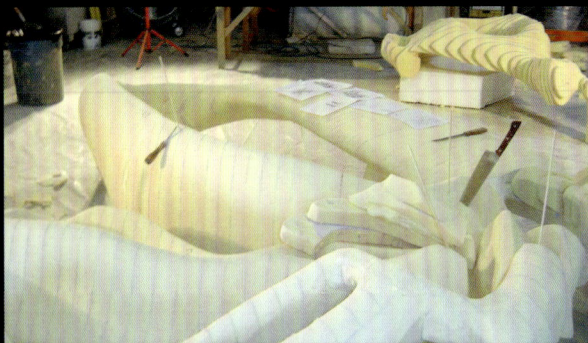

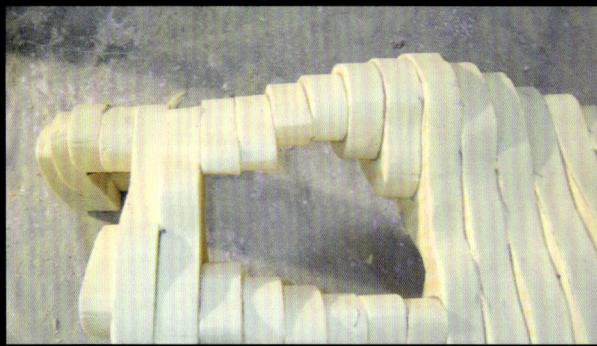

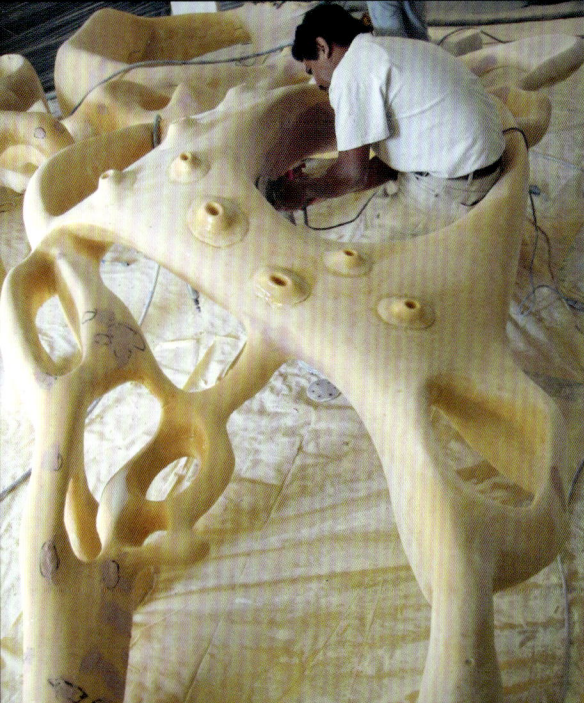

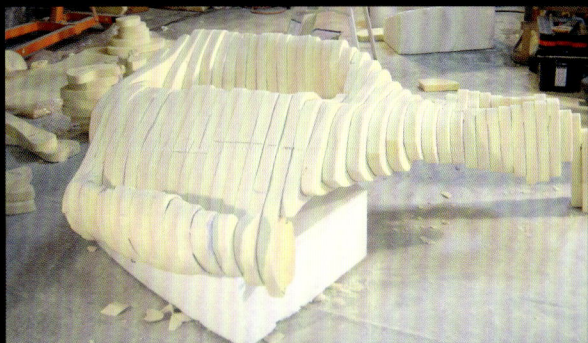

La Chaise Grotesque

Commissioned by Joseph Rosa, John H. Bryan curator and head of architecture and design at the Art Institute of Chicago, for the exhibition *Hyperlinks: Architecture and Design*, our design for a chair is a mutation of Charles and Ray Eames' iconic 'La Chaise' (1948). It uses algorithms, aesthetics and the grotesque to work with contemporary paradigms of sampling and distortions, in the manner of electronic music, or the way that a DJ might work. It took 72 hours to complete.

Date: 2012
Programme: Product design

Related projects
Sangre, 2006 (p. 34)
X-Plosion, 2008 (p. 60)
Miami Ritz Sculpture 1.0, 2011 (p. 66)
Pitch Black, 2008/2016 (p. 164)

HYPER
XEFIROTARCH
LINKS

HYPERACTIVE
HYPERDIGITAL
HYPERDIMENSIONAL
HYPERFUNCTIONAL
HYPERNARRATIVE
HYPERHARDWIRED
HYPERMOBILE
HYPERREAL
HYPERSOCIAL
HYPERSUSTAINABLE

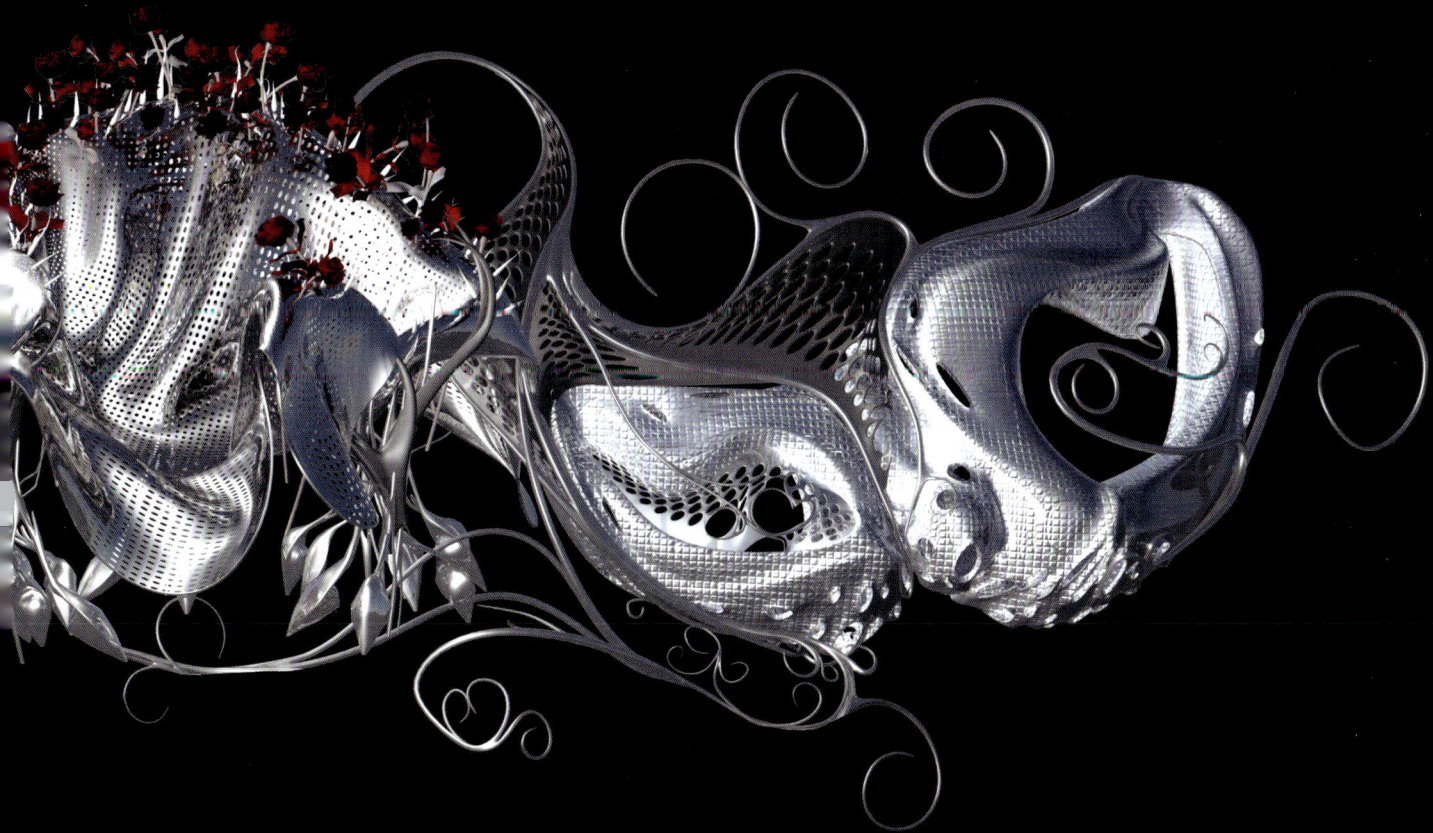

ORNAMENT

Rose Chair

This chair design translates synthetic organism techniques into formal topological ones, creating complex taxonomies of a structure-system that generates new species of formal behaviour. It is not about the mimetic career of biology and structure into and onto architecture, but rather the transference of multiple physiological scales into the production of form. Michel Foucault's history of medicine is simultaneously a history of vision. The species becomes – in the modern regime of medical surveillance – an animated corpse, an assemblage of organs into which diagnoses are invested and installed. The inside becomes the outside, or more precisely, the insides become an interior structural condition to be understood in relation to another exterior structural condition: an epidermal membrane.

Date: 2010
Programme: Product design

Related projects
Mexican Funeral, 2010 (p. 54)
Seroussi Bench, 2010 (p. 226)
TBA 21_1.0, 2011 (p. 234)

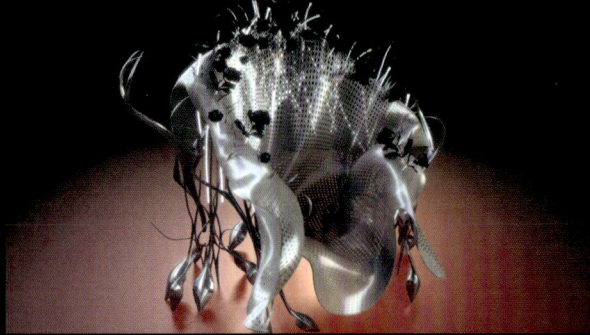

Mexican Funeral

There is an incontrovertible mythology
attached to darkness that combines allure
and unspeakable fear. This fear has been
immutable through time; the only things that
change are the monsters we create, who lurk
under our beds, in our closets, down in the
basement and in our garages. Yet through
all the angst the darkness has caused, there
remains an undeniable fascination – in young
and old – with what lurks within. Monsters
have always been used to explain what we
cannot. Our proposal is a series of displays
that glow in the dark, representing
a particular ontology in the field of
architecture that regards the image as
a form of production, using the grotesque,
the horrific and the misfit as a new condition
of arousal.

Location: Los Angeles, California
Date: 2010

Related projects
Rose Chair, 2010 (p. 50)
Seroussi Bench, 2010 (p. 226)
TBA 21_1.0, 2011 (p. 234)

X-Plosion

One of my favourite characteristics of
architectural design is that it is a discipline
that is weak, in the best sense of the word,
meaning that projects are always in flux, on
the edge of being something else or trying
to be something else – in this case, trying to
be art. With this installation, we were echoing
pieces and genes from other projects, such
as the Maison Seroussi (p. 176). Here, we were
attempting to create a family of projects born
of similar cells of origins and similar formal
vocabularies. In a sense, X-Plosion, like many
of our other projects, operates as a proto-
laboratory for architectural thinking.

Date: 2008
Programme: Window display

Related projects
Sangre, 2006 (p. 34)
La Chaise Grotesque, 2012 (p. 42)
Miami Ritz Sculpture 1.0, 2011 (p. 66)
Pitch Black, 2008/2016 (p. 164)

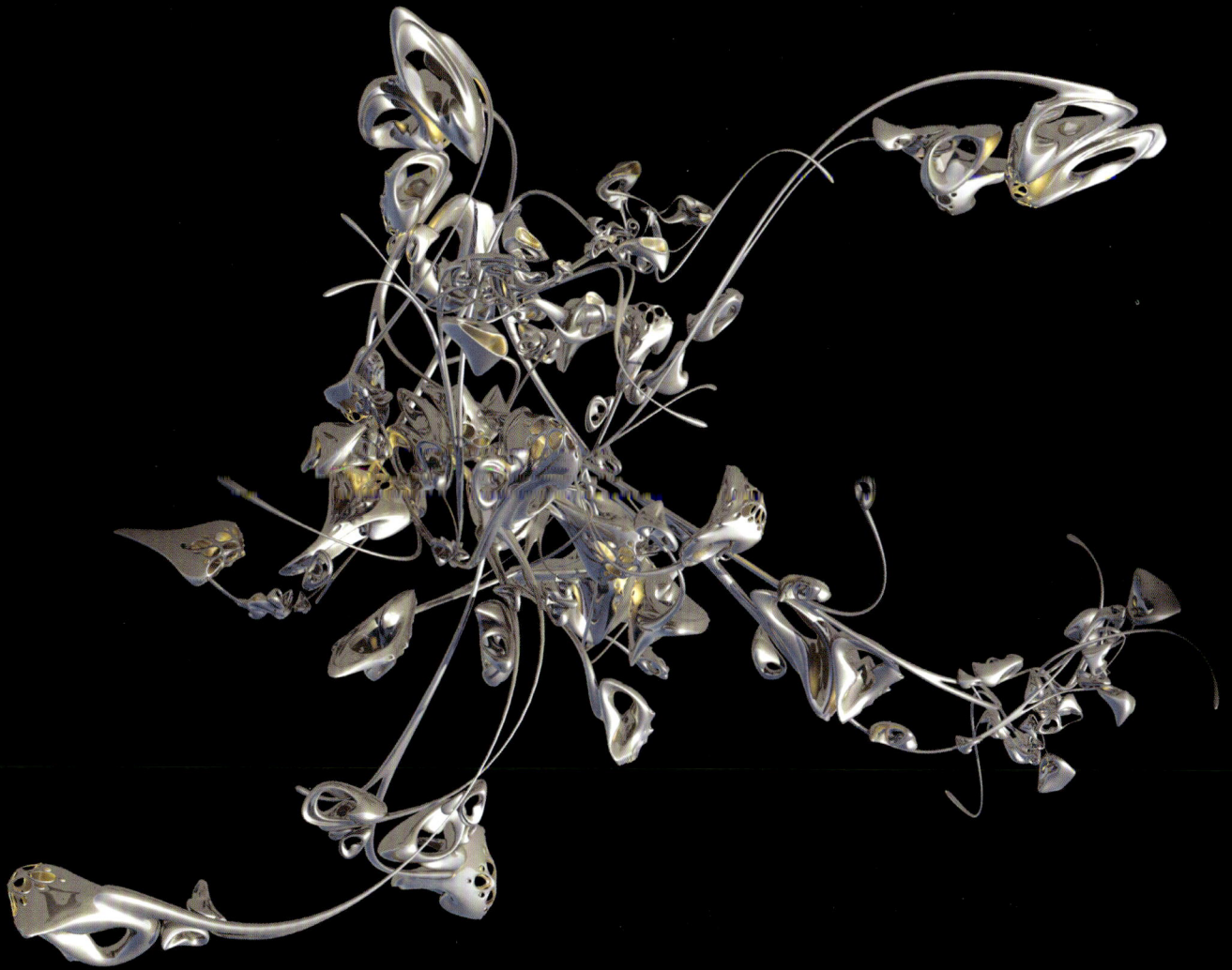

ORCHARD STREET (20B)

OXFORD STREET (20A)

610

1420

200

4250

1790

1460

200

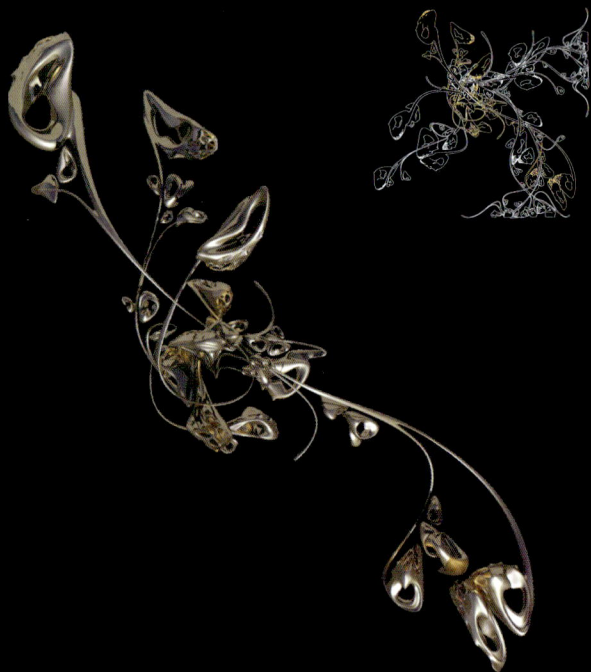

Organ 001

Organ 002

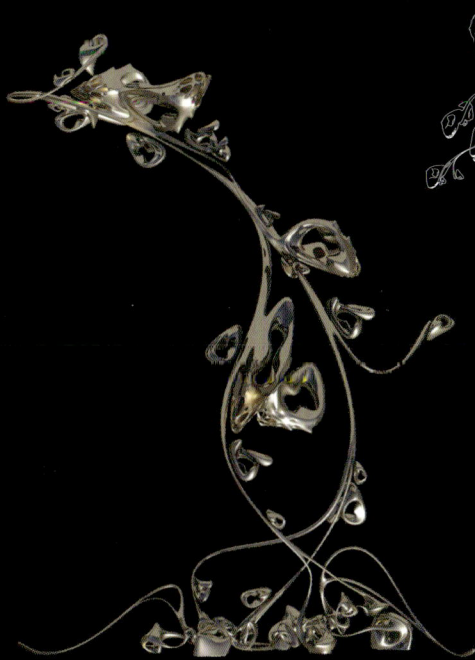

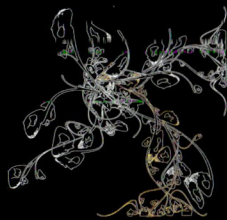

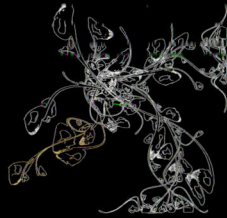

Organ 003

Organ 004

Miami Ritz Sculpture 1.0

In the field of architecture, design operates in accumulations. Novelty is impossible, but innovation can come through the compounding of mutations, long lineages of genetic modifications. This installation is an artificial mutation of a tree, a reconfiguration and editing of its tendencies, which evolves and disrupts the type without destroying it. It is also a mutation of the genetic code running through other projects we were developing at the time, feeding back into our practice. Nothing exists in isolation.

Location: Miami Beach, Florida
Date: 2011
Programme: Artwork

Related projects
Sangre, 2006 (p. 34)
La Chaise Grotesque, 2012 (p. 42)
X-Plosion, 2008 (p. 60)
Pitch Black, 2008/2016 (p. 164)

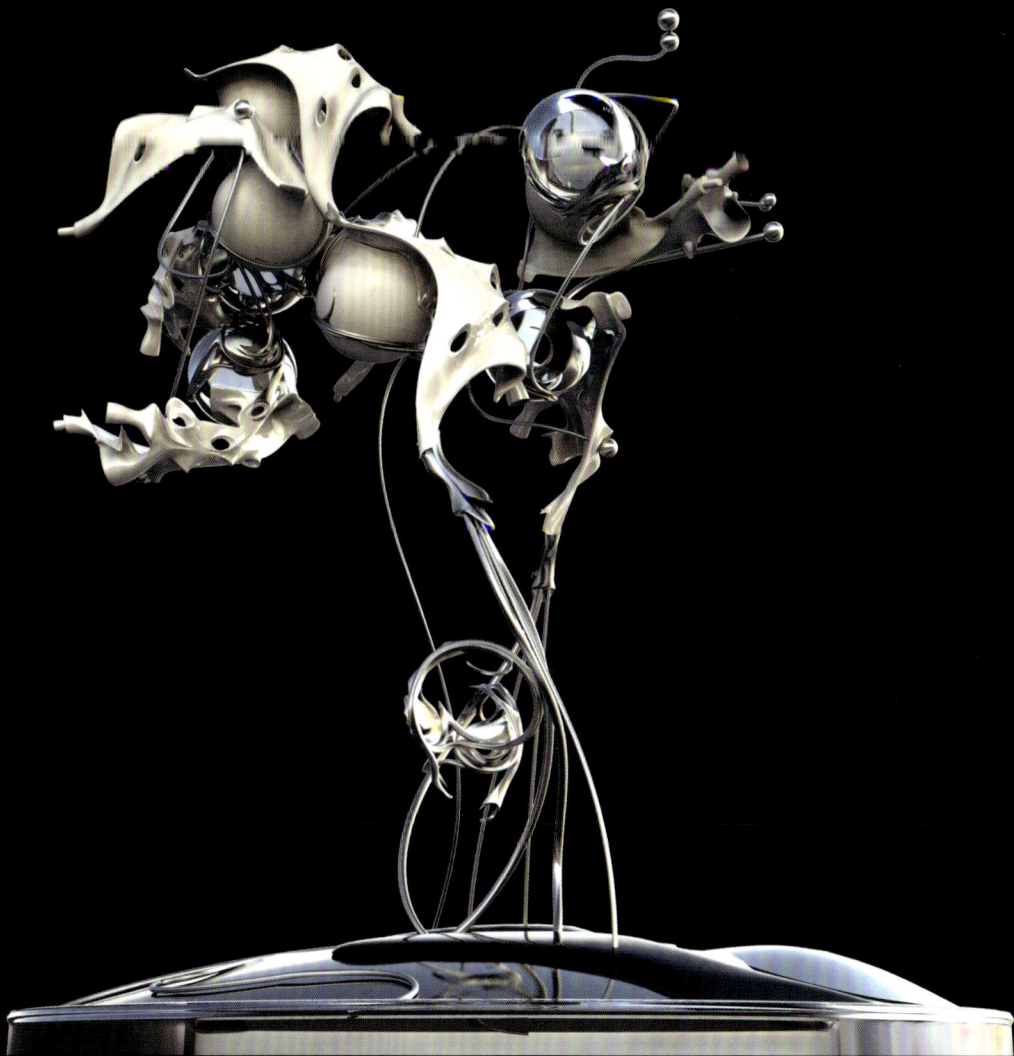

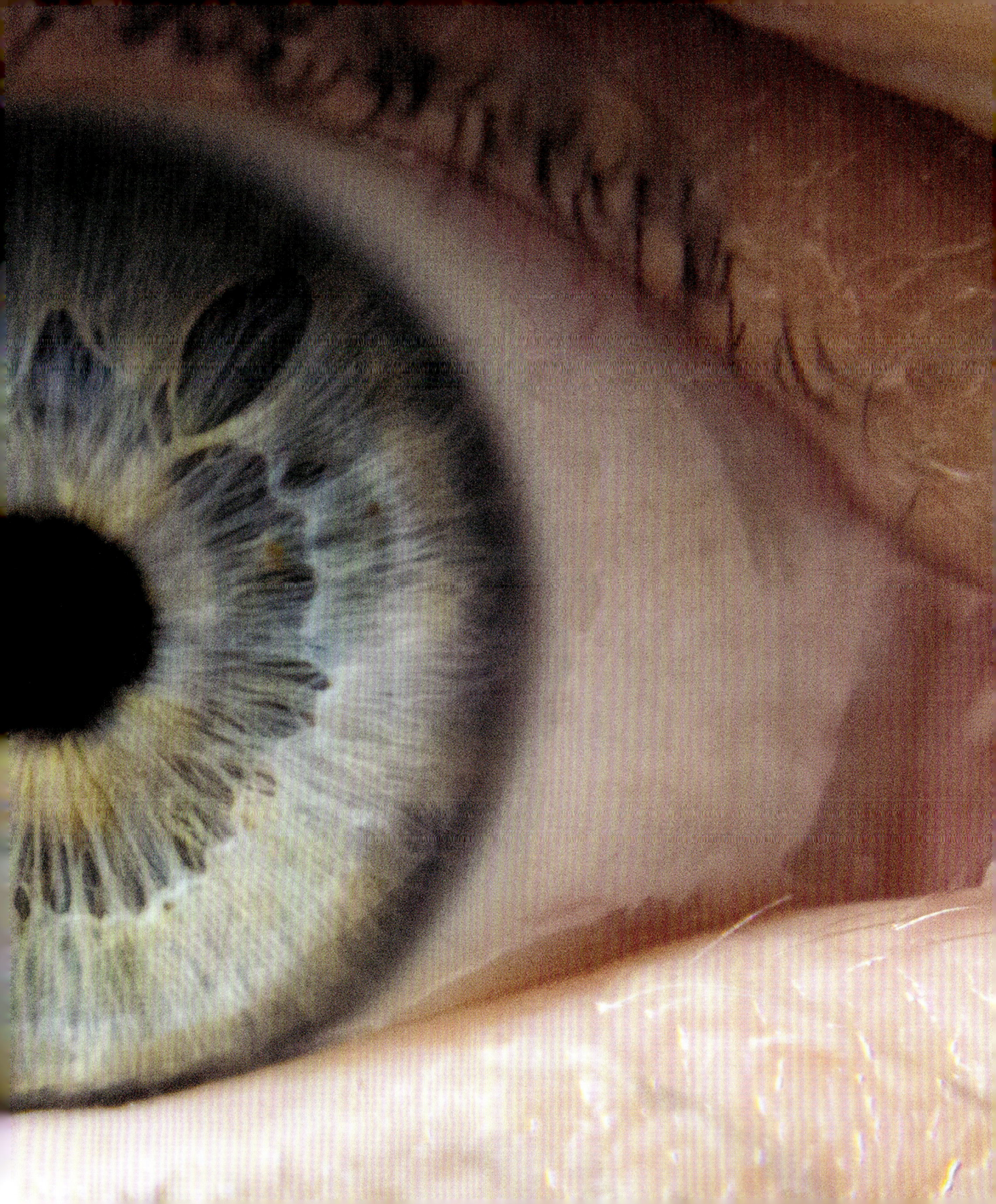

Helsinki Library

This project for a library activates the effects and sensations of the city, creating a feeling of playful urban organization and absorption. As a jewelled elegance, the space intensifies mood and play, becoming dense and textured through contortion and exuberance. Our design serves to aestheticize that process, so that we might understand the complex city of Helsinki as a living entity – one that is supple, dynamic, responsive and cohesive, allowing for a mix of cultures and ideas. The image, and the image of architecture itself, plays an integral part in this process. Our ambition is clear: to produce beauty in terms of the future, and not in a condition that we already know. A city like Helsinki is always surprising.

Location: Helsinki, Finland
Date: 2012
Programme: Competition

Related projects
Taichung Cultural Centre, 2013 (p. 90)
Guggenheim Helsinki, 2014 (p. 98)

1.1 Service spaces
1.2 Main lobby
1.3 Meeting and lounge area
1.4 Public toilets
1.5 Central public service space

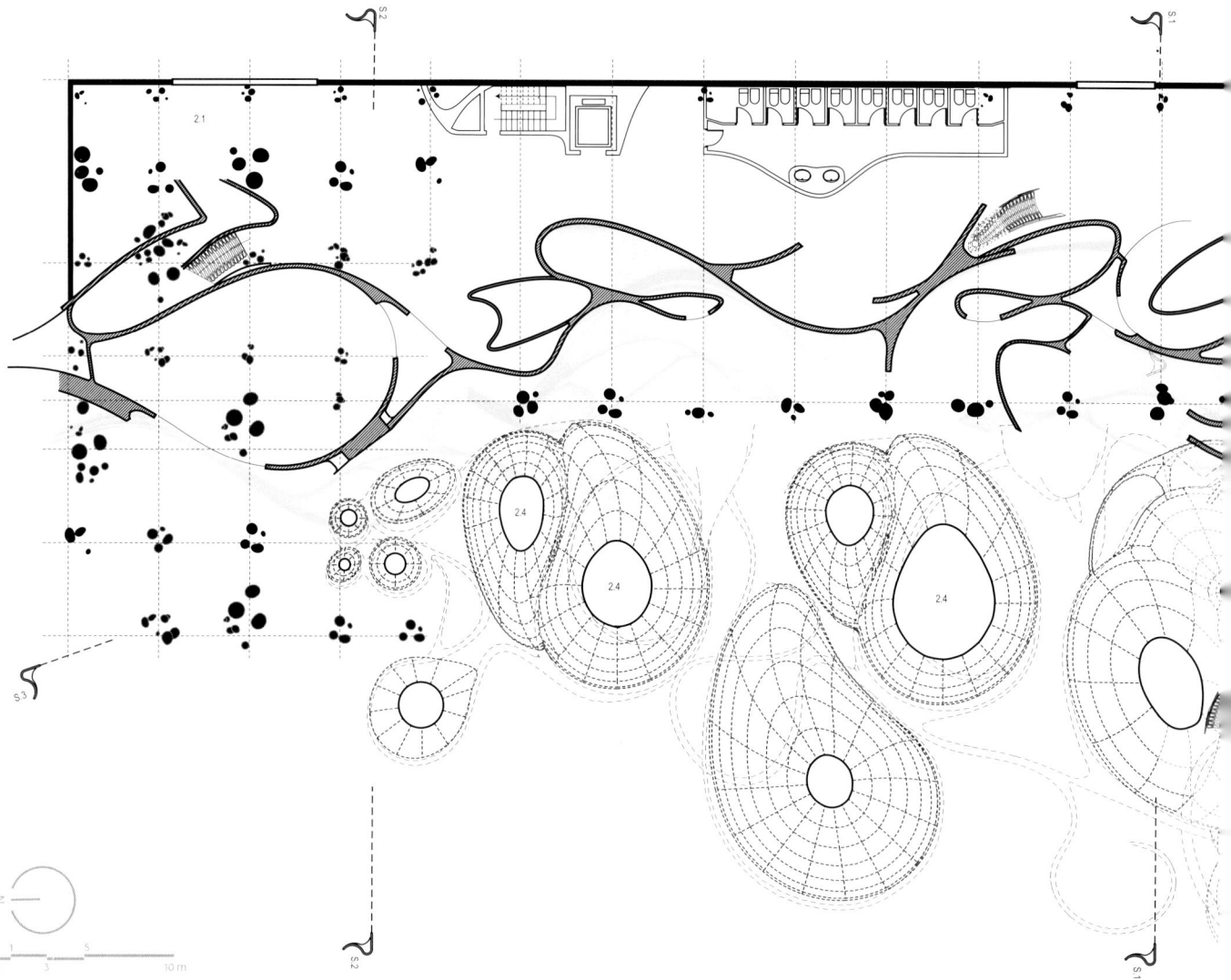

Floorplan – Level 1

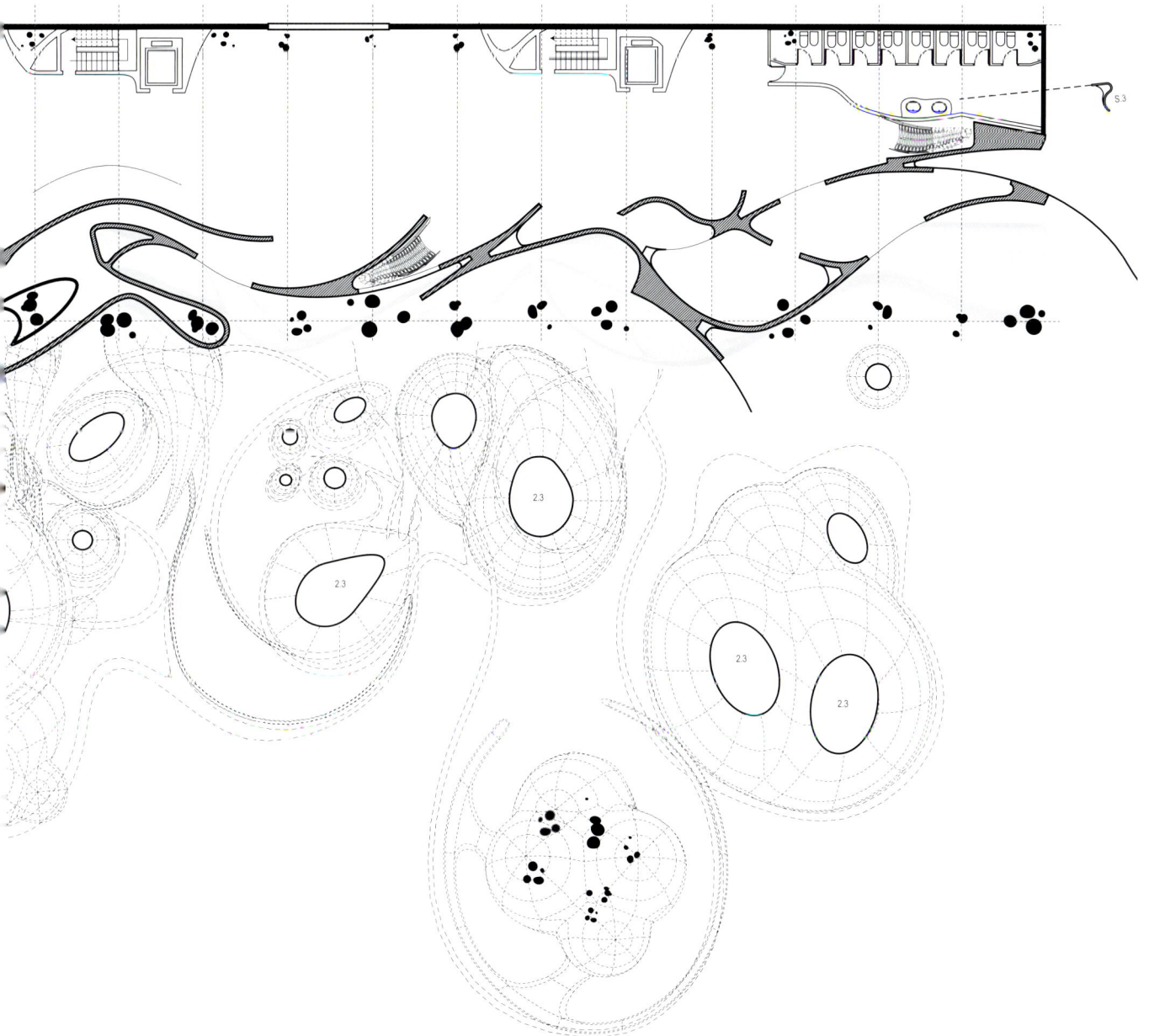

S.3

2.1   Library area
2.2   Interactive spaces
2.3   Lounge spaces
2.4   Quiet spaces

2.5   Public toilets
2.6   Library collection storage
2.7   Multipurpose hall

S2

S1

2.5

2.7

2.1

2.4

2.2

2.2

S3

S2

S1

N

0   1   5   10 m

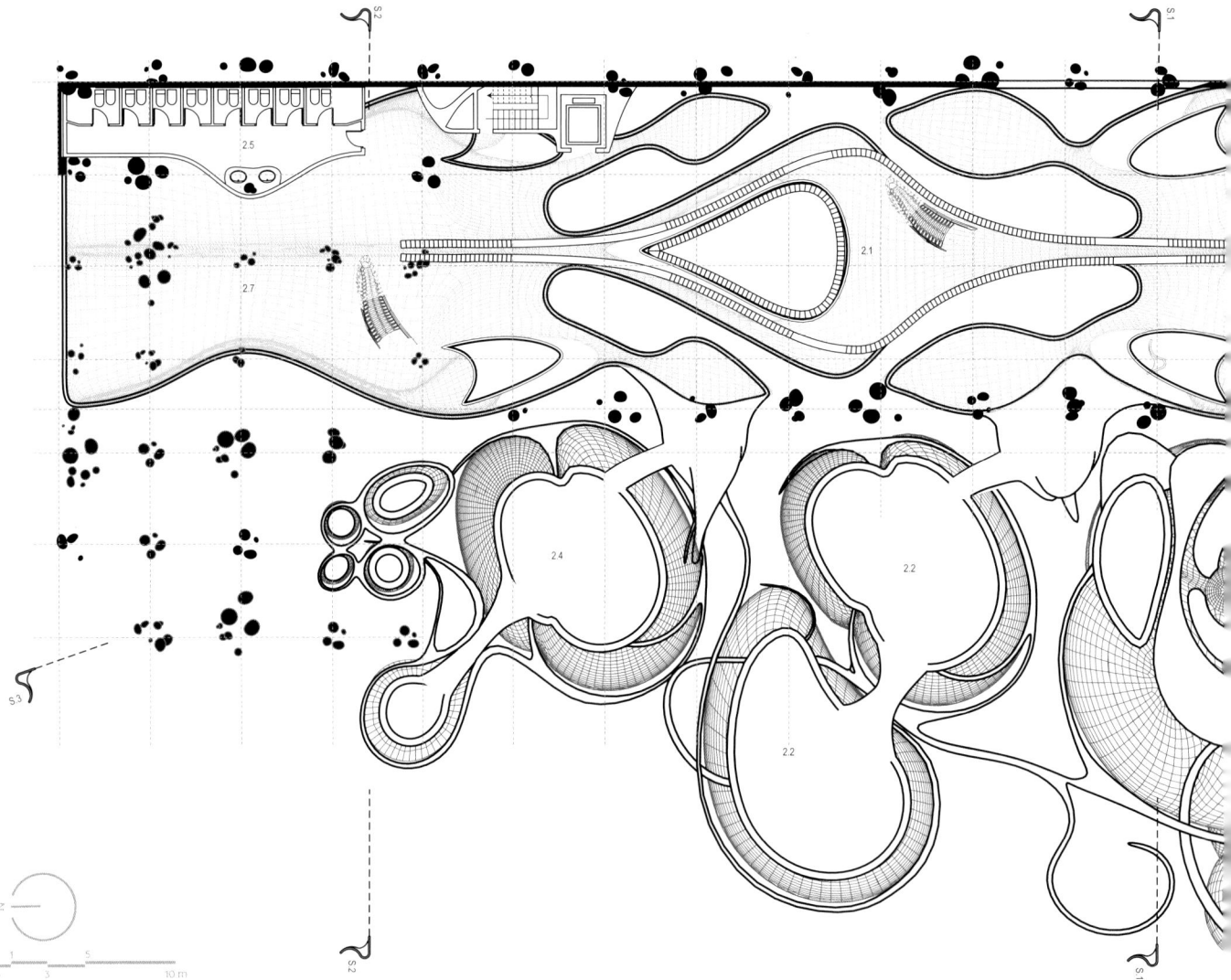

Floorplan – Level 2

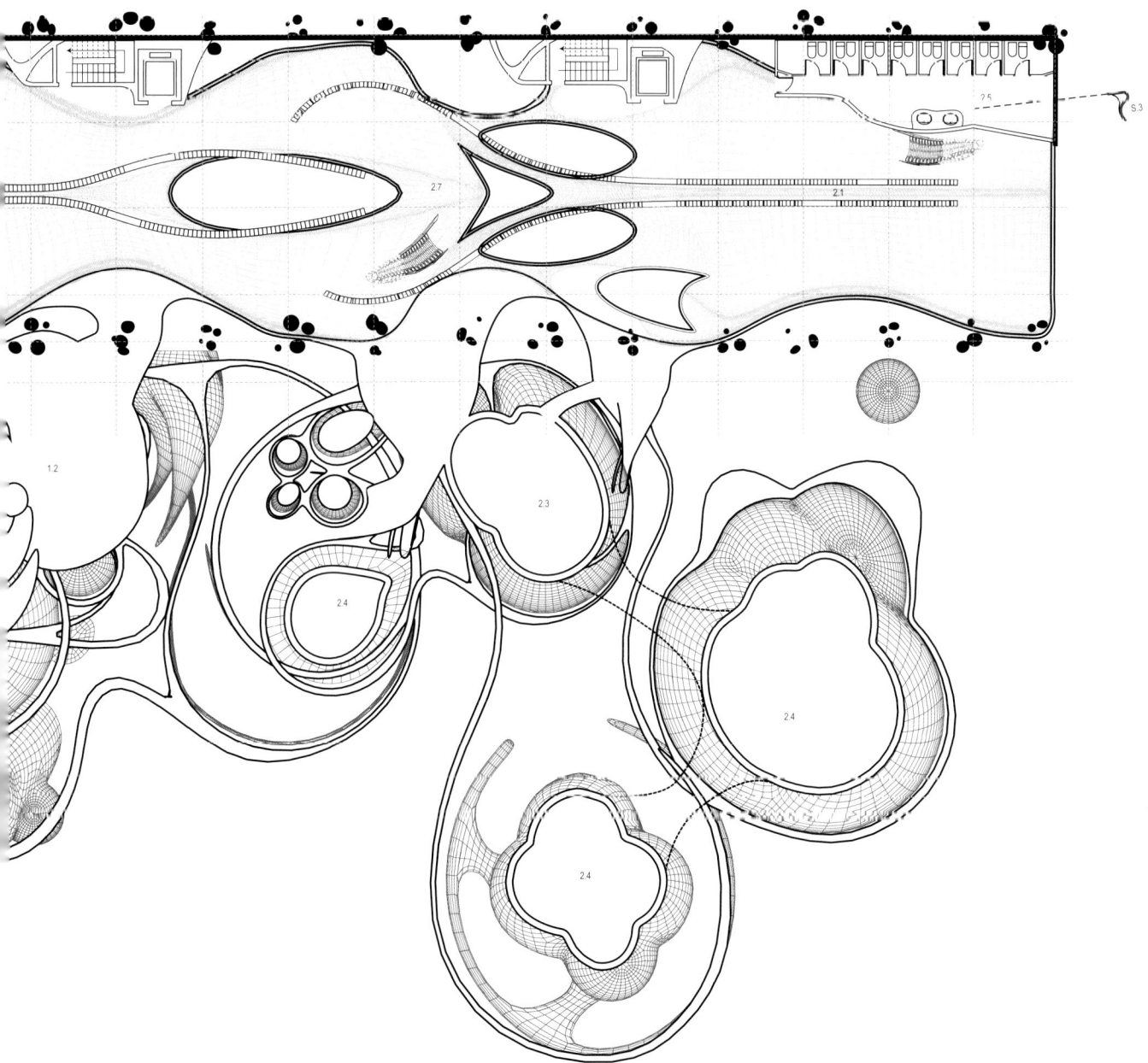

2.5

S.3

2.7

2.1

1.2

2.3

2.4

2.4

2.4

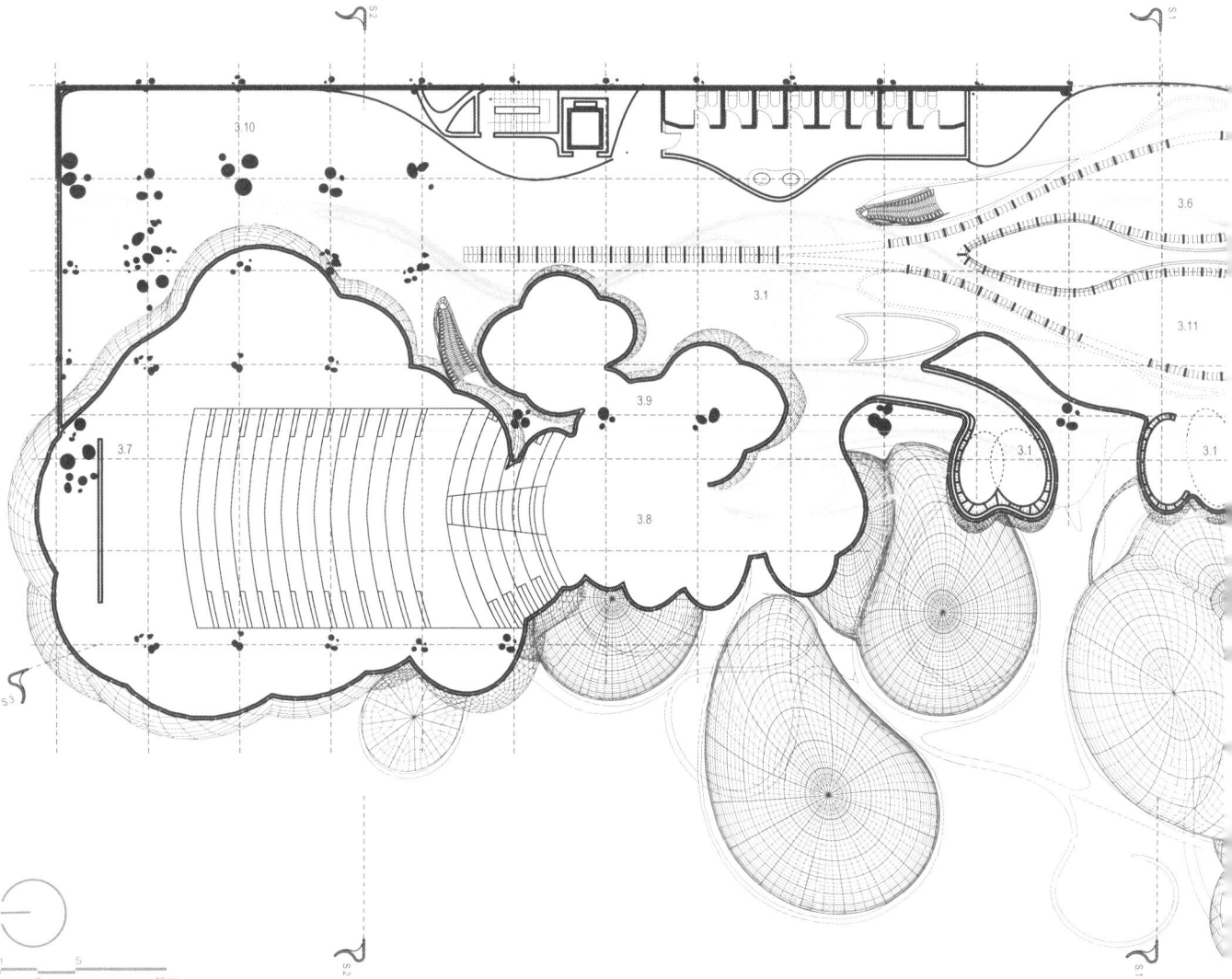

3.10

3.6

3.1

3.11

3.9

3.7

3.8

3.1

3.1

N

S

0   3   10 m

Floorplan – Level 3

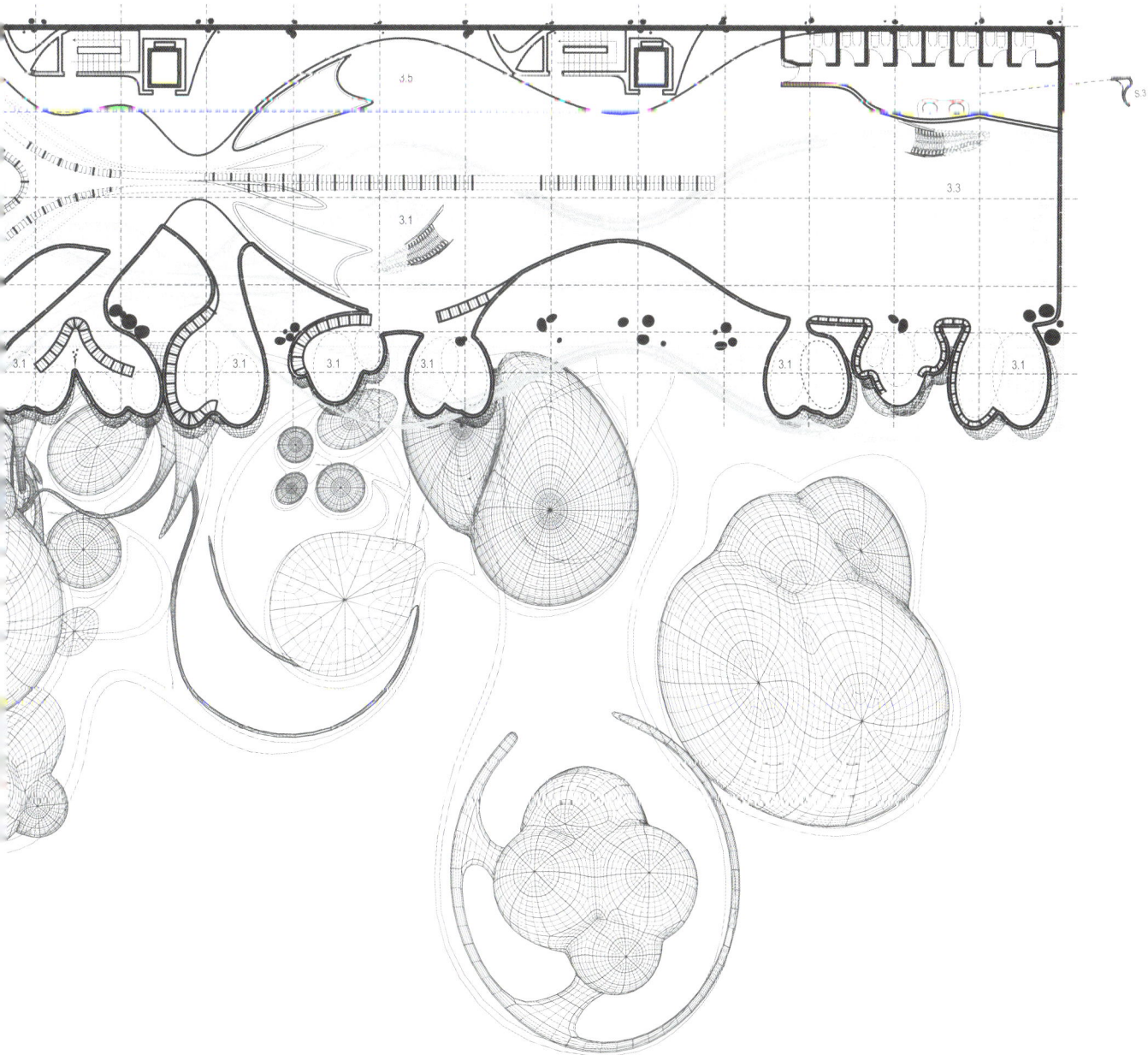

3.5

3.3

3.1

3.1

3.1

3.1

3.1

3.1

3.1

S.3

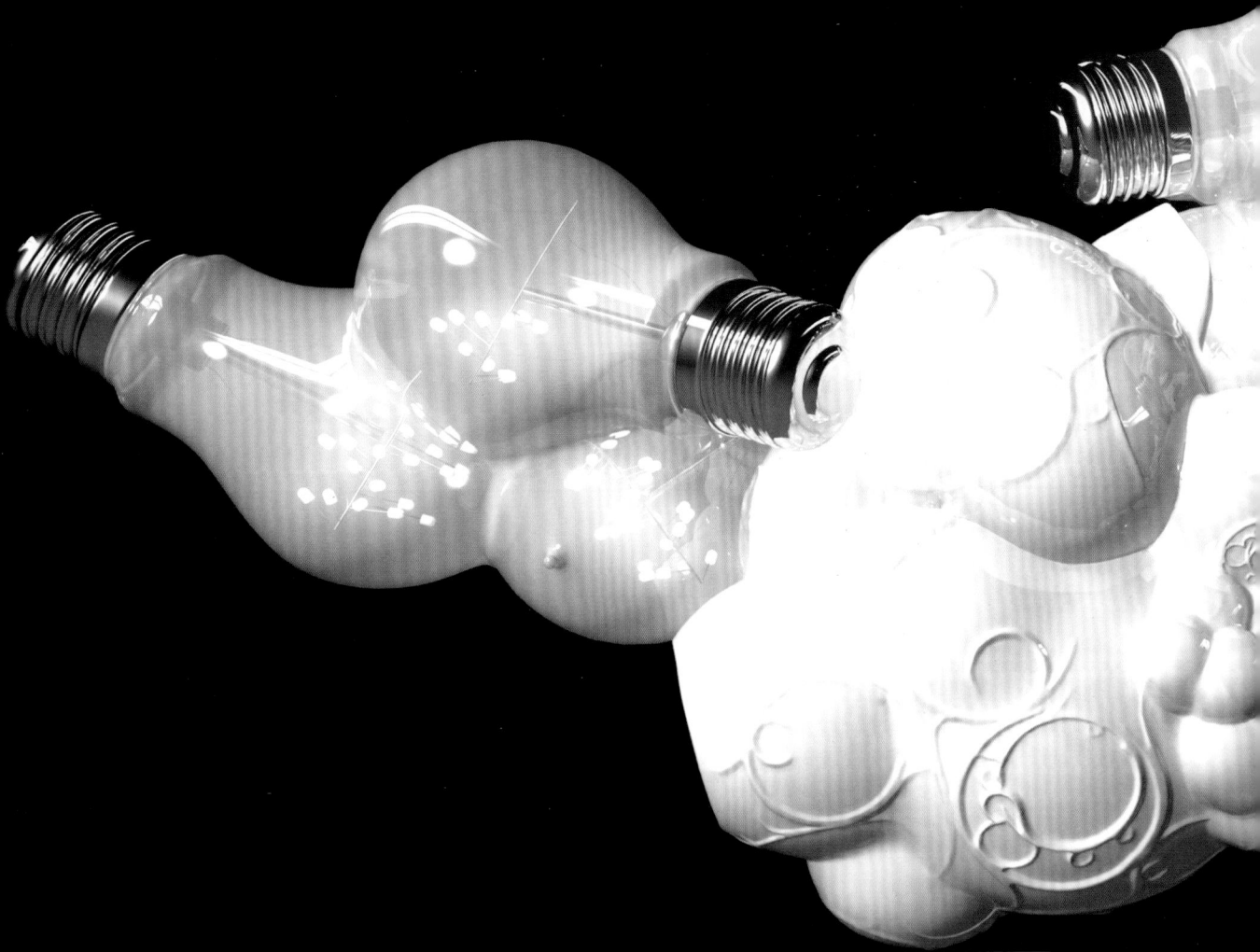

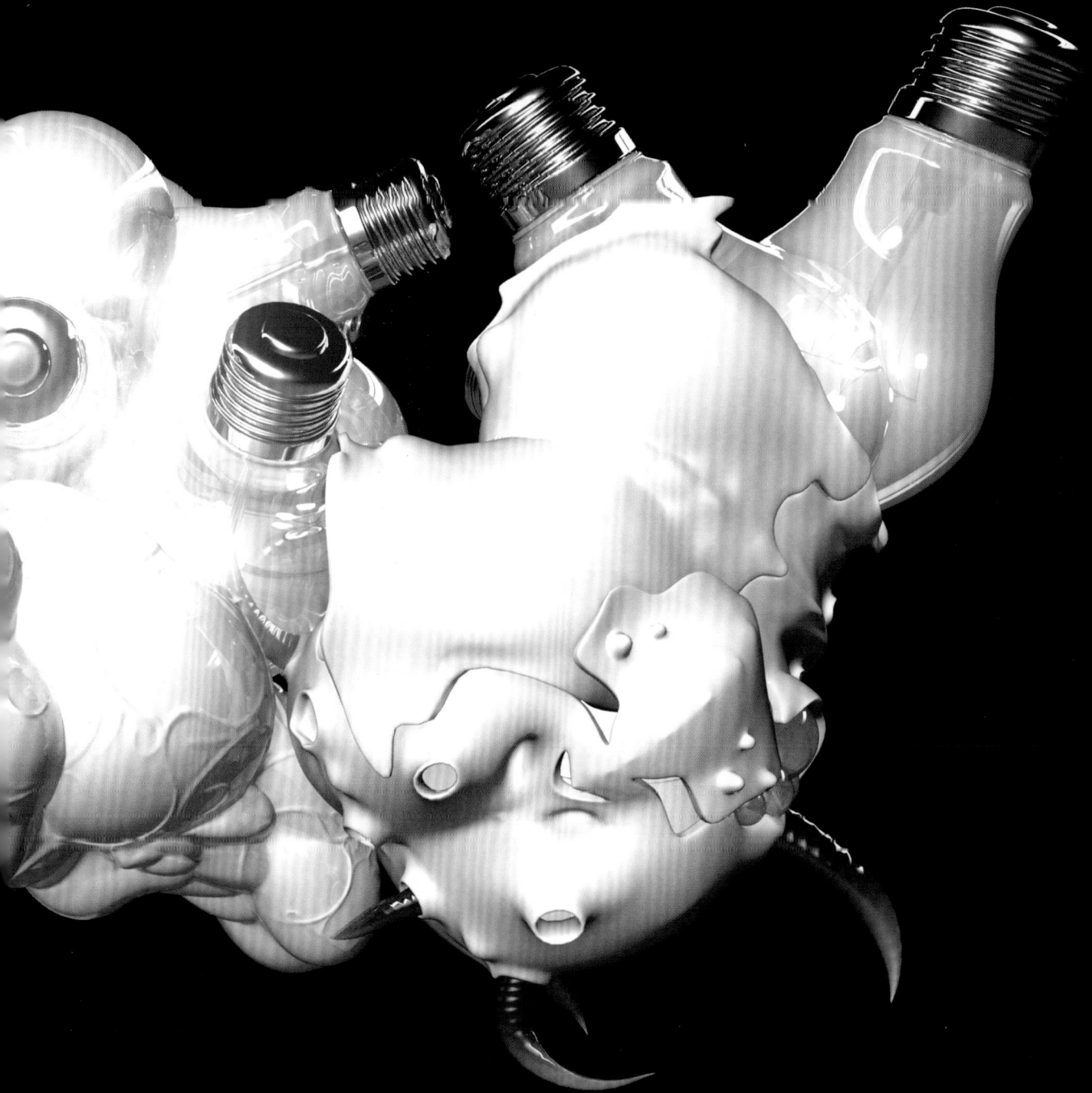

Taichung Cultural Centre

The image and the digital environment are vehicles for the production of form. The silver biological masses of the Taichung Culture Centre simultaneously erode the twin-tower typology, carving away large chunks, and digest it into a more evolved form that reconciles its two contradictory types through the implication of digestive motion. The material artificiality of metallic biological forms draws an inextricable link between the speculative, virtual realm from which the form emerges and its physical manifestations.

Location: Taichung, Taiwan
Date: 2013
Programme: Competition

Related projects
Helsinki Library, 2012 (p. 70)
Guggenheim Helsinki, 2014 (p. 98)

Level 3
1   Core
2   Ticketing
3   Museum lobby
4   Security

Level 5
1   Core
2   Library café
3   Reading room
4   Reading room
5   Reading area
6   Reading room

Level 6
1   Core
2   Bar
3   Restaurant lobby
4   Security
5   Dining
6   Private dining
7   Restaurant lobby
8   Kitchen
9   Theatre lobby
10 Theatre
11 Lounge

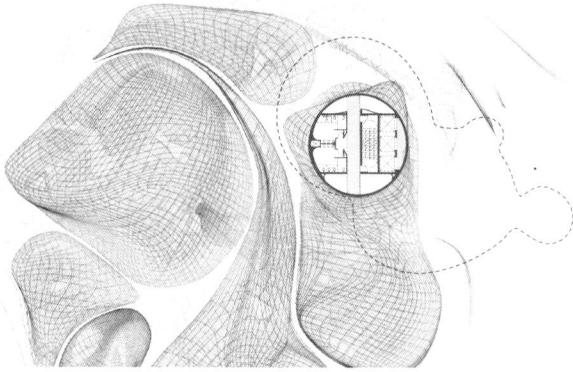

Floorplan – Level 3

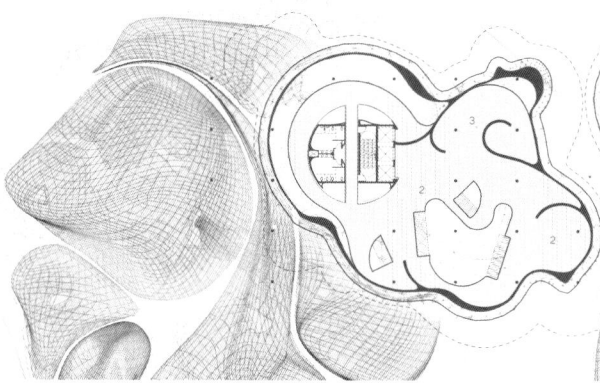

Floorplan – Level 5

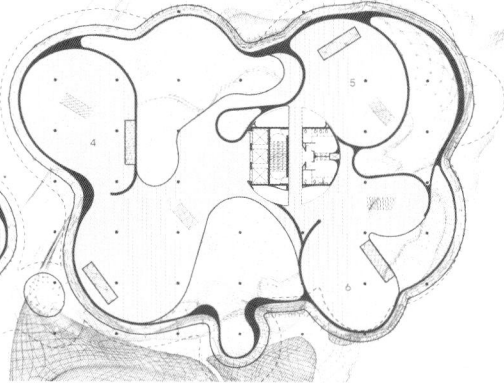

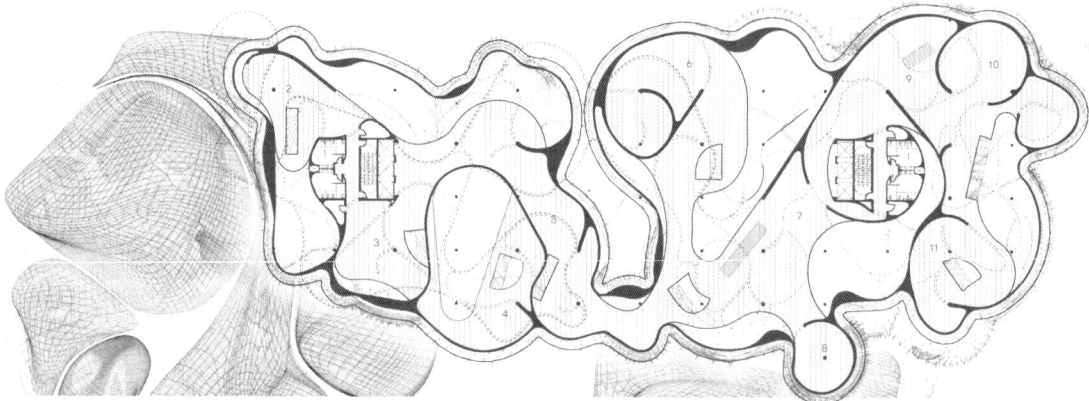

Floorplan – Level 6

Level 8
1   Core
2   Reading area
3   Reading rooms
4   Reading area

5   Senior reading room
6   Reading rooms
7   Young Adult reading room
8   Children's reading room
9   Young Adult reading room

Level 9
1   Core
2   Literature stacks
3   Storage
4   Special exhibition

Level 10
1   Core
2   Social science stacks
3   Special exhibition
4   Storage

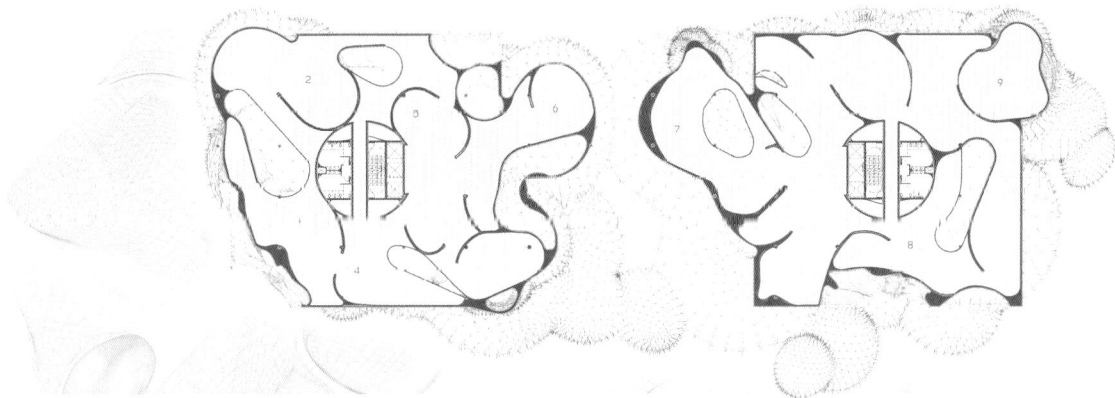

Floorplan – Level 8

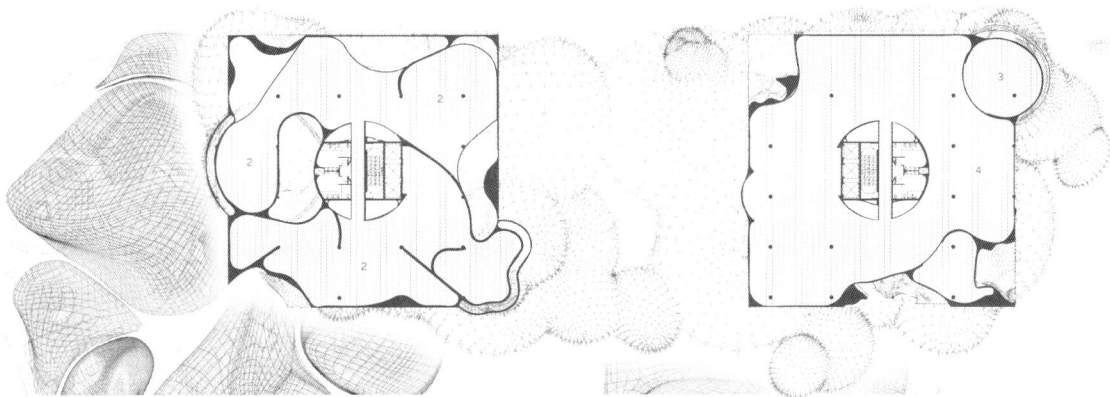

Floorplan – Level 9

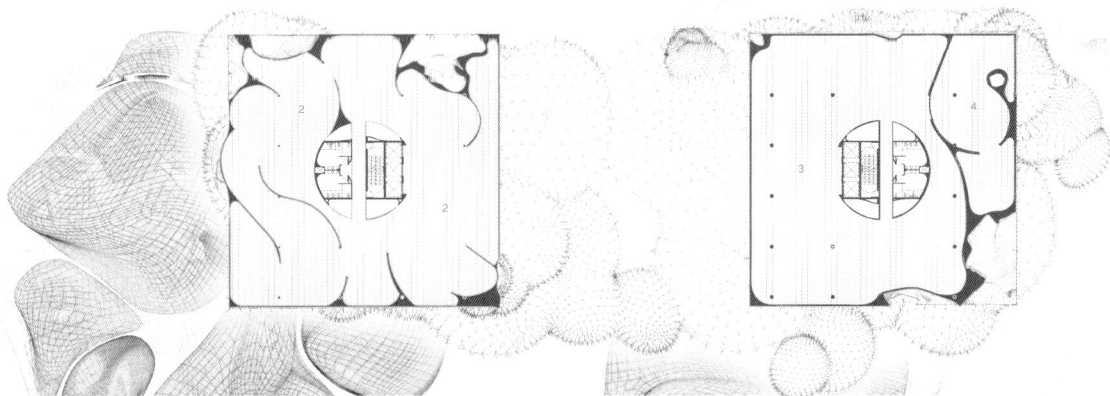

Floorplan – Level 10

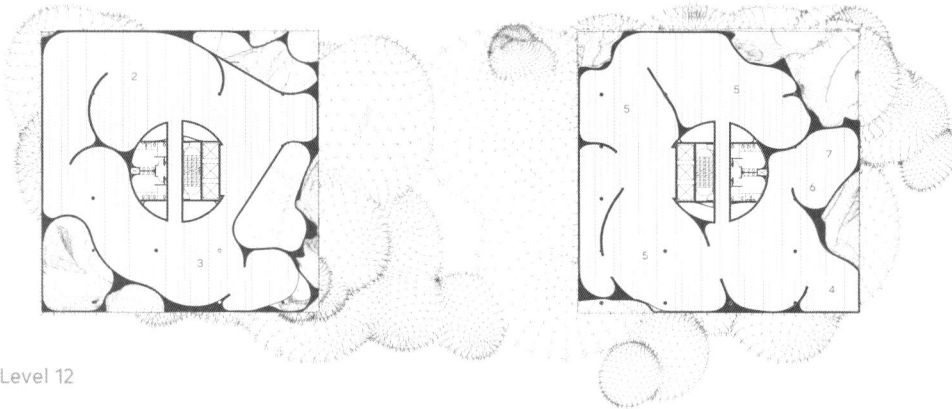

Floorplan – Level 12

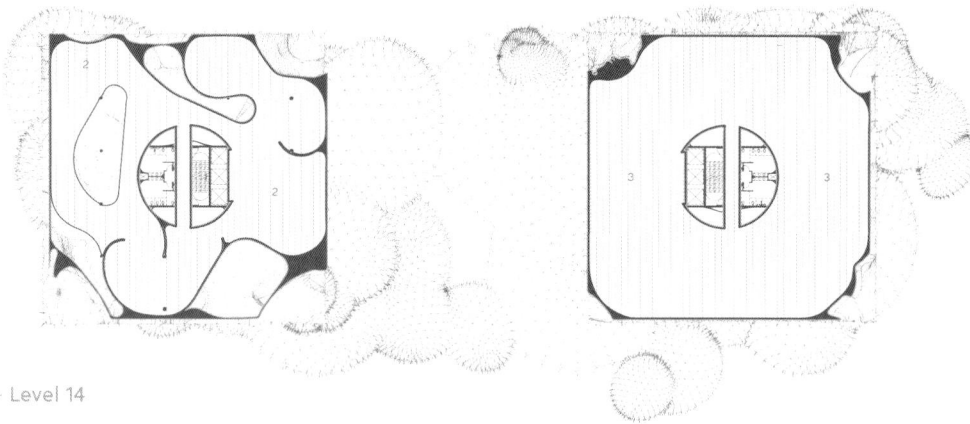

Floorplan – Level 14

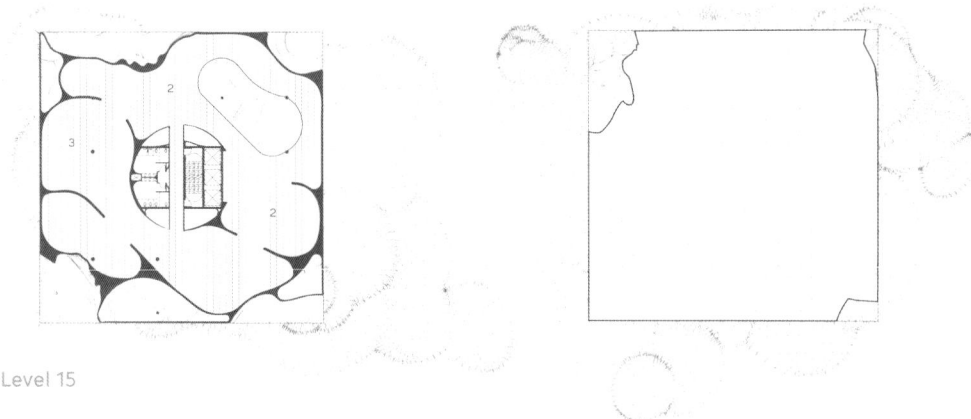

Floorplan – Level 15

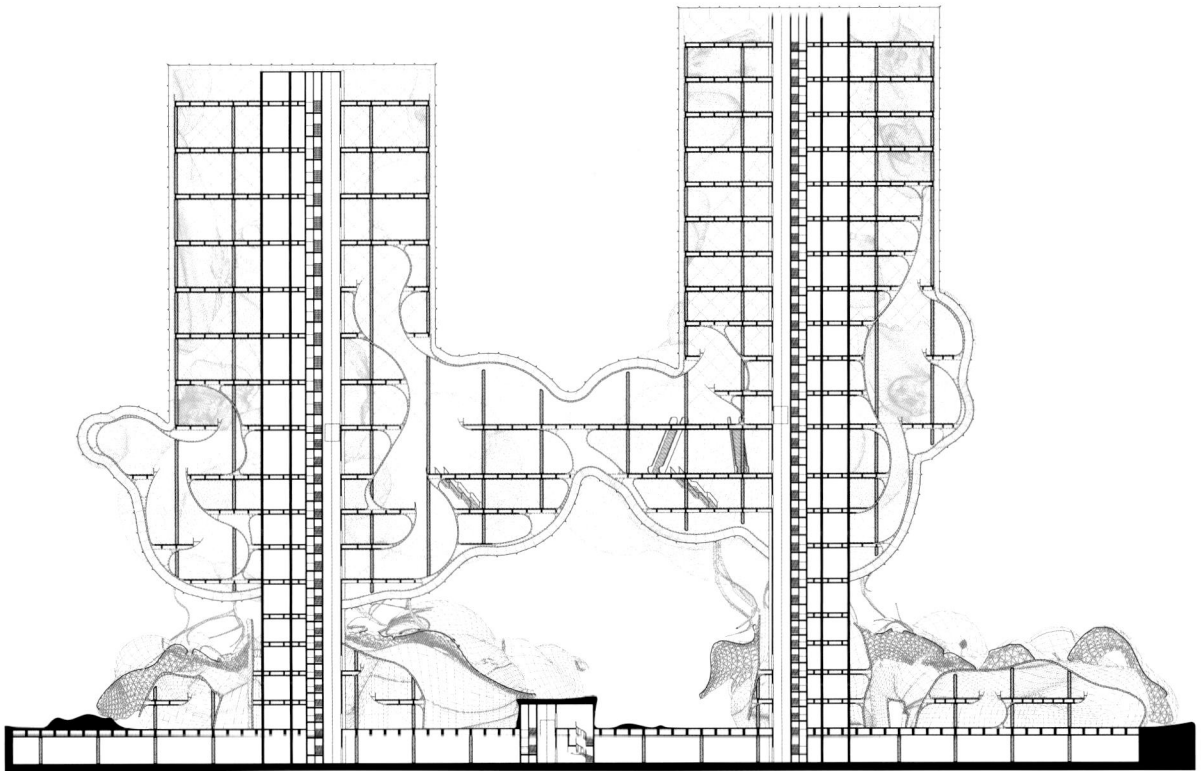

Section

Guggenheim Helsinki

The role of an art museum is to be not just a museum, but also a beacon of a society and its culture, achievements and aspirations. It represents a city, a country, a history and a future. This proposal for the Guggenheim Helsinki, therefore, aspires to be a permanent seismographer of society and its culture – in this way, architecture can be updated, revisited, modified. The notion of permanence tells us less about buildings and more about the societies that believe they are permanent when they are not. The collection of wooden display cases and glass boxes are part of this notion of architecture – what is captured is time itself, being tracked.

Location: Helsinki, Finland
Date: 2014
Programme: Competition

Related projects
Helsinki Library, 2012 (p. 70)
Taichung Cultural Centre, 2013 (p. 90)

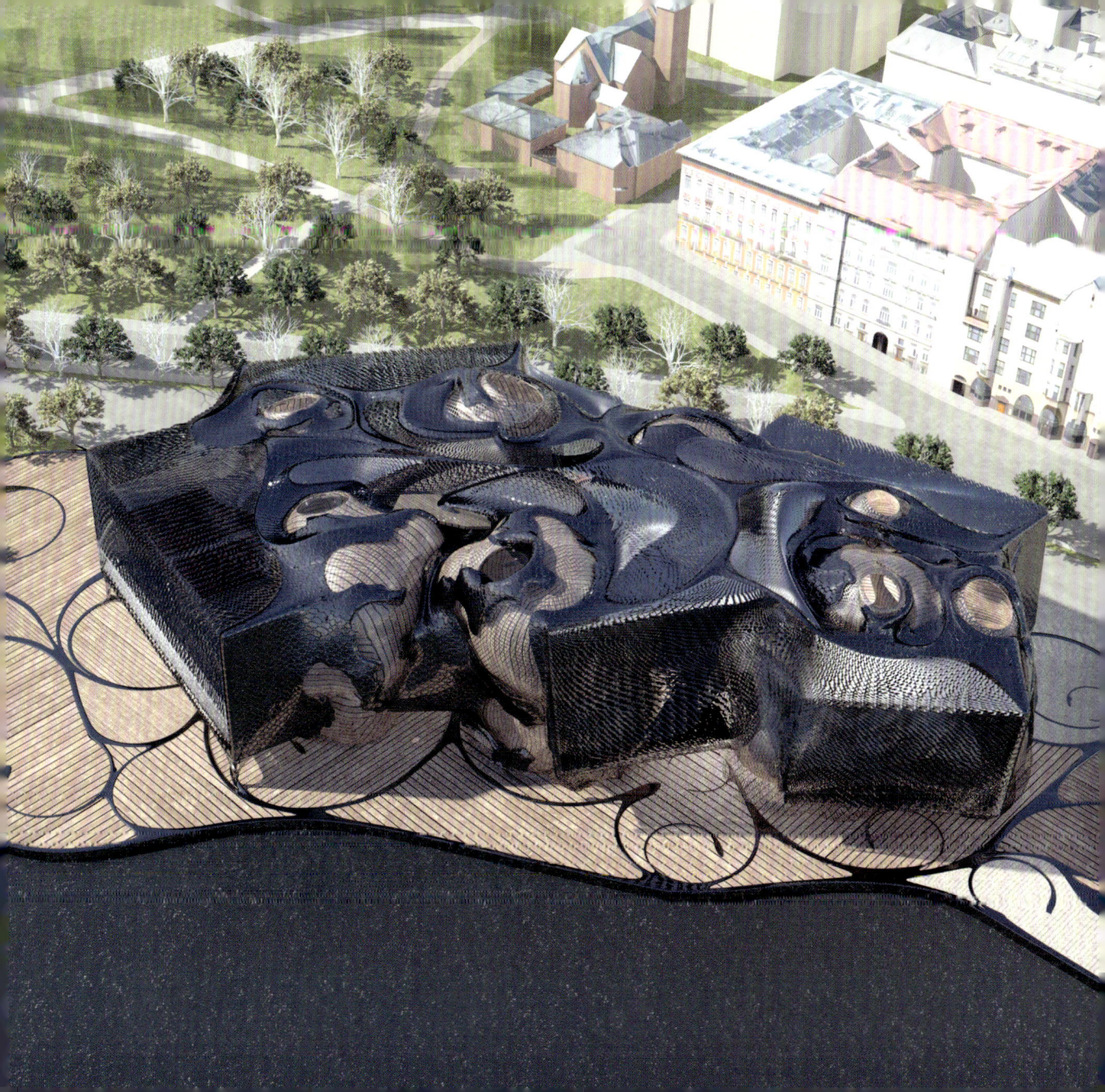

1 Garden
2 Gallery
3 Kitchen
4 Café

5 Atrium
6 Auditorium/theatre
7 Foyer
8 Restrooms

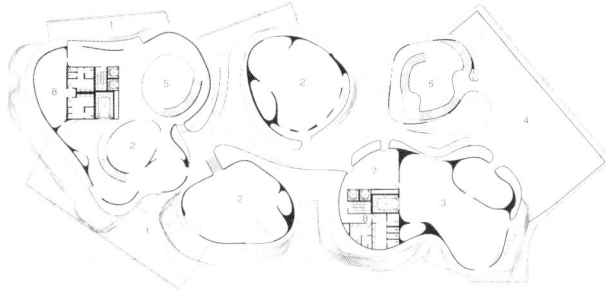

Floorplan – Level 2

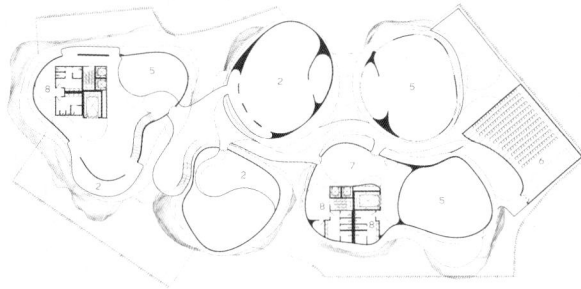

Floorplan – Level 4

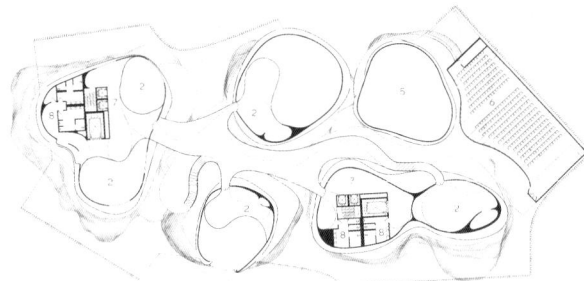

Floorplan – Level 5

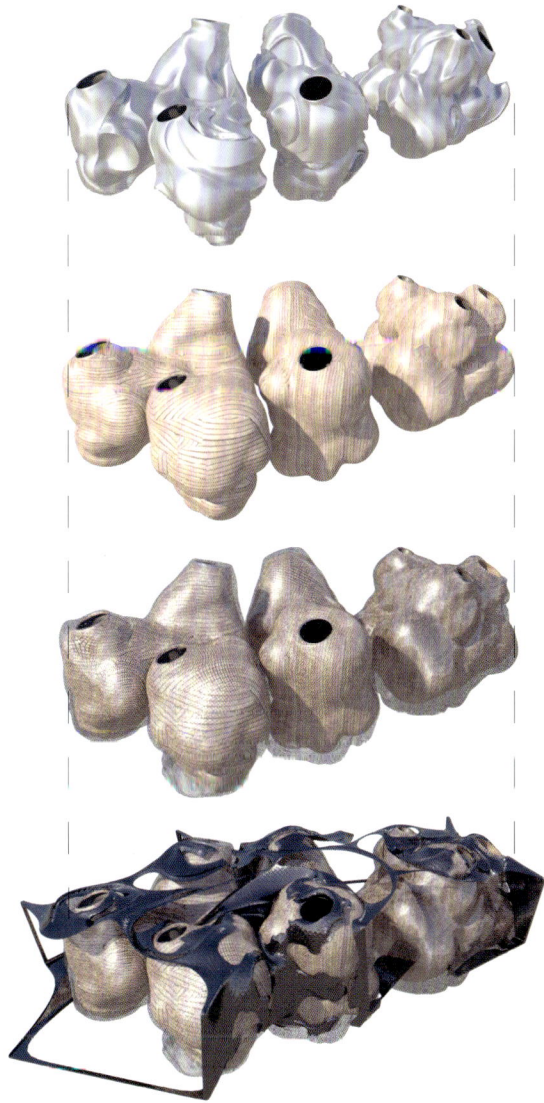

Instruments of Manner, 2009

Architecture has the power to modify and recode social behaviour. Form is not shaped by behaviour – rather, the opposite is true – so that design is always in the process of contaminating our rituals and daily routines. Formal mutations, like genetic distortions to familiar species, force us to rethink our everyday actions and to confront their inherent grotesqueness.

Date: 2009
Programme: Product design
Client: Alessi

Related projects
Instruments of Manner, 2010 (p. 108)
Instruments of Manner, 2012 (p. 124)
JP Morgan Chase Remote, 2013 (p. 126)

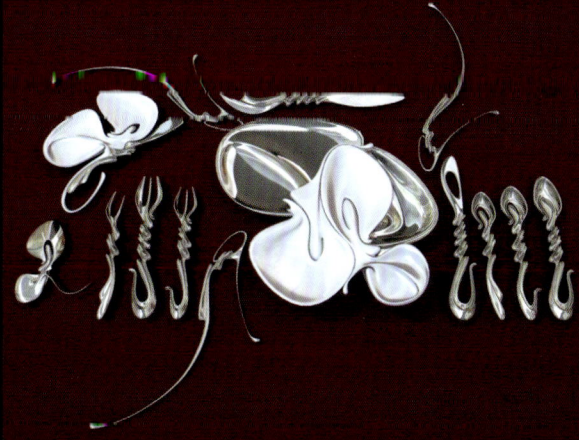

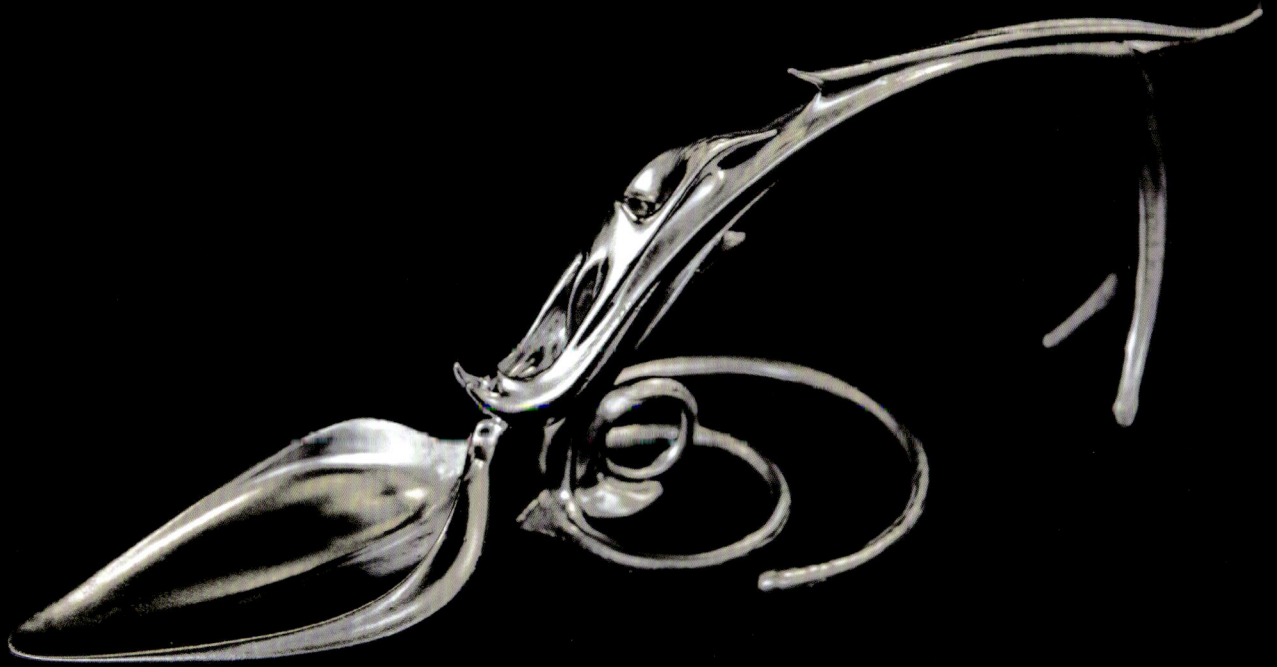

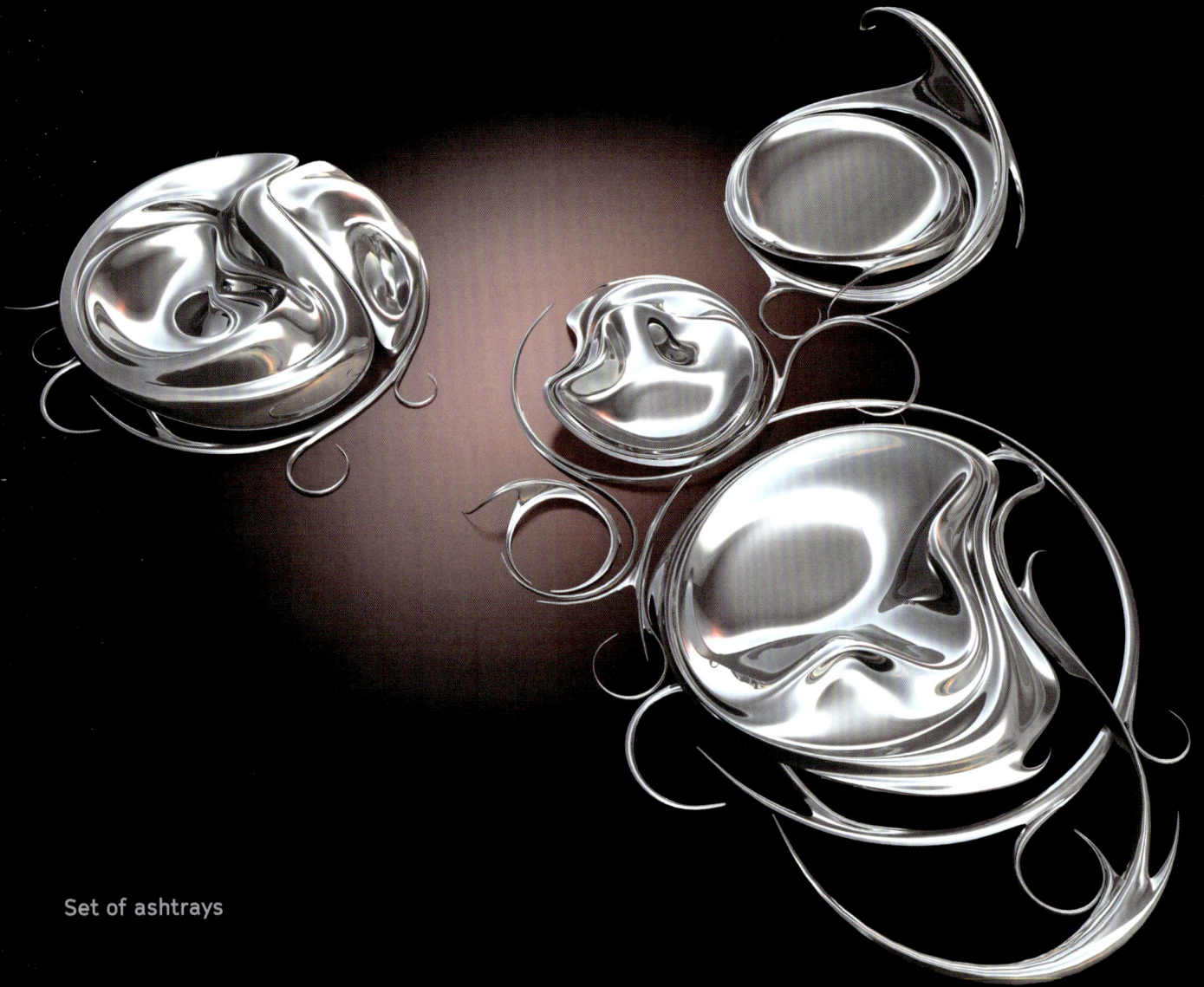

Set of ashtrays

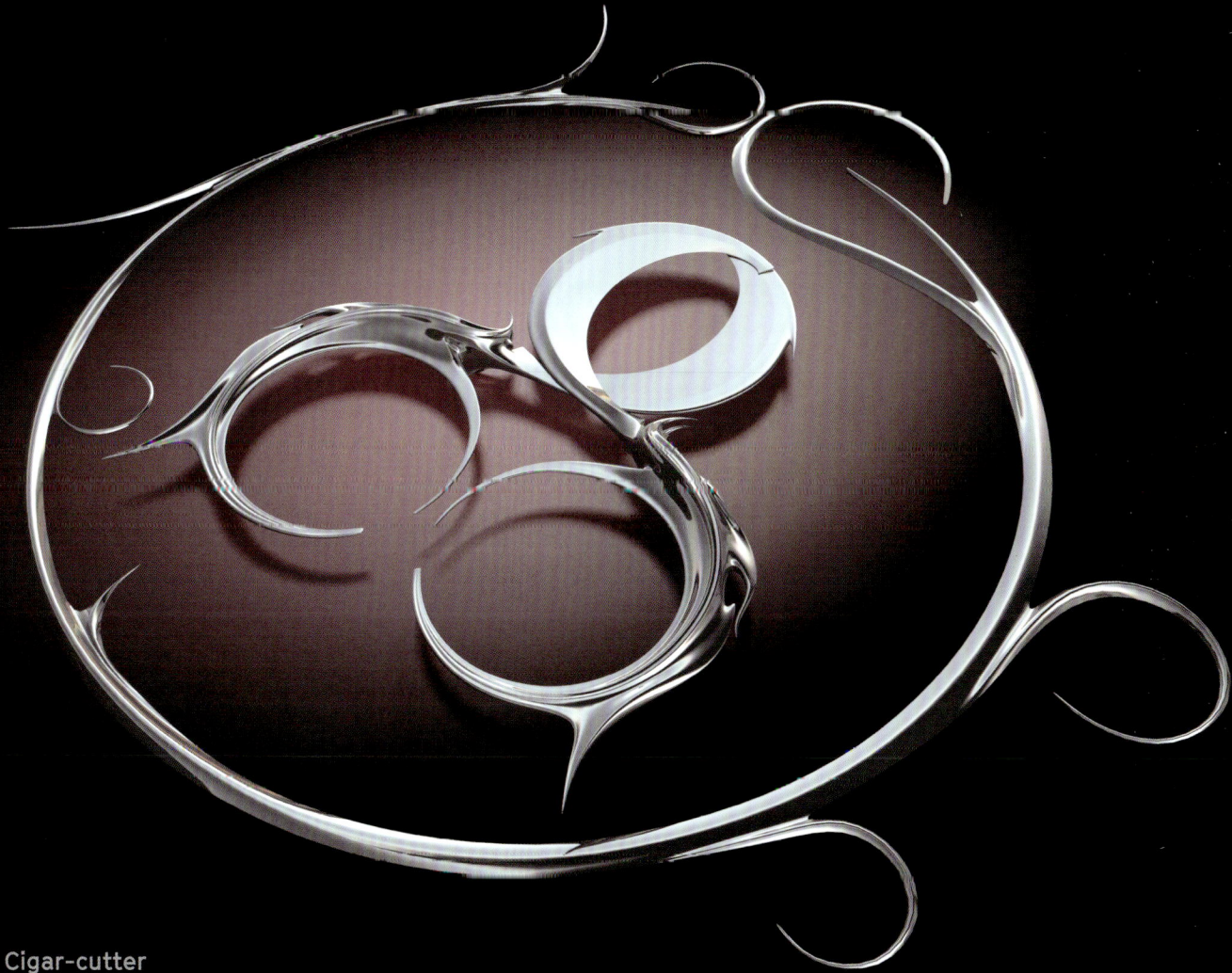

Cigar-cutter

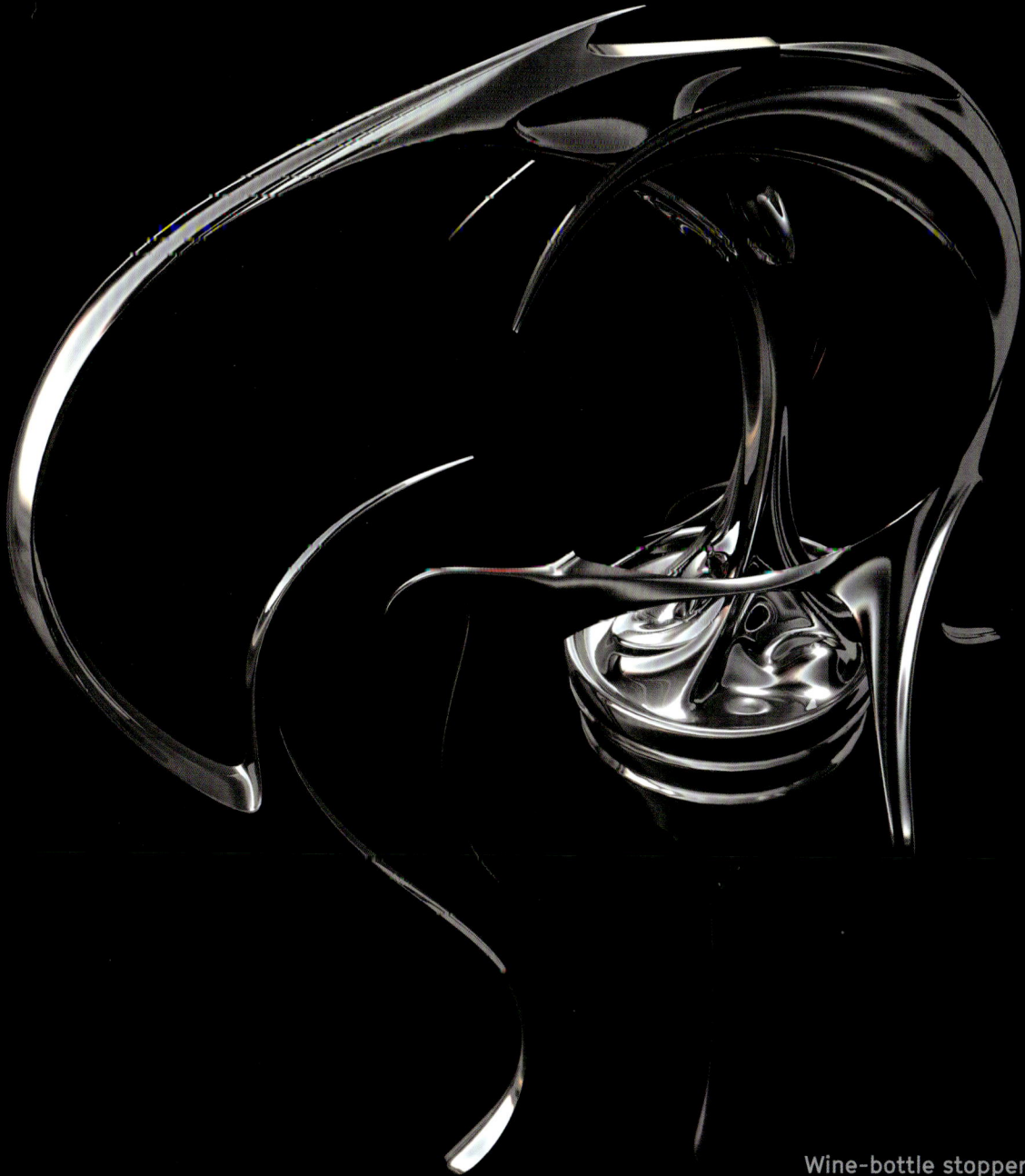

Wine-bottle stopper

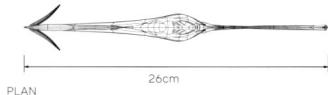

PLAN

26cm

SIDE

FRONT

9.3cm

Butter knife

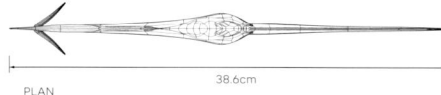

PLAN

38.6cm

SIDE

FRONT

9.3cm

Steak knife

PLAN

19.8cm

SIDE

FRONT

7.5cm

Small fork

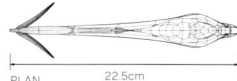

PLAN

22.5cm

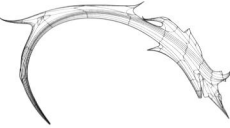

SIDE

FRONT

9.3cm

Dinner fork

PLAN

22.5cm

SIDE

FRONT

9.3cm

Serving spoon

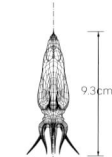

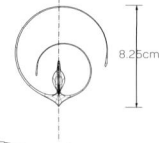

8.25cm

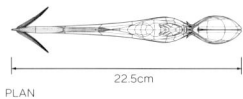

PLAN

22.5cm

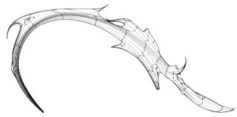

SIDE

FRONT

7.5cm

Olive spoon

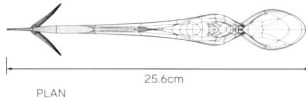

PLAN

25.6cm

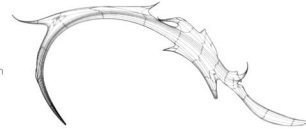

SIDE

FRONT

9.3cm

Spoon

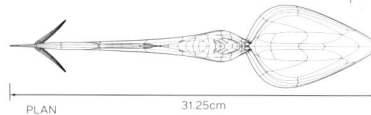

PLAN

31.25cm

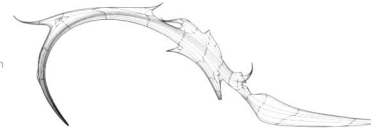

SIDE

FRONT

9.3cm

Serving spoon

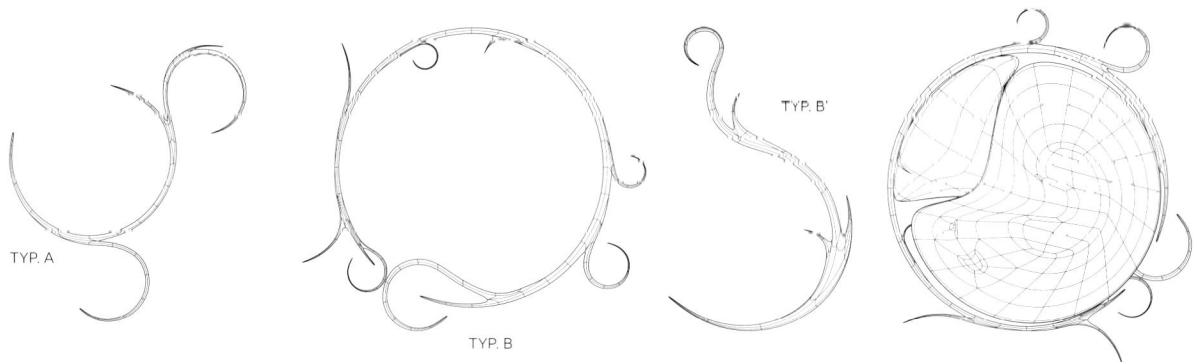

TYP. A

TYP. B

TYP. B'

Table ornament

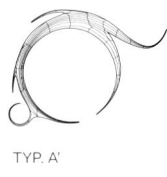

TYP. A'

20.5cm

Tray (open)

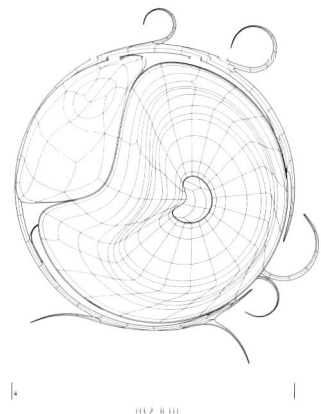

Tray (closed)

Spoon (detail)

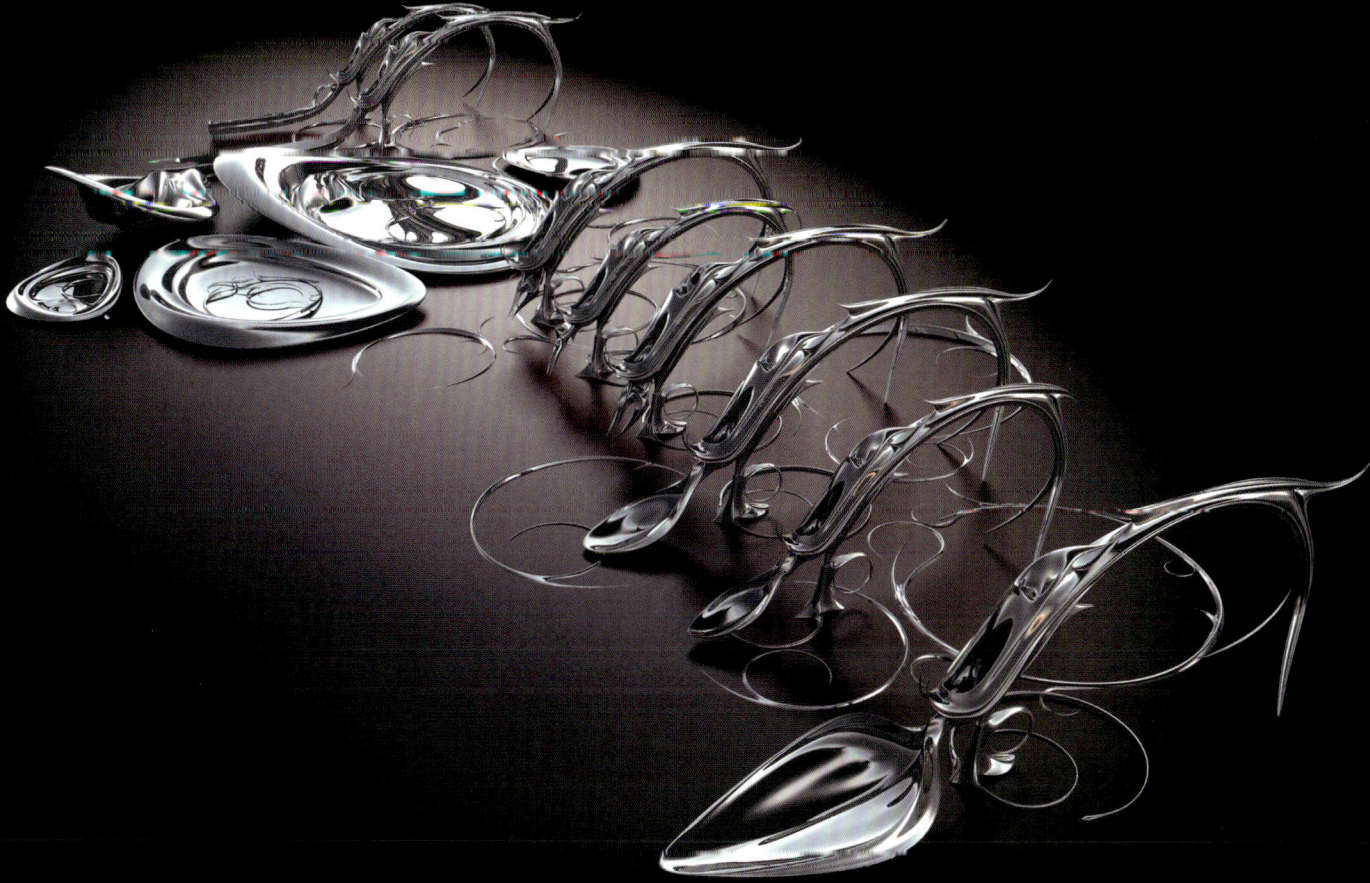

Silverware set

Silverware set

Silverware set

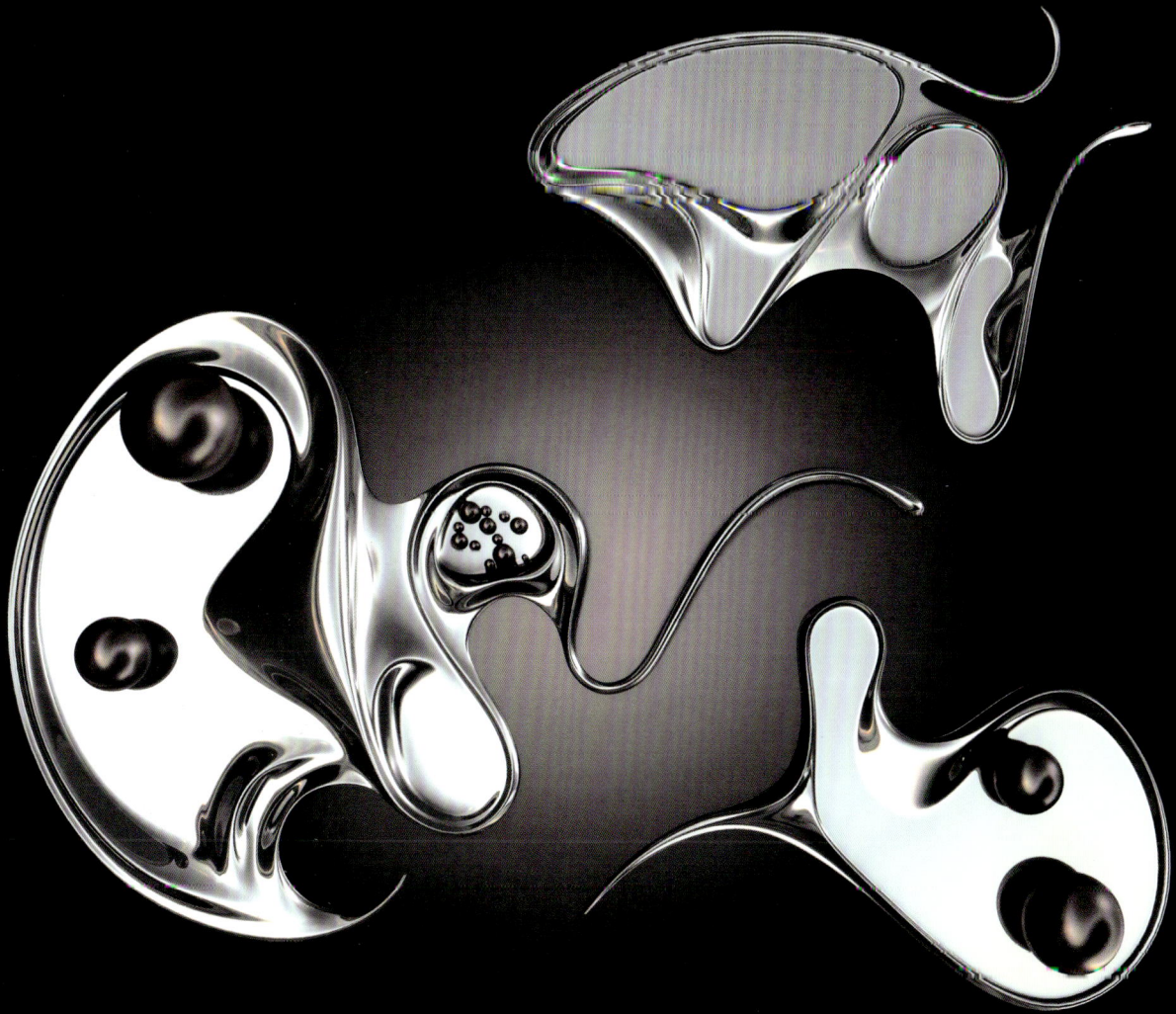

Plate set (open)

REAR

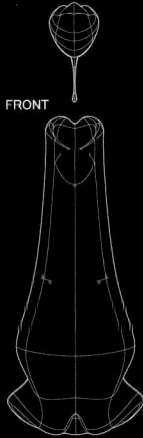

FRONT

SIDE

12.5cm

10.3cm

ELEVATION

PLAN

Cup

FRONT

28.5cm

10.3cm

PLAN

Half-bottle (750 ml)

SIDE

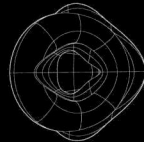

12.3cm

PLAN

FRONT

16.5cm

10.3cm

PLAN

Half-bottle (375 ml)

SIDE

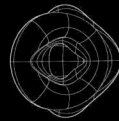

12.3cm

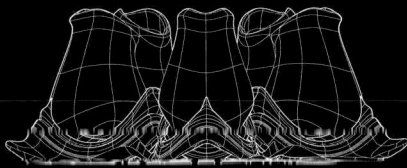

12.5cm

32.5cm

Bottles

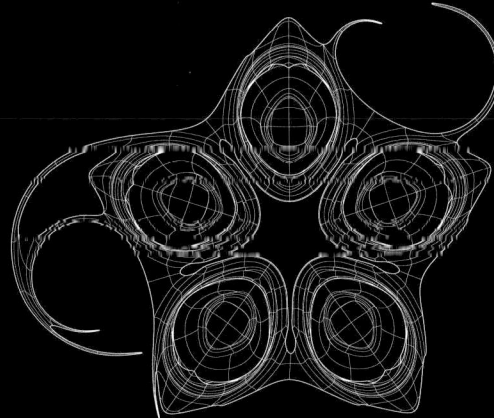

32.5cm

Ornamental base

Instruments of Manner, 2012

This tableware mutation builds on our previous collections for Alessi (pp. 106, 108). It takes on the concept of the 'literal' in a simpler manner of production.

Date: 2012
Programme: Product design
Client: Alessi

Related projects
Instruments of Manner, 2009 (p. 106)
Instruments of Manner, 2010 (p. 108)
JP Morgan Chase Remote, 2013 (p. 126)

JP Morgan Chase Remote

We always try to find a way to design that is not all about efficiency, to make an argument for completely unnecessary and non-functional formal manoeuvres. Design is speculative, so that it is not so much about a single, refined statement as it is about an evolution across time in thought and of form. Each piece of furniture, each cup of coffee, can begin to be developed in a way that is not just about efficiency, but also gives an efficiency of comfort or an efficiency of experience.

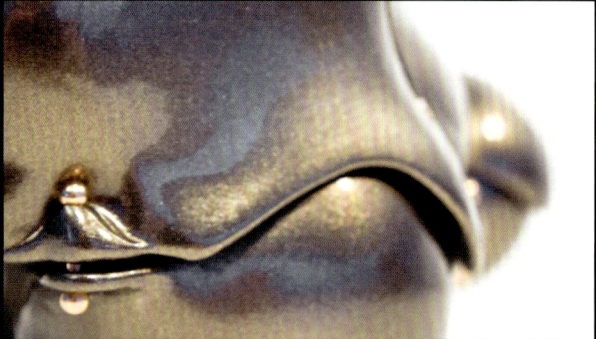

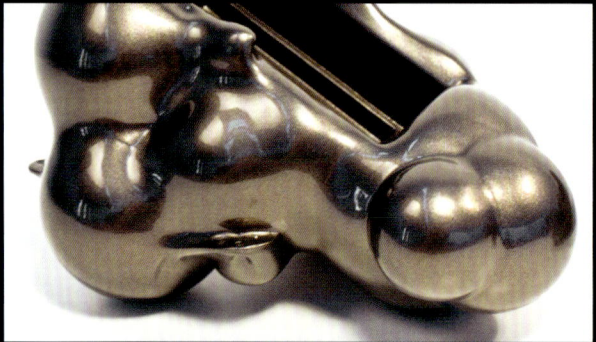

Location: Los Angeles, California
Date: 2013

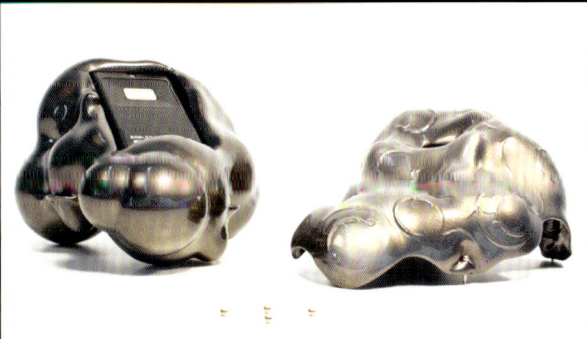

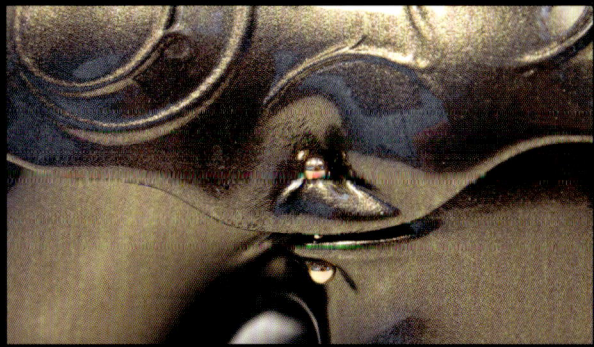

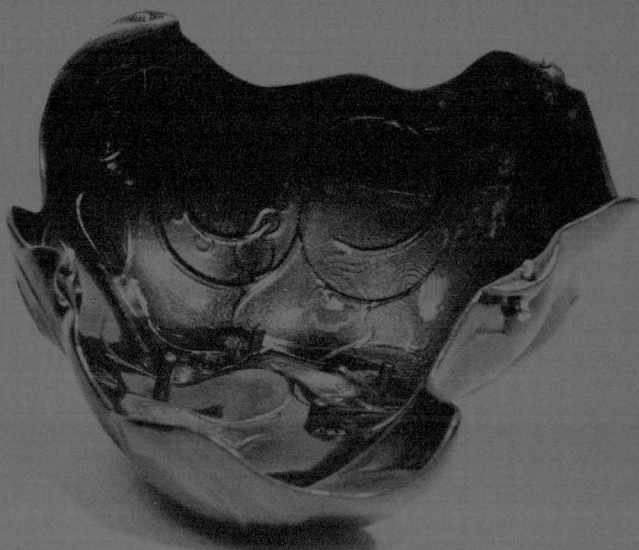

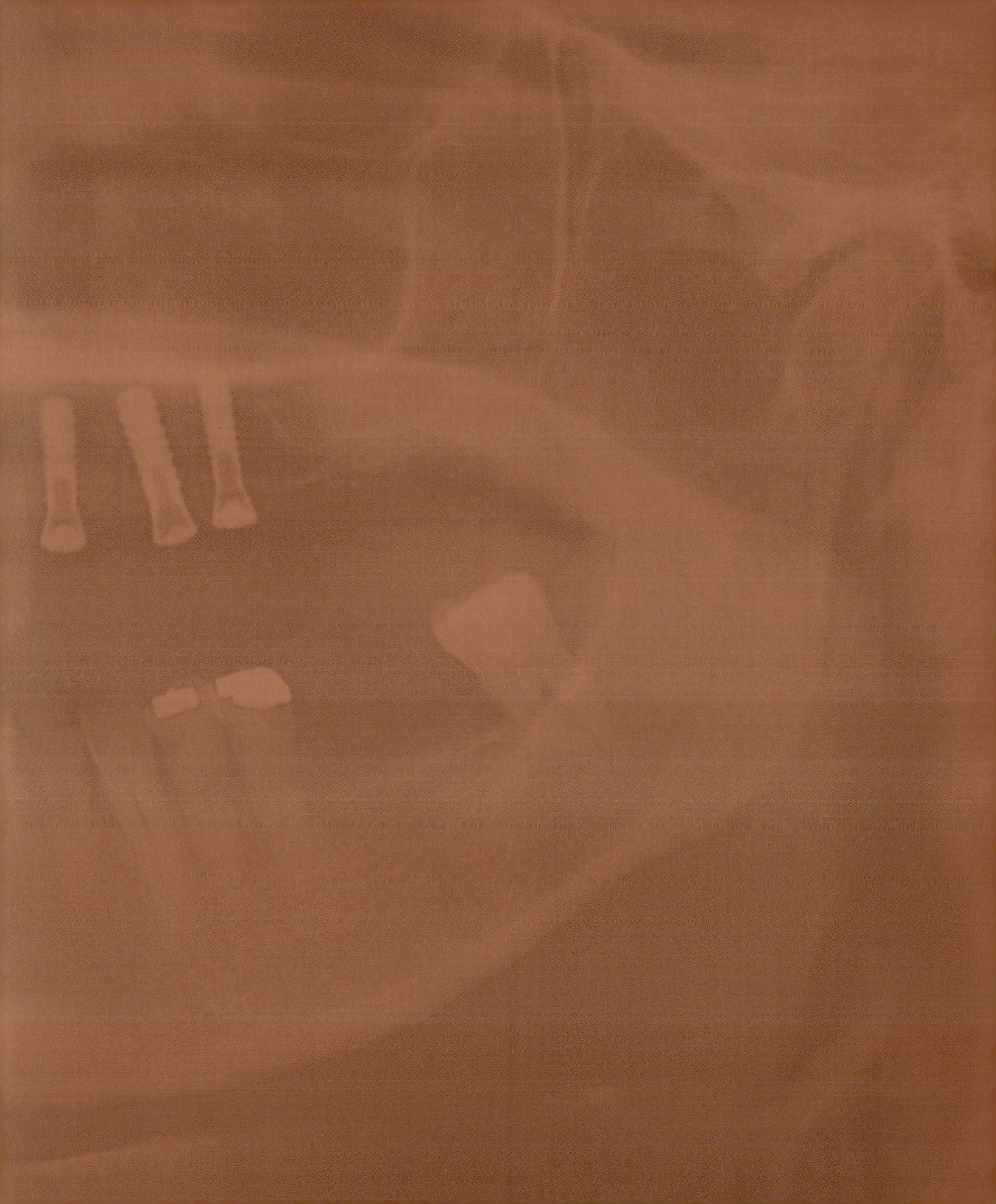

Le Cru et le Cuit:
The Feral Cultivation of HDA-X

Marcelyn Gow & Florencia Pita

The silver ashes and black char set against the orange volcanic glow of a culinary tableau created by Argentinian chef and grill-master Francis Mallmann, the comic darkness that permeates

Origin Myths

the writing of Osvaldo Soriano and the sartorial ferocity of Alexander McQueen's fashion designs form a lineage that draws on formal dexterity coupled with feral cultivation. The architecture of Hernán Díaz Alonso adheres to this lineage,

and exemplifies the contrast between the raw and refined. *Le Cru et Le Cuit* (*The Raw and the Cooked*), the first volume of Claude Lévi-Strauss's *Mythologiques* (1964), is a meditation on how cultivation transforms the raw into something finished or refined. Drawing on a series of opposing qualities, Lévi-Strauss examines the sensory aspects of myth and how we mobilize the instruments we use to form concepts through it. The work of HDA-X shifts the opposition between raw and refined, creating an unlikely admixture of the two that forcefully displays itself in various increments and scales, ranging from the tines of Instruments of Manner (pp. 106–25; awaiting a feast prepared by Mallmann himself, perhaps), the serpentine trajectory of Sant Adrià de Besòs (p. 154) or the ornate stanchions that comprise TDA 21_2.0 (p. 240) and Conexion Barcelona (p. 204) to the shredded volumes of the Teatro Colon (p. 282).

The origin myths that linger in the studio's projects conjure scenes in which monsters repose in Pitch Black (p. 164), and the inert still life as the rendition of a possible reality is traded for the sanguine quality of Still Flesh (p. 304). The tropes of the classical still life become animated and populate the imagination with creatures that simultaneously reside in the architecture, and are the architecture itself. Similar to the manner in which Soriano moulds his characters to appear at various turns as comic or tragic, HDA-X's characters resurface in different guises as they migrate from one site to another. A scythe-like hook that is the scale of a claw or beak in the corkscrew or cigar-cutter from Instruments of Manner, 2010 (p. 108) metamorphoses into a room-sized enclosure in TBA 21_2.0. A piece extracted from the jungle of sinewy forms that encase Sant Adrià de Besòs transmutes into a series of columnar protrusions in the Rusuupuisto extension (p. 246). The tendrils of the Seroussi Bench (p. 226) could also take on a more domesticated mien at the dining table as the silverware set from Instruments of Manner.

Convulsive Beauty

In *L'Amour fou* (1937), André Breton declared that the 'convulsive beauty' exhibited by Surrealist works owed in no small degree to what he called the *explosante-fixe*, or the qualities of a fixed explosion of movement. Such movement arrested in the act of becoming animates the buoyant spaces of the Helsinki Library (p. 70), through a detached gaze that falls on its reflective surfaces. Refracted images of the building's host city mingle with details of the architecture itself. The overall impression is one of *explosante-fixe*. The levitating act performed by the Taichung Cultural Centre (p. 90) produces the impression that the buildings are only tenuously anchored to their physical site, and will drift away like helium-filled balloons. The Budapest Museum (p. 270) is a building that literally effervesces out of the landscape in which it sits. All of these projects emanate the convulsive qualities that make us pause to reconsider the ways in which we inhabit and move through the world.

Barbecue & Rituals

The Patagonian barbecue prepared by Francis Mallmann is indelibly marked both by his training in the culinary arts in the kitchens of Paris and by his profound knowledge of indigenous cooking techniques. The ritual of cooking the food not only transforms it or renders it finished for consumption, but the act of cooking also becomes part of the meal itself. Ritual is also evoked by Díaz Alonso's architectural creations. The act of *preparing* the architecture can be traced through the precision of cutting, cleaving, inflating, aerating and rupturing to produce forms that are the literal yield of these procedures. The ashes that remain after the feast are a transmutation of raw into refined, and back again. The coexistence of these seemingly opposed qualities in HDA-X's work occurs as an architectural vision that is processed through a technological lens using disciplinary expertise. An architecture emerges that appears to be undomesticated yet refined, cultivated yet feral.

Technology / Craft

SPECULATION

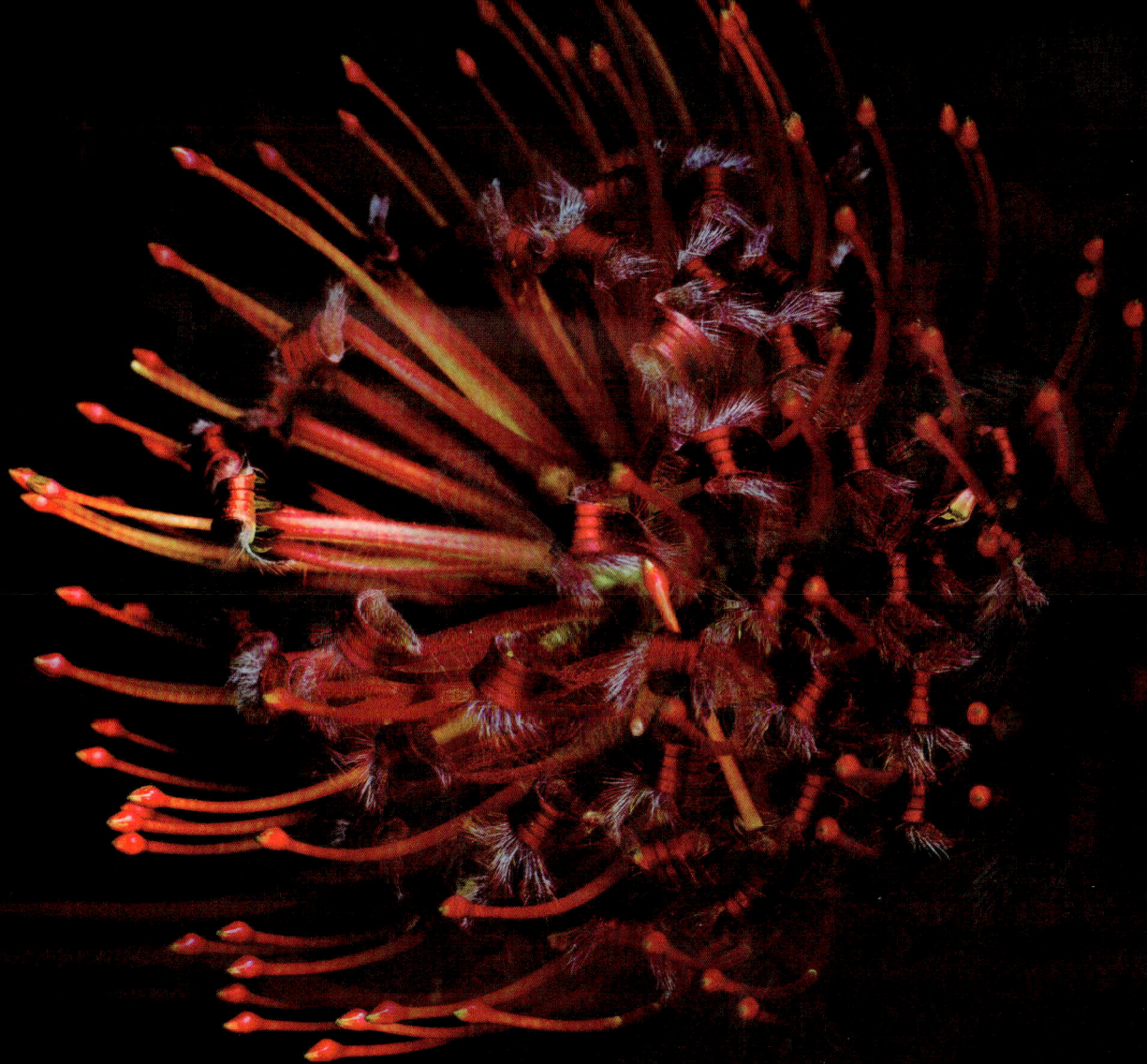

Tabakalera

The International Competition for the Architectural Renovation of Tabakalera was launched in 2008, with the aim of converting the former tobacco factory in San Sebastián into an International Centre of Contemporary Culture specializing in audiovisual culture. Rather than working from the idea of building types, we developed the concept of 'species', creating a new, dynamic logic that allows the project and the city to develop a playful relationship. Our design is not based on an organization of functions, but on the generation of sensations through cells that are the multiplying producer for the building. The addition also operates as a prosthesis – adding, transforming, but not replacing – producing a dialogue between history and the past.

Location: San Sebastián, Spain
Date: 2008
Programme: Museum

Related projects
PS1 MoMA, 2005 (p. 28)
Sant Adrià de Besòs, 2014 (p. 154)
Rusuupuisto, 2015 (p. 246)

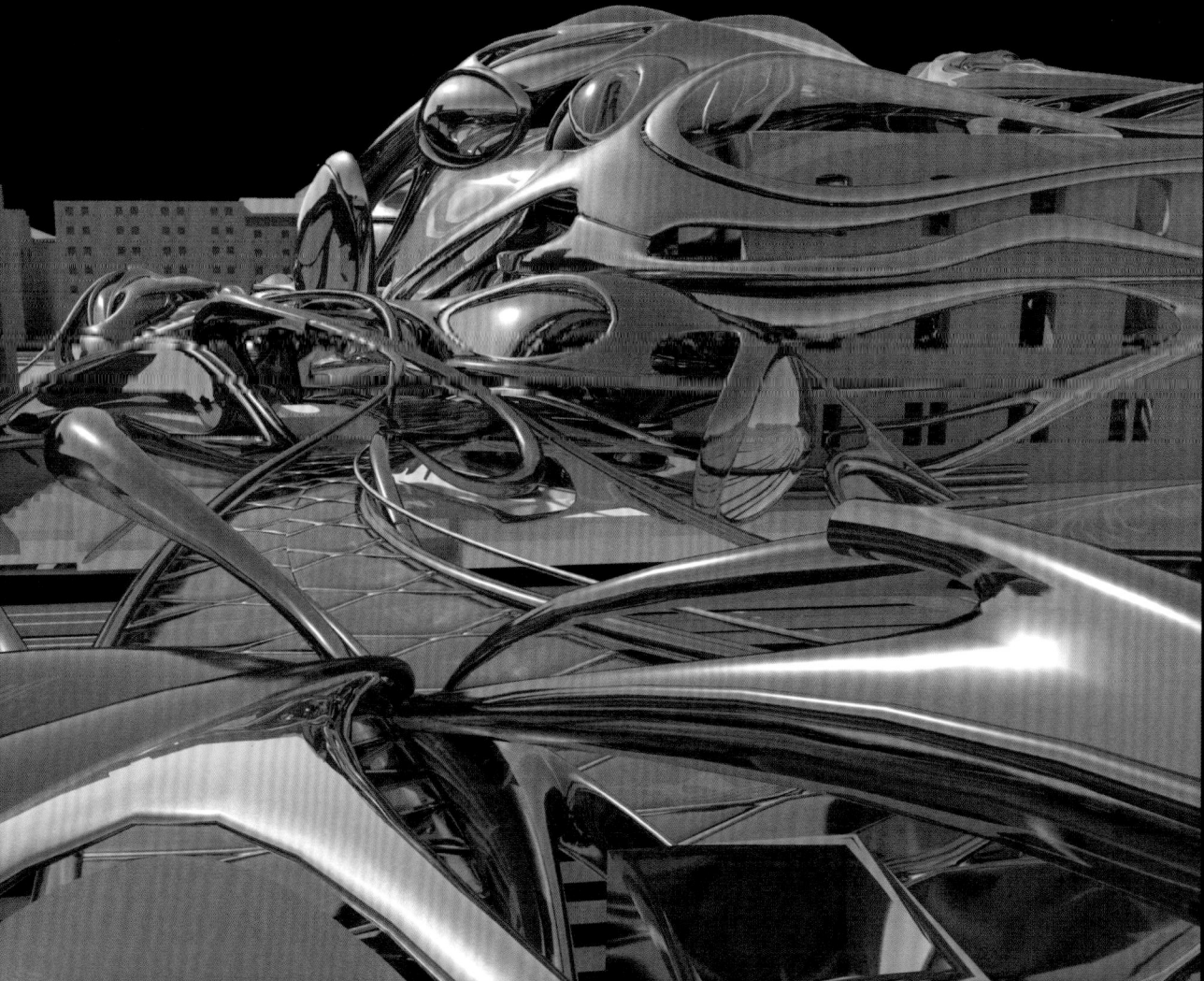

Sequence_A   0.1   0.2   0.3

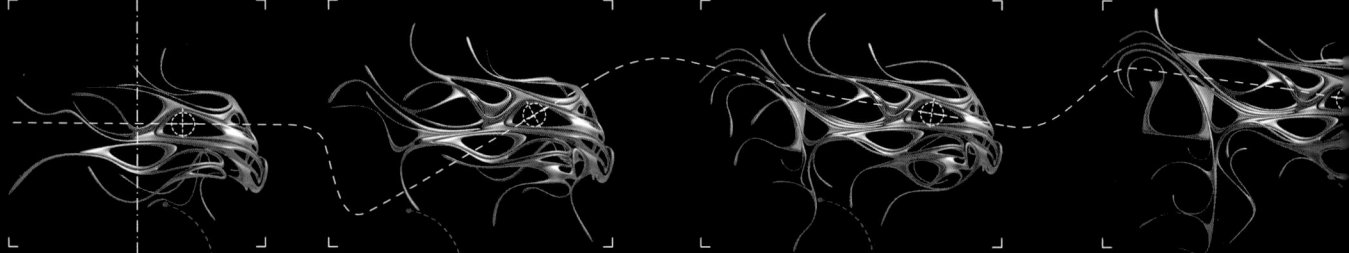

Sequence_B   0.1   0.2   0.3

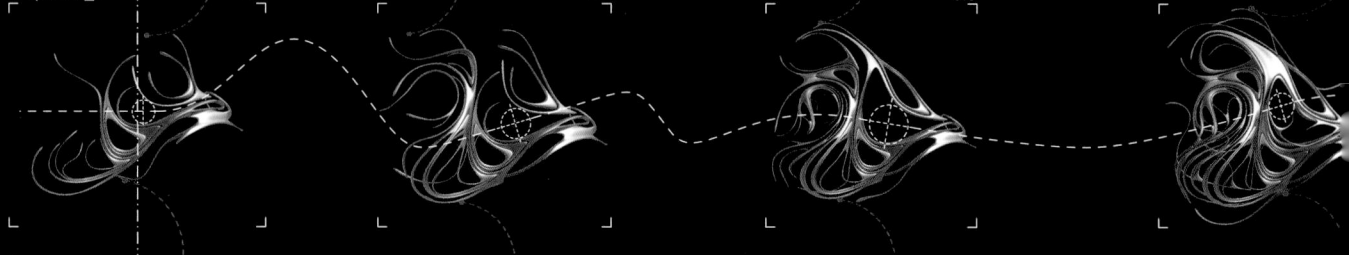

Sequence_C   0.1   0.2   0.3

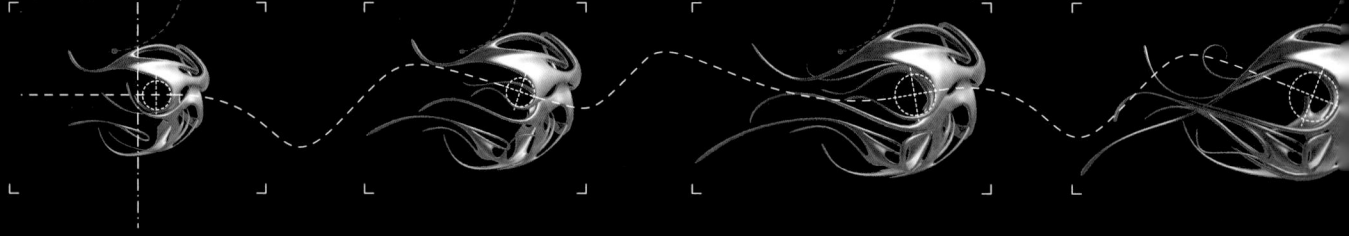

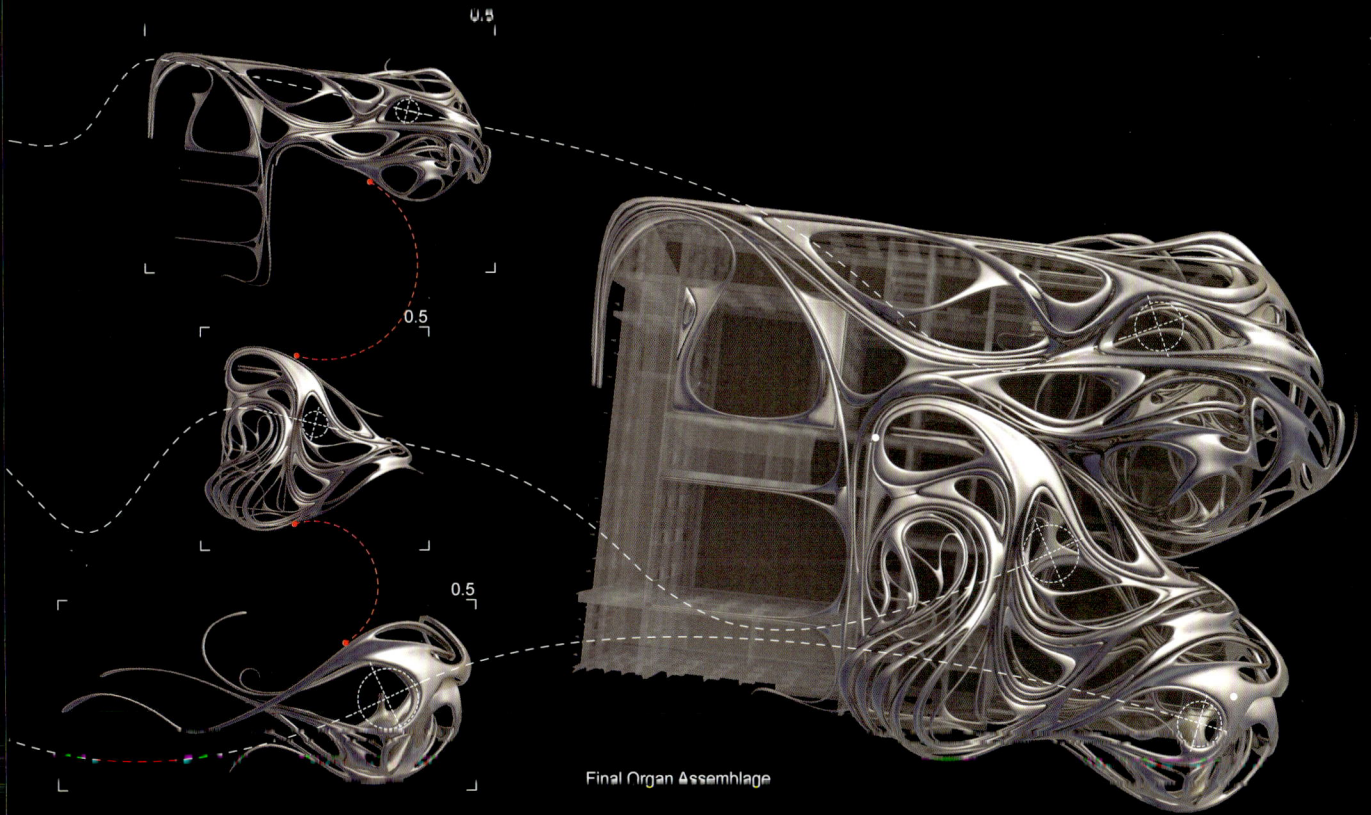

0.5

0.5

0.5

Final Organ Assemblage

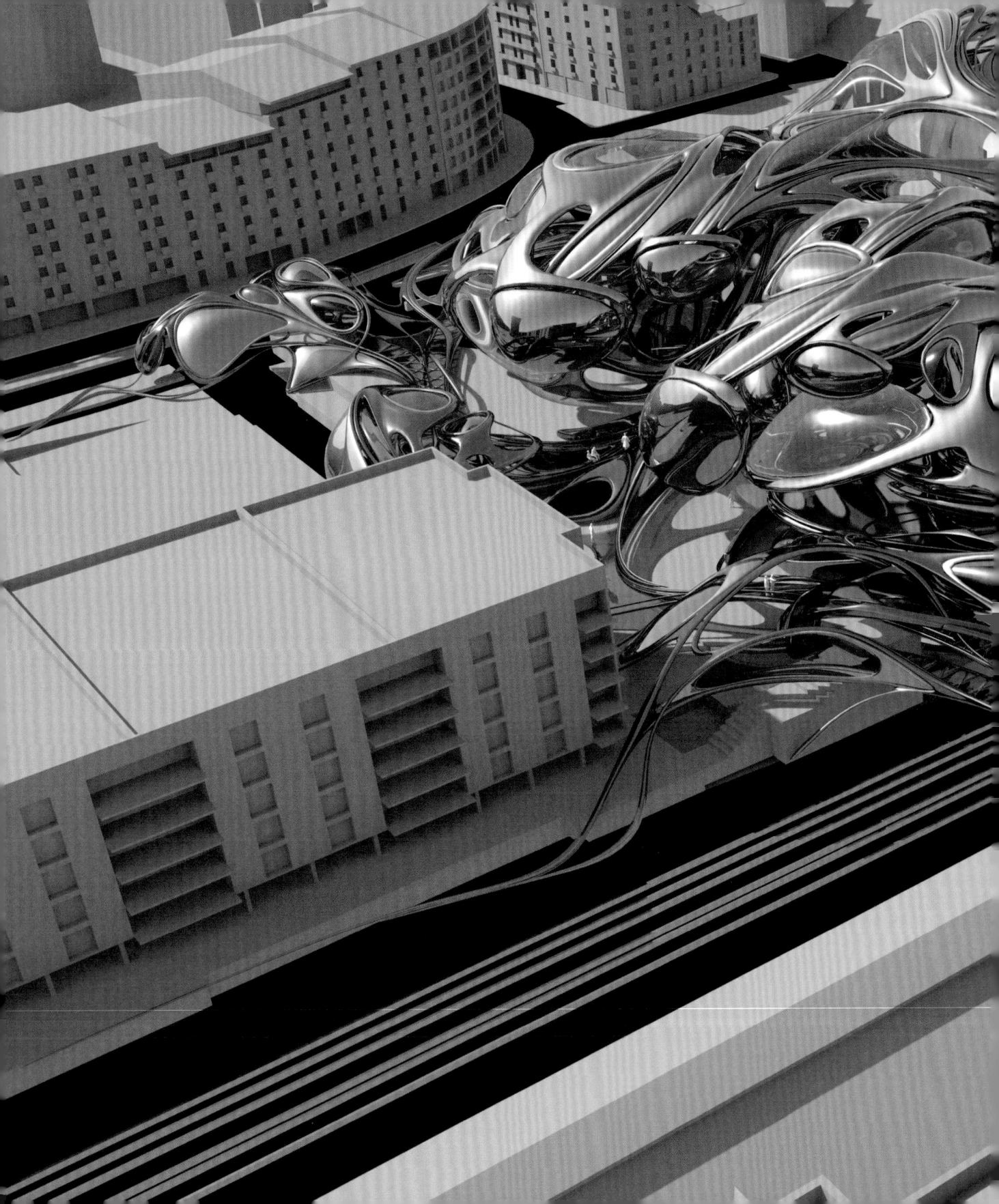

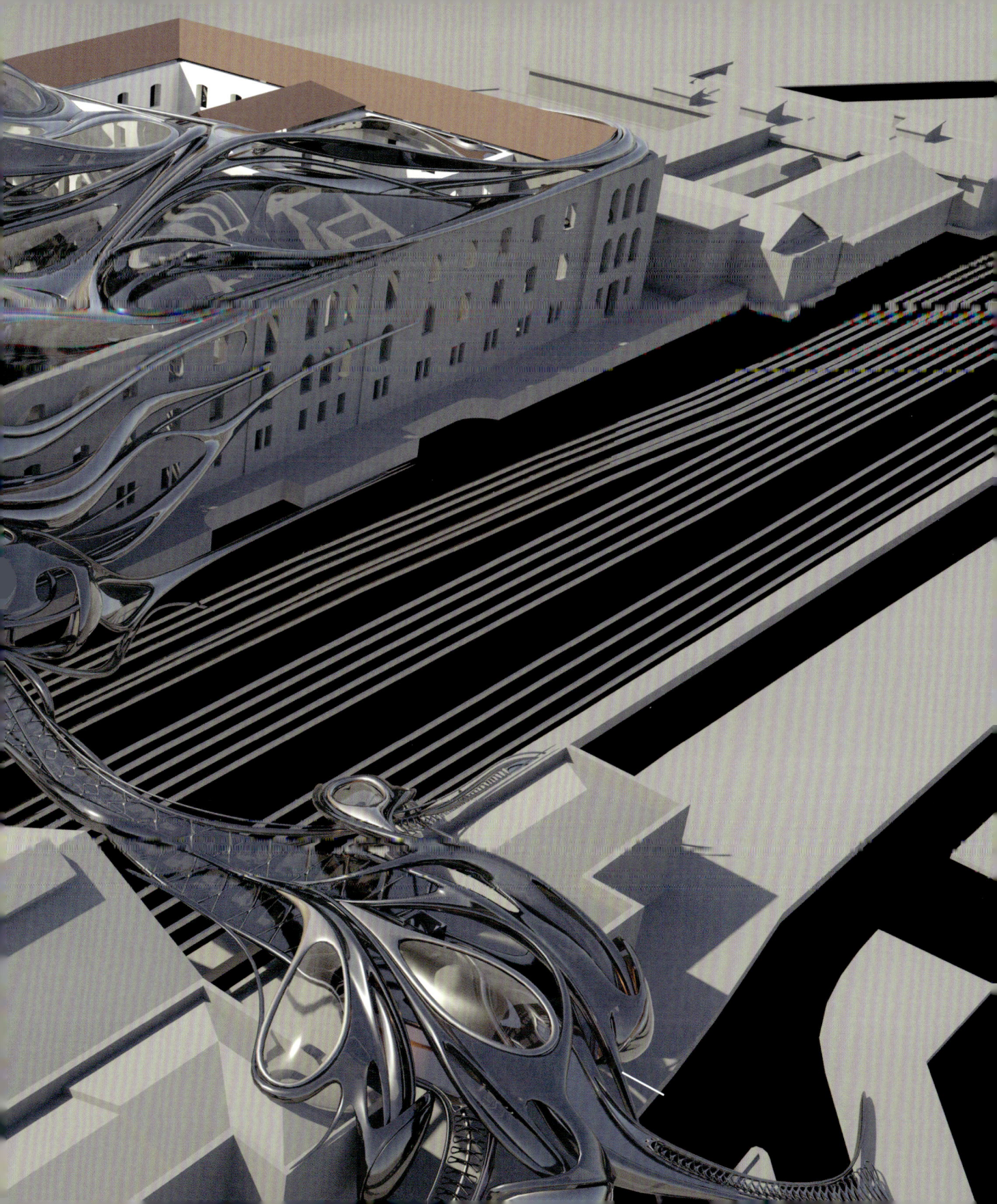

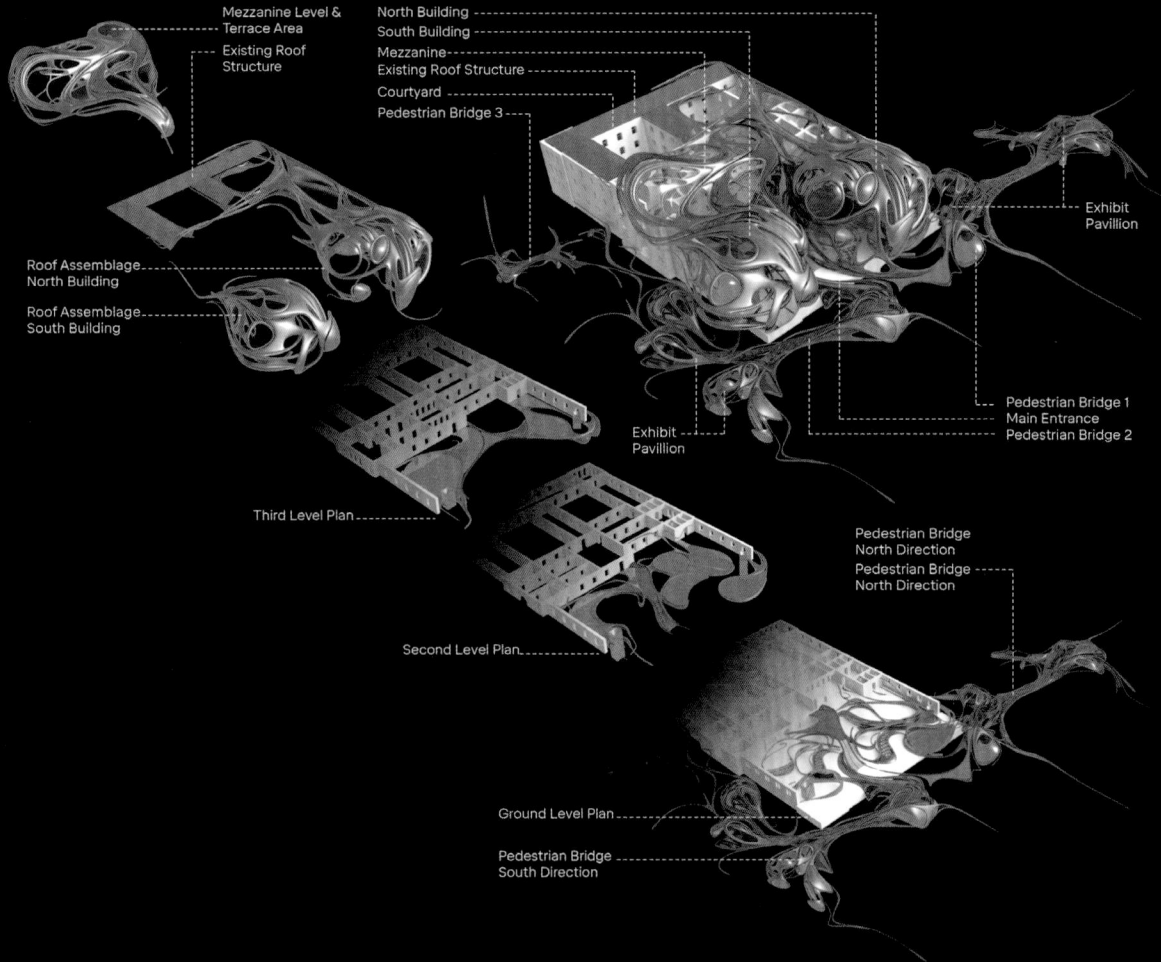

Mezzanine Level &
Terrace Area

Existing Roof
Structure

North Building

South Building

Mezzanine

Existing Roof Structure

Courtyard

Pedestrian Bridge 3

Roof Assemblage
North Building

Roof Assemblage
South Building

Exhibit
Pavillion

Pedestrian Bridge 1

Main Entrance

Pedestrian Bridge 2

Exhibit
Pavillion

Third Level Plan

Pedestrian Bridge
North Direction

Pedestrian Bridge
North Direction

Second Level Plan

Ground Level Plan

Pedestrian Bridge
South Direction

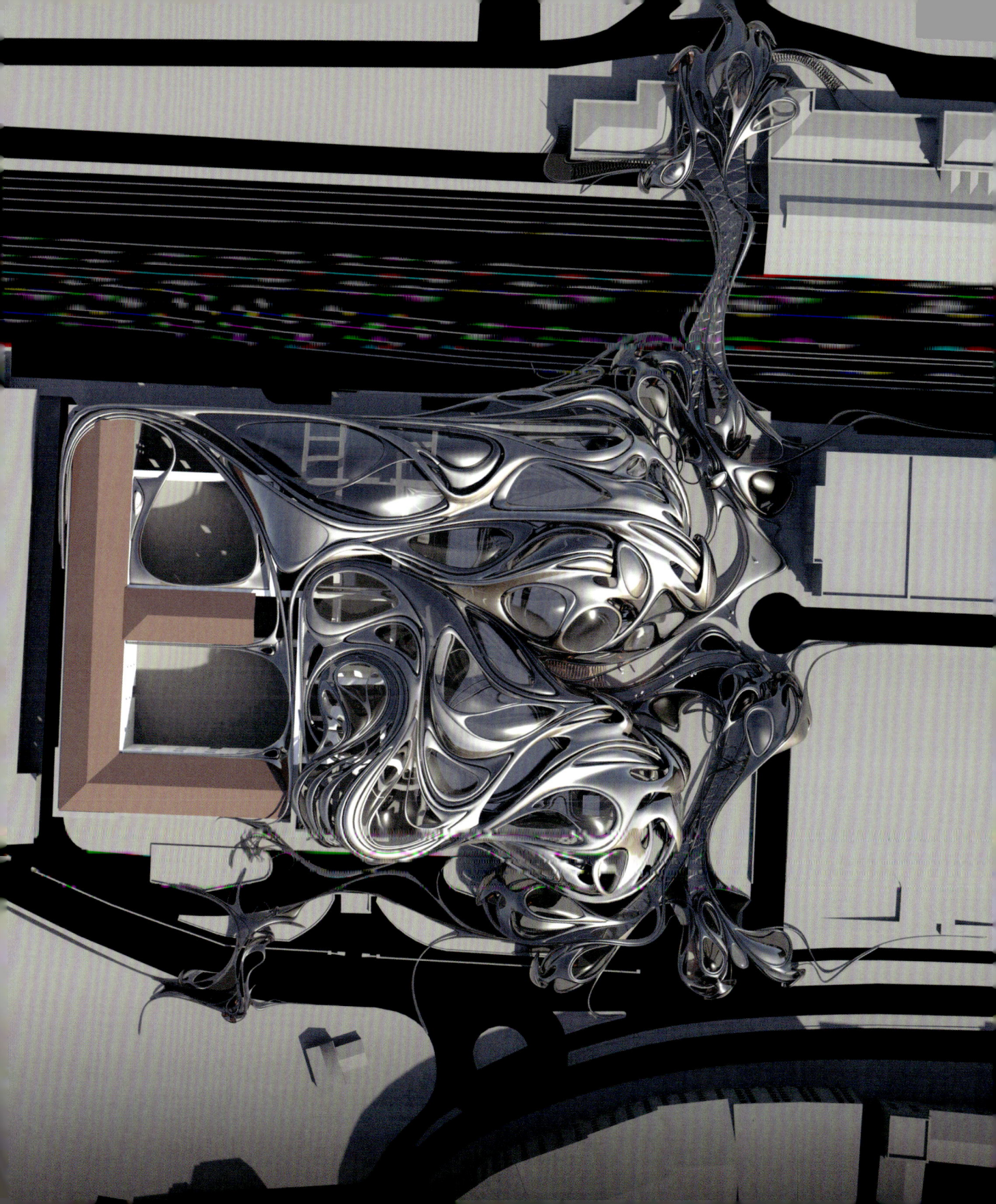

1.1   Multipurpose room   1.9   Storage
1.2   Dressing rooms   1.10 Auditorium
1.3   Control rooms   1.11 Project booth
1.4   Offices   1.12 Interpretation booth
1.5   Current news   1.13 Classrooms
1.6   Snack bar   1.14 Free consultation area
1.7   Catering space   1.15 Consultation stations
1.8   TB café   1.16 Silent zone

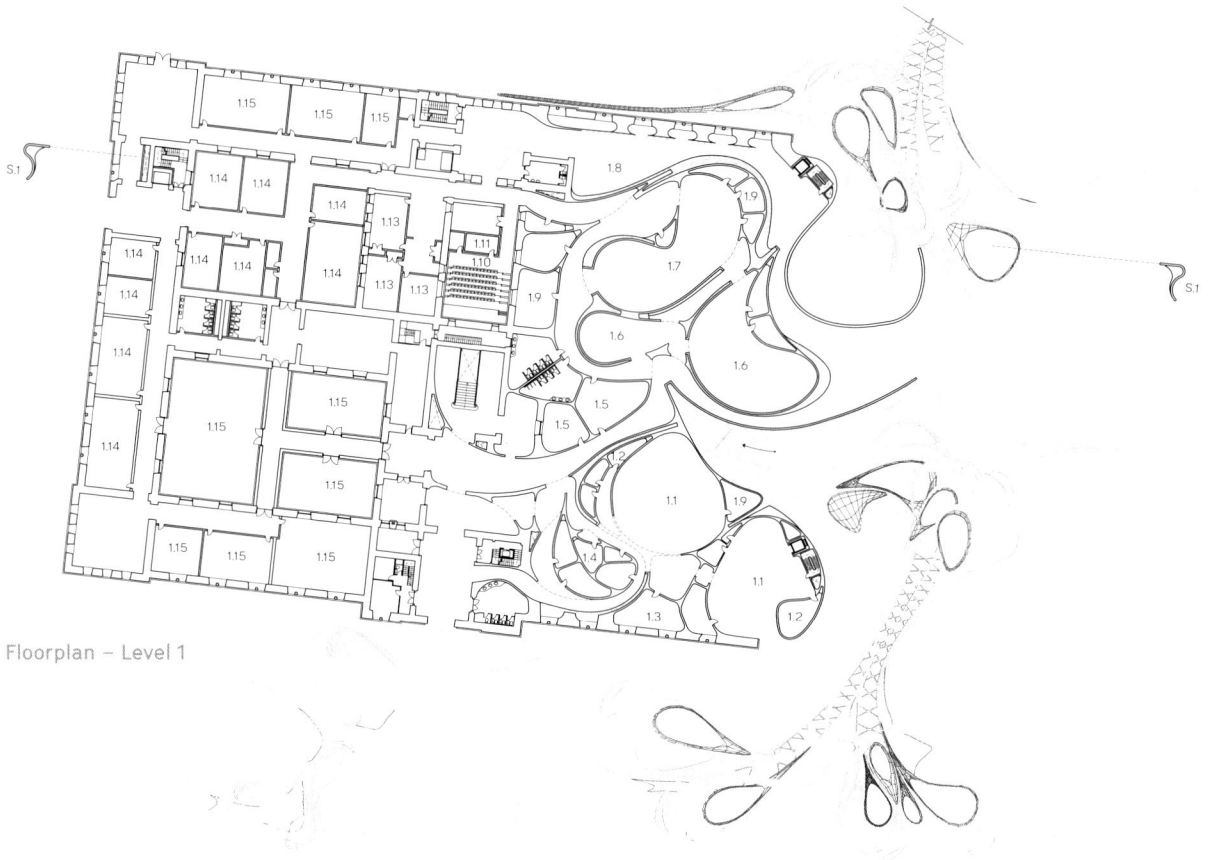

Floorplan – Level 1

3.1   Exhibition galleries
3.2   Storage
3.3   Library / documentation
3.4   Tech / restoration area
3.5   Archives
3.6   General management

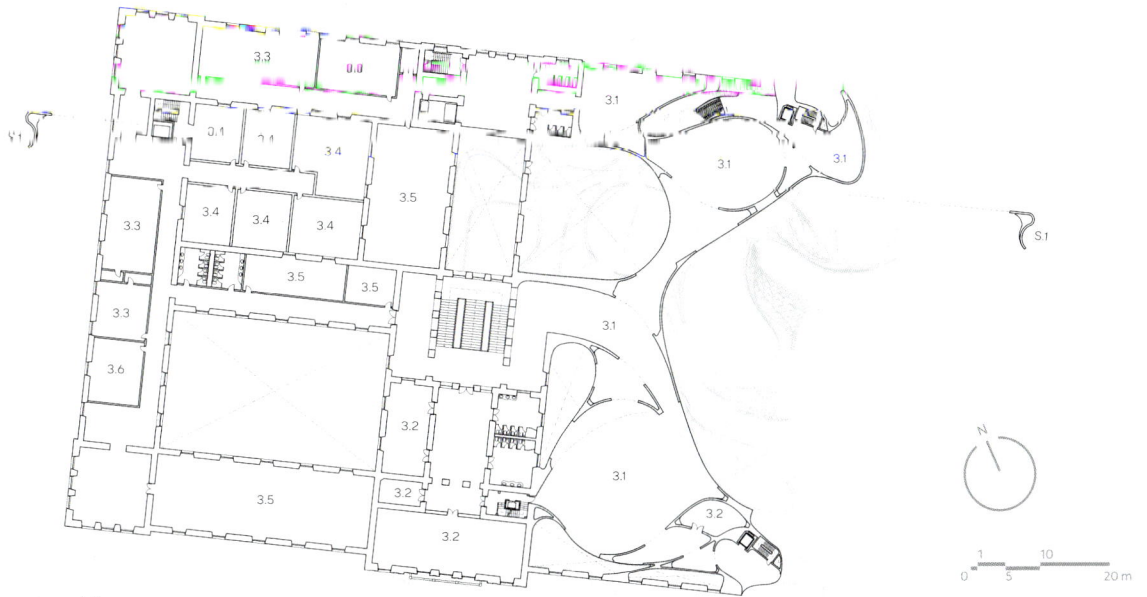

Floorplan – Level 3

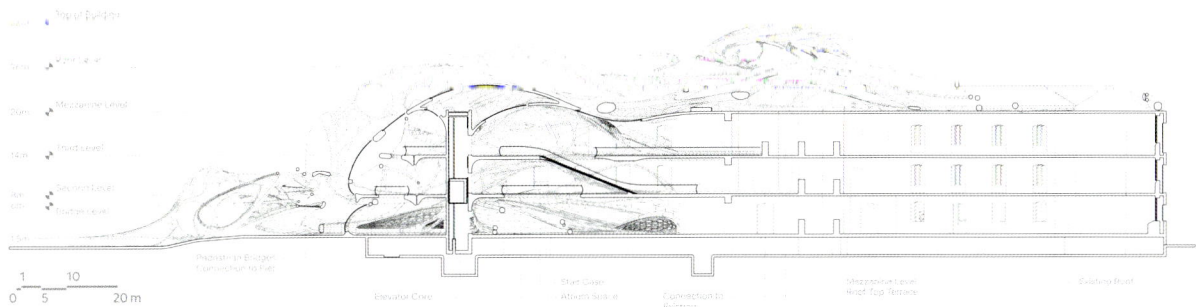

Section

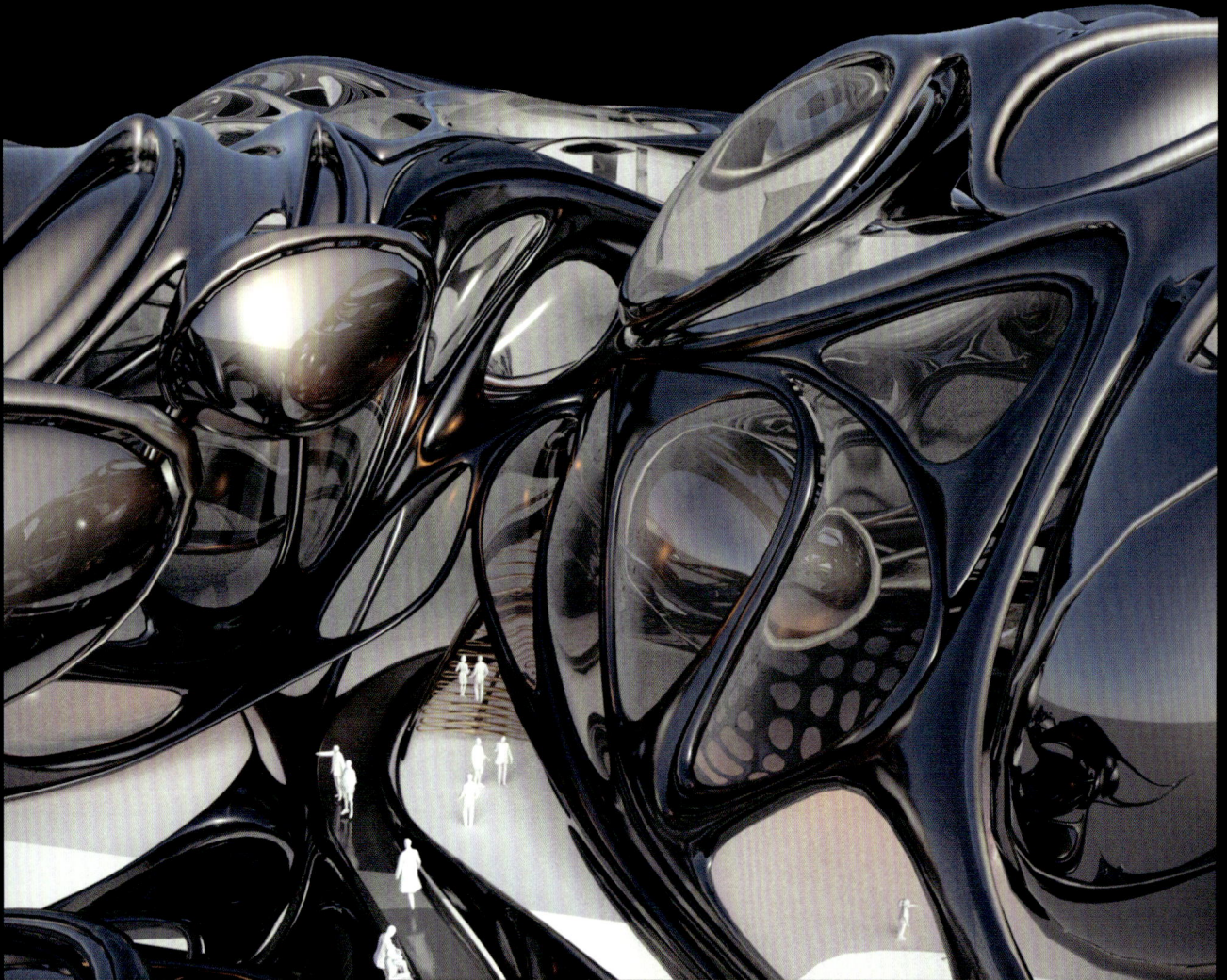

DR: Let's talk about humour. You are one of the funniest people I know. What is the function of humour in your work?

HDA: I don't think there is humour in my work. I think there is humour in me. I don't find architecture that attempts humour to be appealing, and have always thought that architects take themselves too seriously. I understand why that is, but have never entirely agreed with it. I have experienced some dark moments in my life, especially recently, and like everyone else, need humour to cope with difficult things. To be serious all the time, and to somehow be professionally obligated to be humourless, seems exhausting. I think we all need a healthy appreciation of life's absurdity.

Humorous architecture, on the other hand, depends on irony, and most of the time relies on inside jokes that only other architects understand. This seems kind of academic and elitist, and is probably why I dislike PoMo. I would like my work to be something that anyone can appreciate directly without it ever being some game that requires insider knowledge.

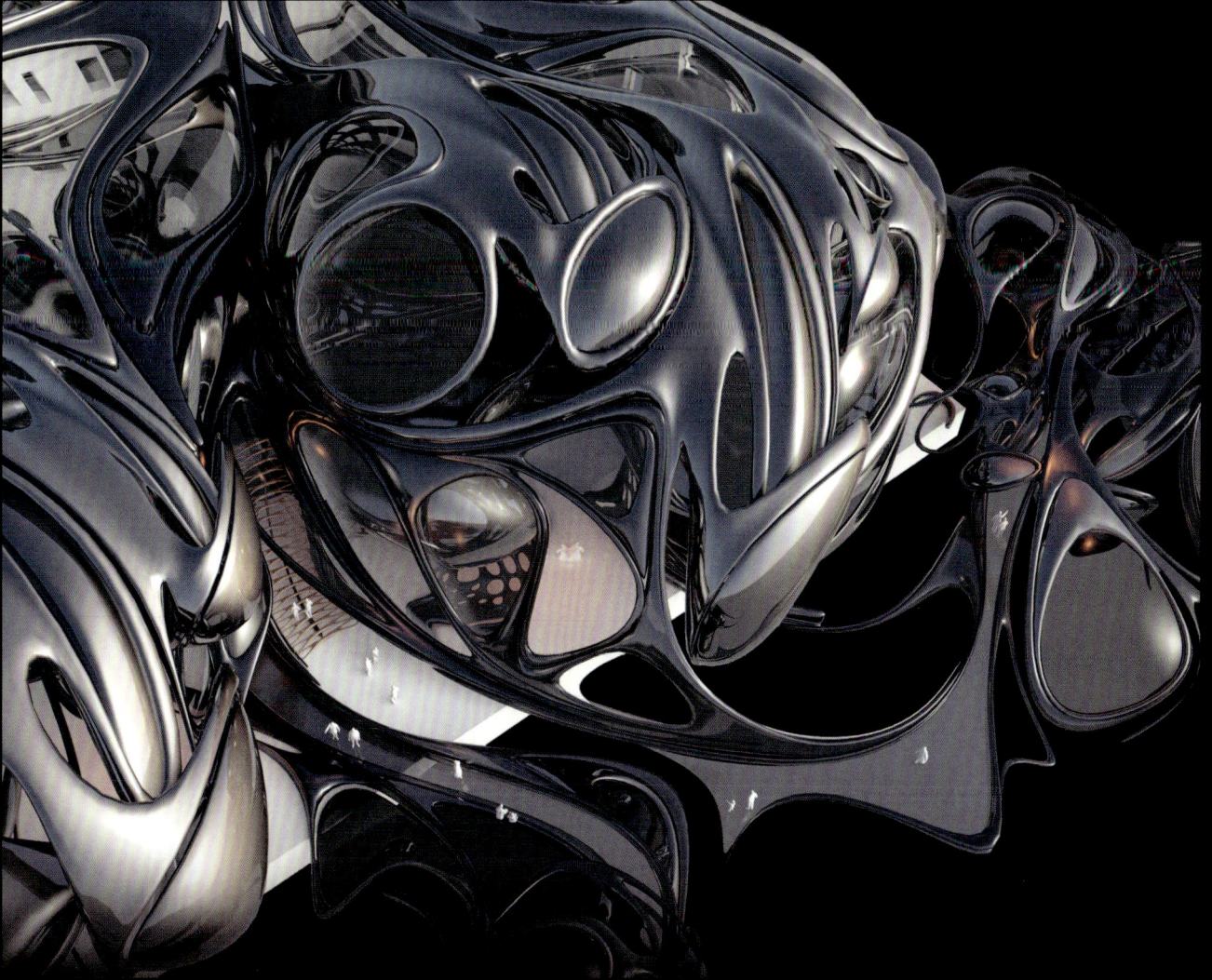

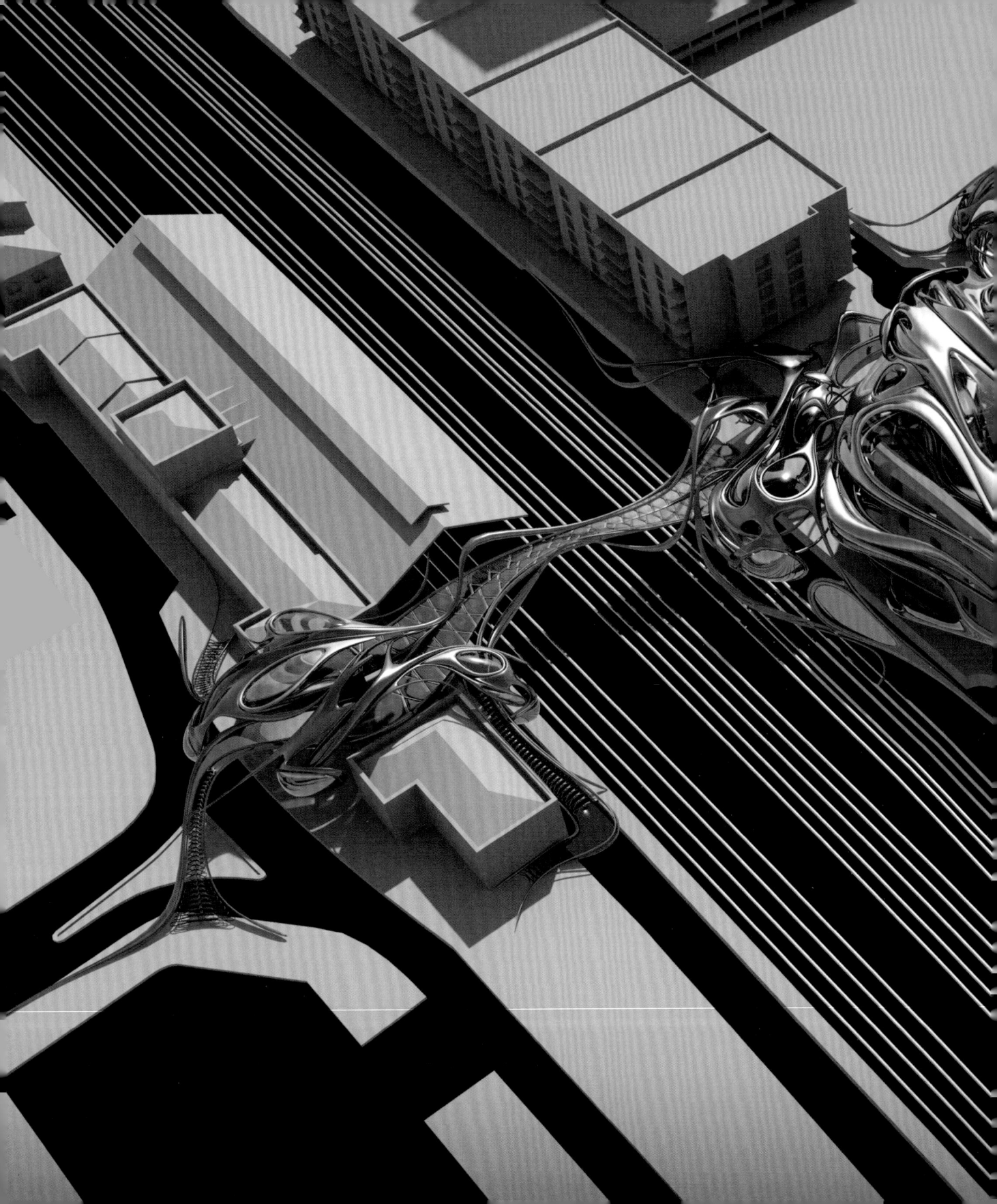

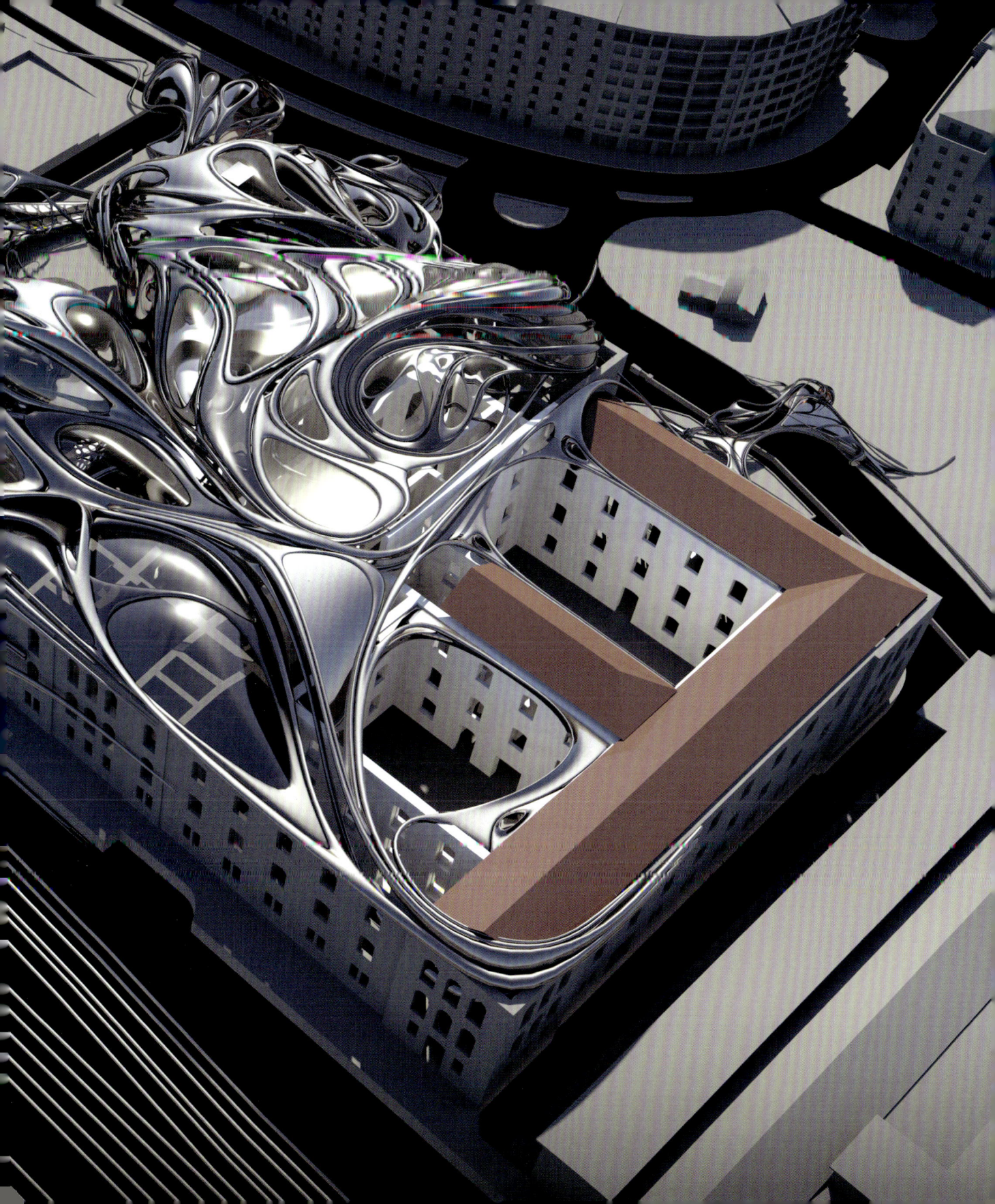

Sant Adrià de Besòs

The challenge here was to connect two cities in Catalonia: Barcelona and Sant Adrià de Besòs. Spanning the river Besòs, this connection serves as more than just a bridge, but as a destination, triggering a new relationship between the cities. As part of a larger masterplan to redevelop the riverside pathways, the design finds inspiration in Catalonian culture, the snake as a mythical animal and in the rich construction methods of the area, which emphasize rudimentary assemblies to create a high level of sophistication. The design of the bridge, which is mostly pedestrian, is based on the notion of standardized pieces that, by a simple manoeuvre of rotation, create the effect of singularity while reducing cost. As the pathways reach halfway across the river, a series of viewing and activity platforms break the rhythm to generate moments for stopping, thinking and absorbing one's surroundings – places for visitors to admire the site's position on the waterfront, facing the sea over a natural preservation region.

Location: Sant Adrià de Besòs, Spain
Date: 2014
Programme: Bridge
Client: Barcelona Regional

Related projects
Barcelona Park, 2014 (p. 194)
Budapest Museum, 2014 (p. 270)
Lip Chair, 2013 (p. 310)

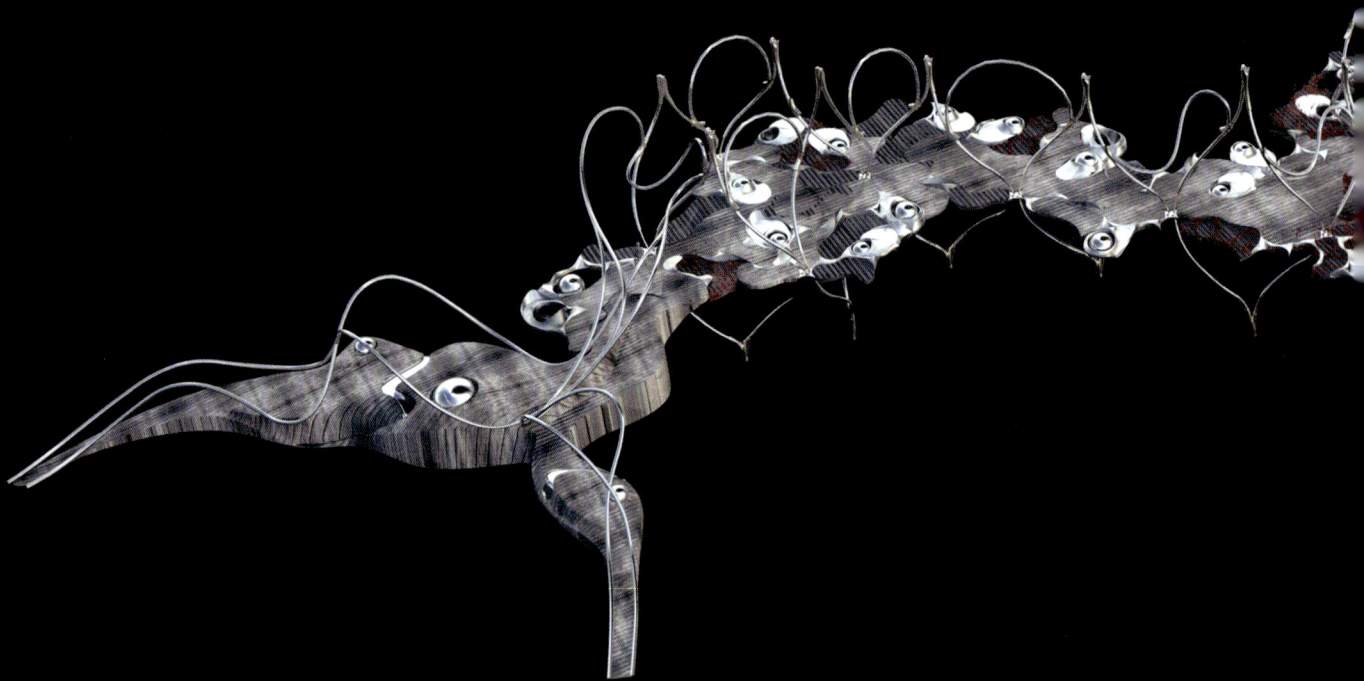

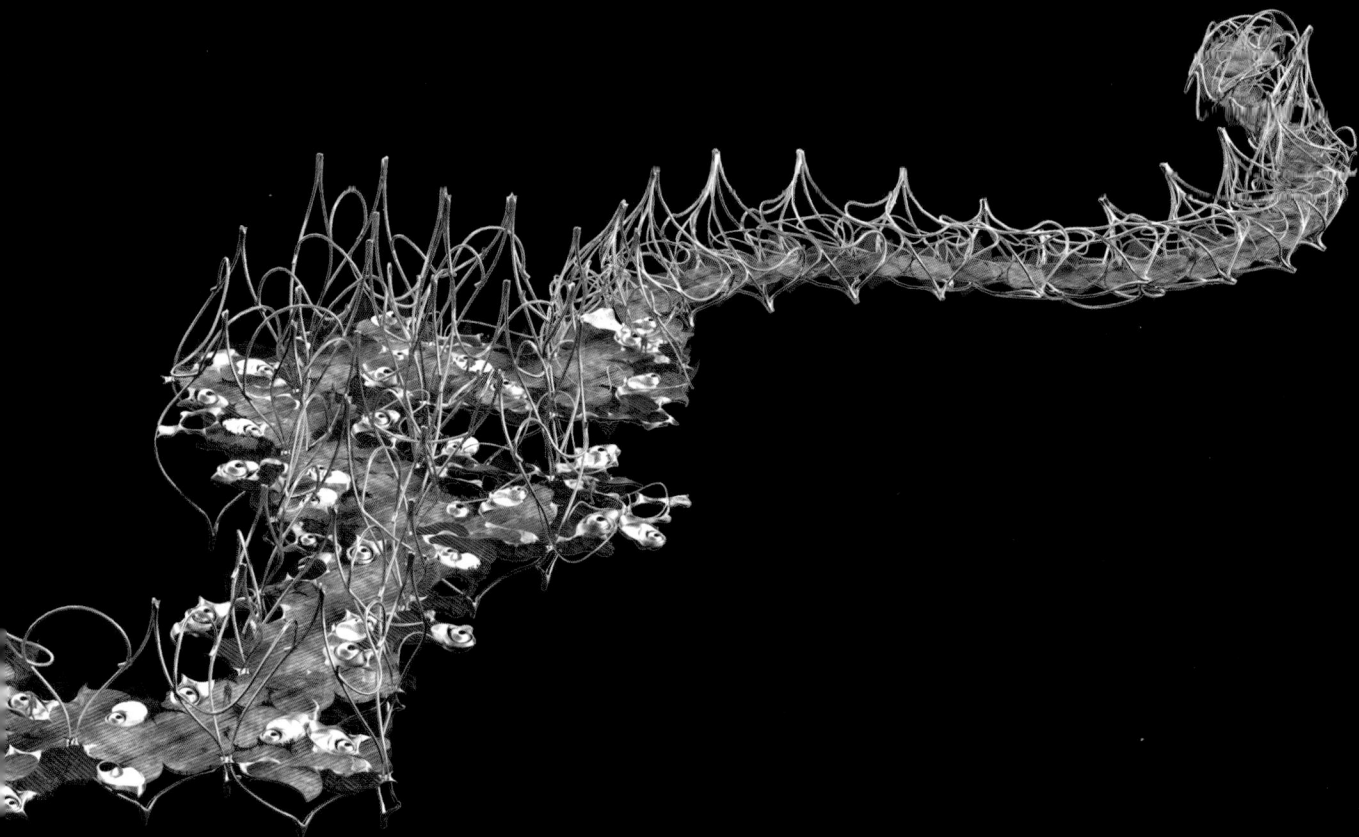

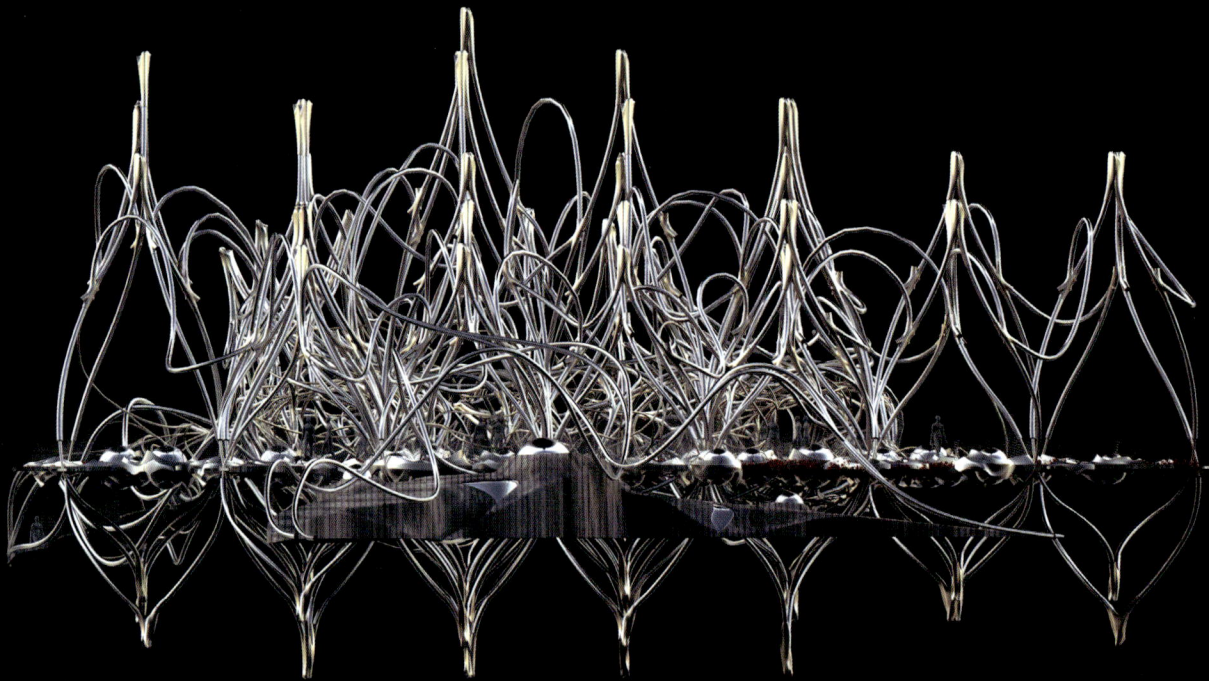

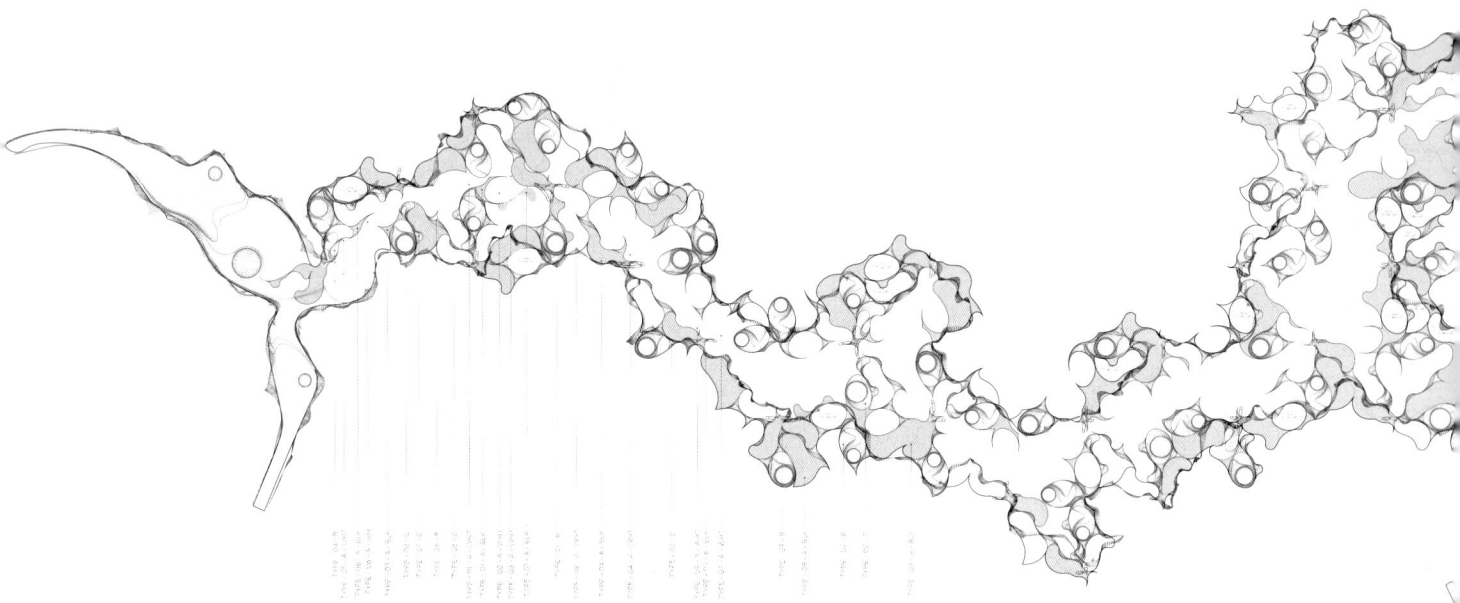

Plan

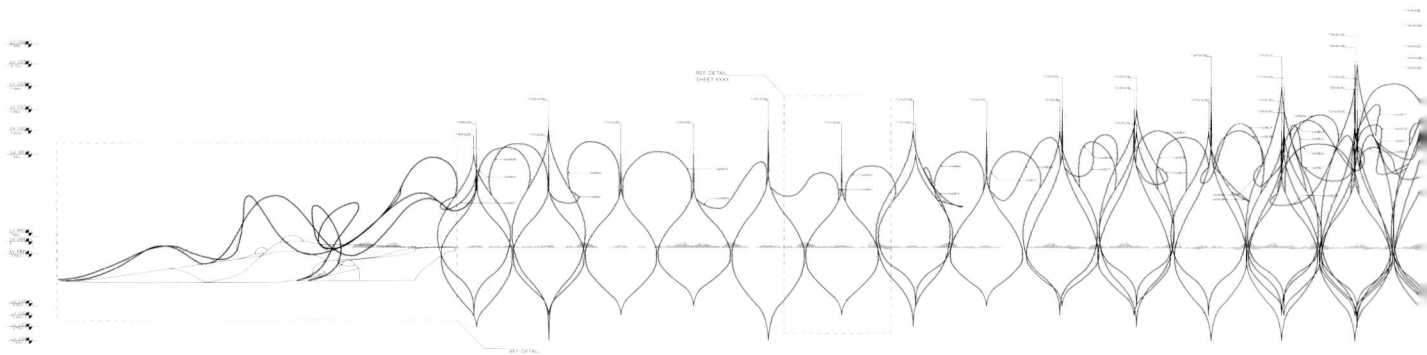

Structural modules – elevation

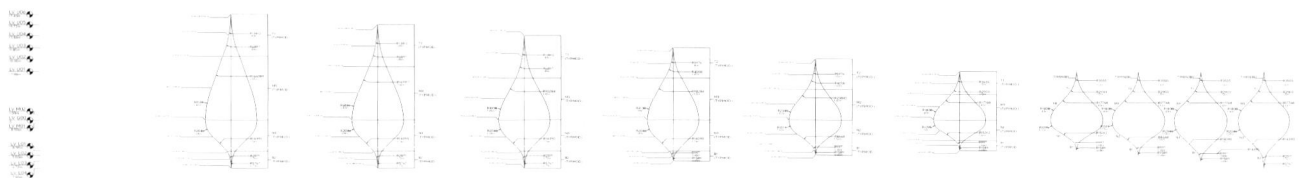

Structural modules

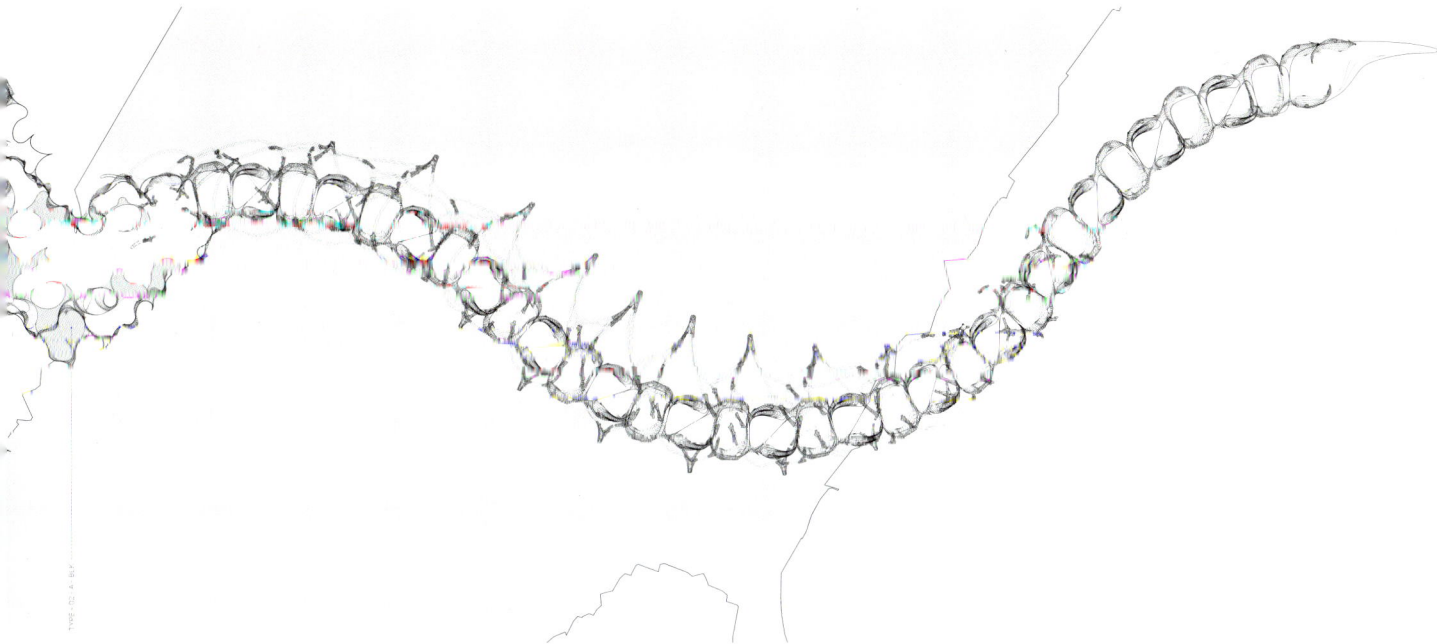

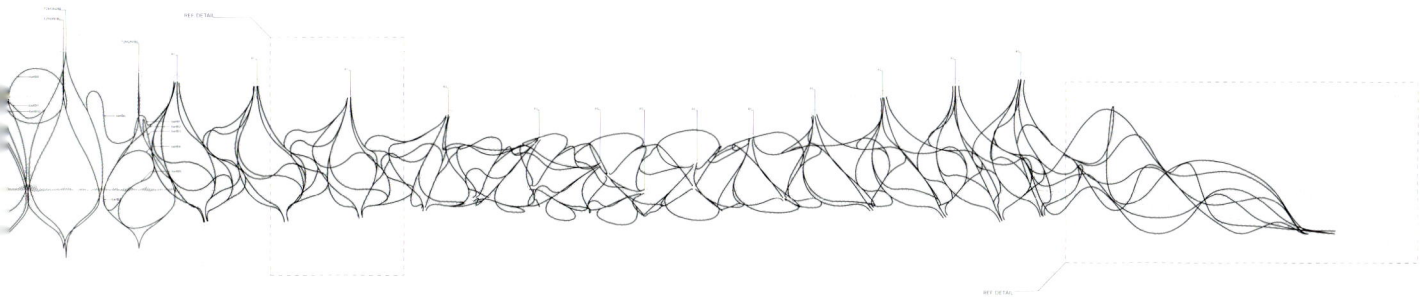

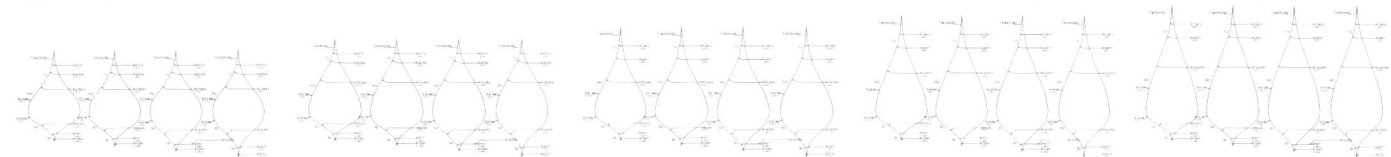

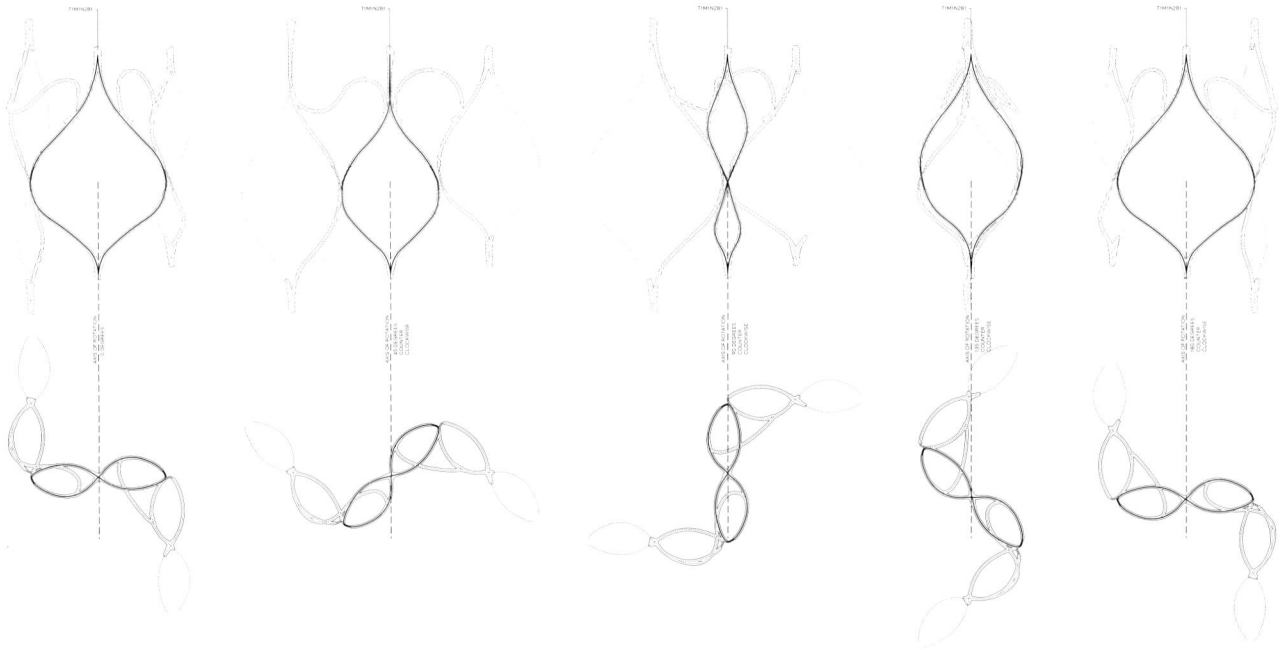

Typical structural modules – Elevations and plans

Typical structural modules – Side B

Pitch Black

How boring has perfection become? Our design obsessions are based on an appreciation for the perversity of mutant form, a taste learned from the movies and put into practice in architecture. It is produced in the act of design, in the focused sensation of pointing and clicking. Here, that sensation is more like painting than engineering. Image-forms are the product of speed up and slow down, slice and blend, fuse and separate – repetitions of scenic rhythms learned from a lifetime of being awed by cinematic effect.

Location: Vienna, Austria / Shanghai, China
Date: 2008 / 2016
Programme: Exhibition

Related projects
Sangre, 2006 (p. 34)
La Chaise Grotesque, 2012 (p. 42)
X-Plosion, 2008 (p. 60)
Miami Ritz Sculpture 1.0, 2011 (p. 66)

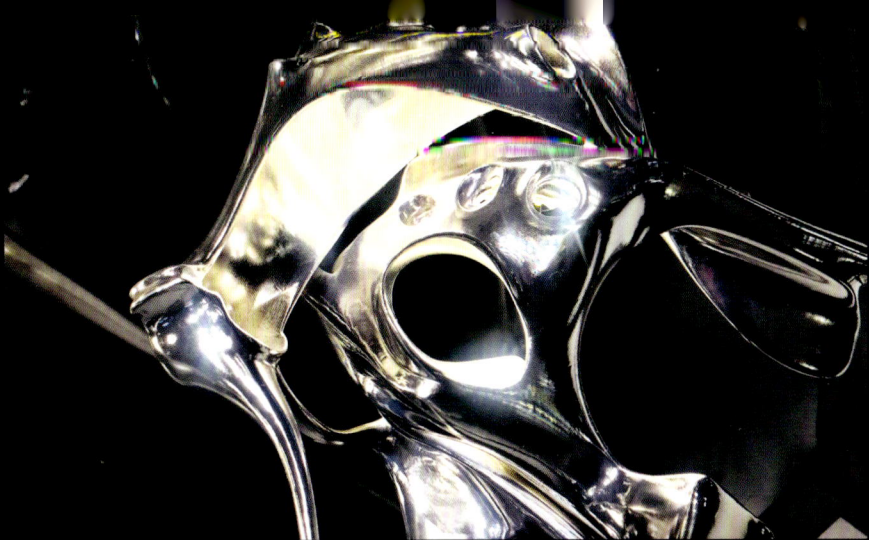
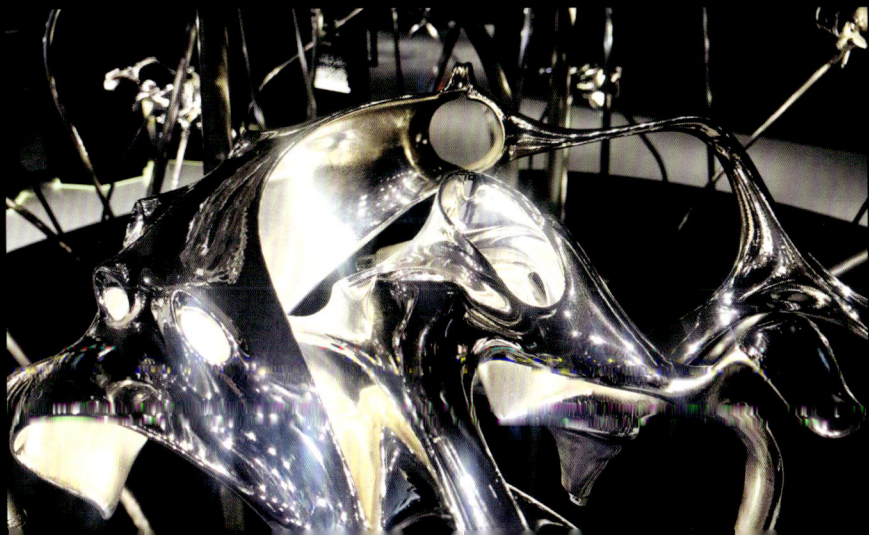

HDA: Although my work is not humorous, I think it is playful, which I hope comes through when looking at it. Some might find my work surprising, but I find it incredibly happy and optimistic, in the way that children might view monsters. It is serious play that can serve an important purpose on some level.

The architects that I like and the artists that I love all tend to bring some sort of serious play to their work. Even though it might not be the first thing that comes to your mind when you look at a painting by Francis Bacon, when I see one of his works I see a master engaged in deadly serious play.

DR: I find it fascinating that you use the term 'serious play', because it mirrors aspects of Romanticism from the late 18th and early 19th centuries, especially Friedrich Schiller's ideas about aesthetic education as a counterpoint to rationalism. For him, the drive towards play is what mediates between the material and formal drives. The instinct to play, or *spieltrieb*, is the source of creation and beauty. I think there is something very true about this. Perhaps we are suspicious of moralizing architecture because we're both romantics at heart.

HDA: I hate the idea that architecture is on a higher moral ground than other creative disciplines. I think all the moralizing of social-justice projects has created a distance between architecture and its audience. I'm very interested in pop culture. I'm very interested in how things operate. I'm very interested in the now.

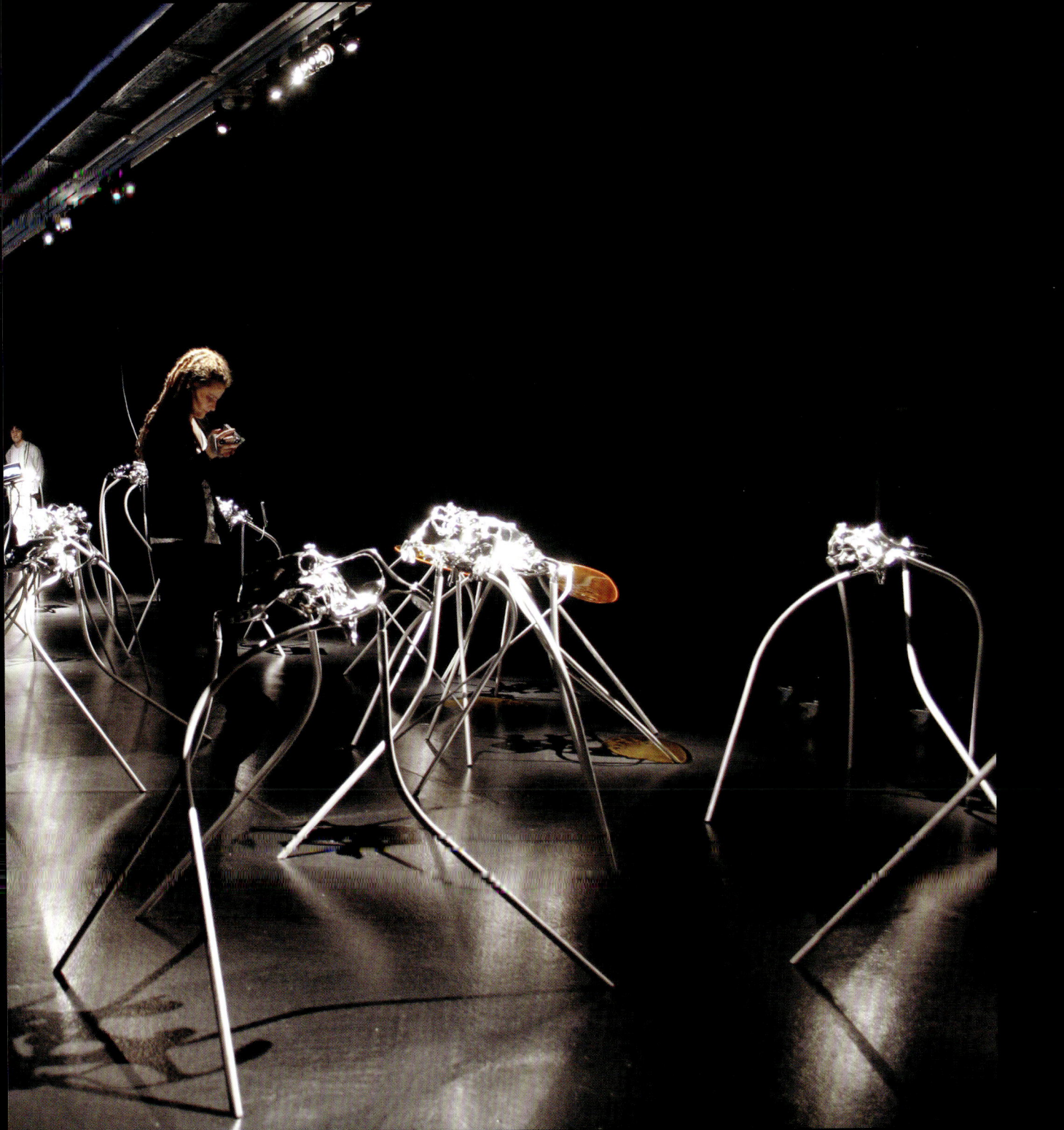

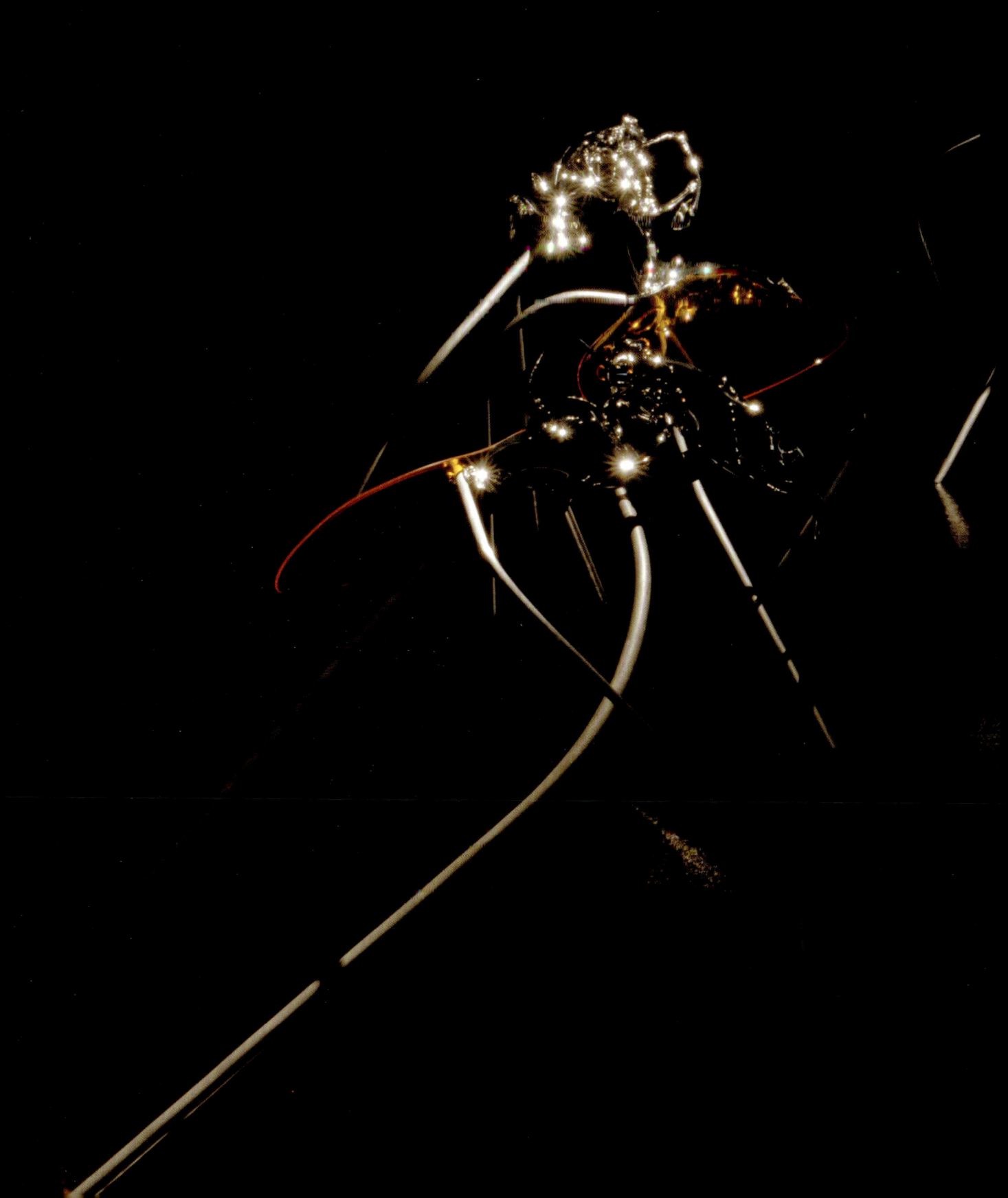

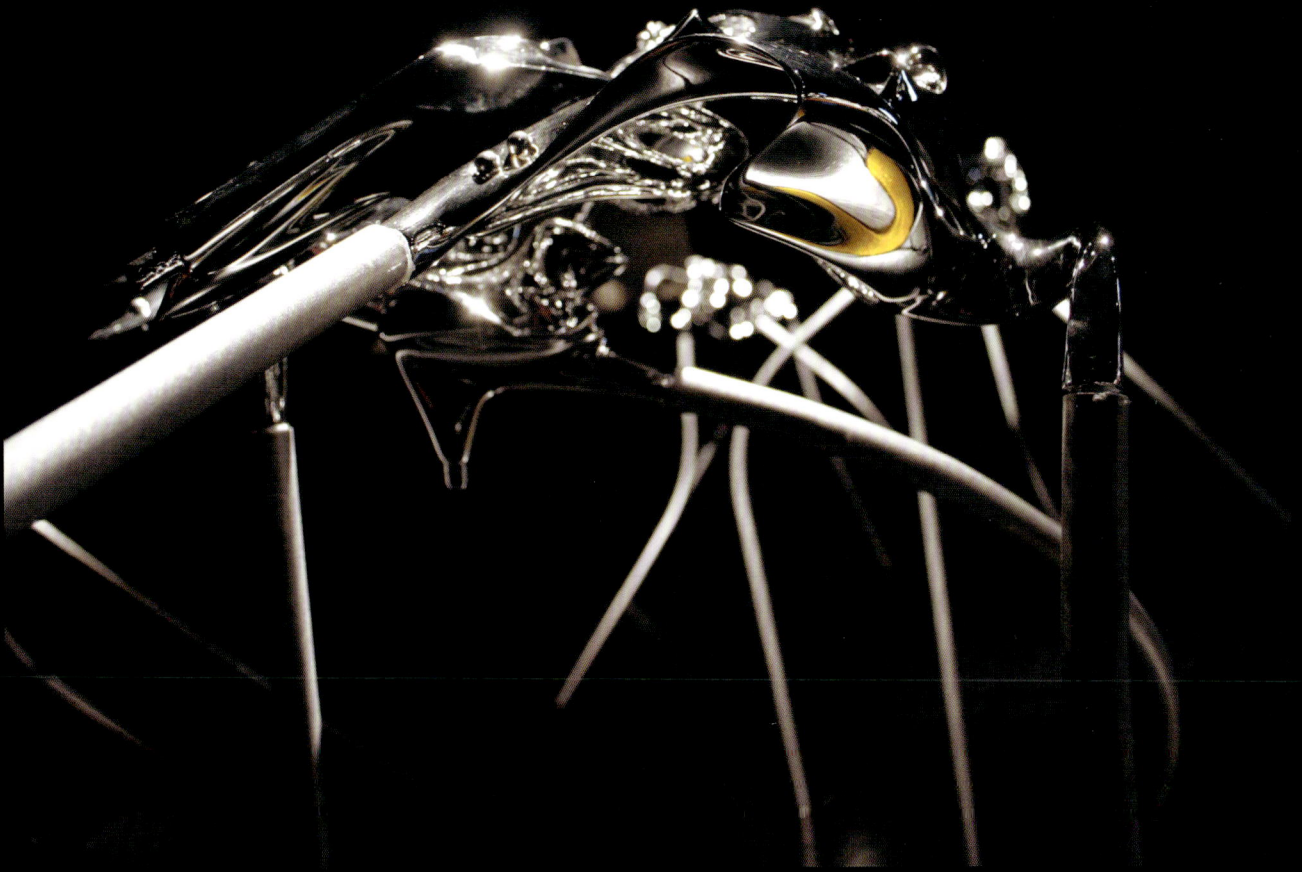

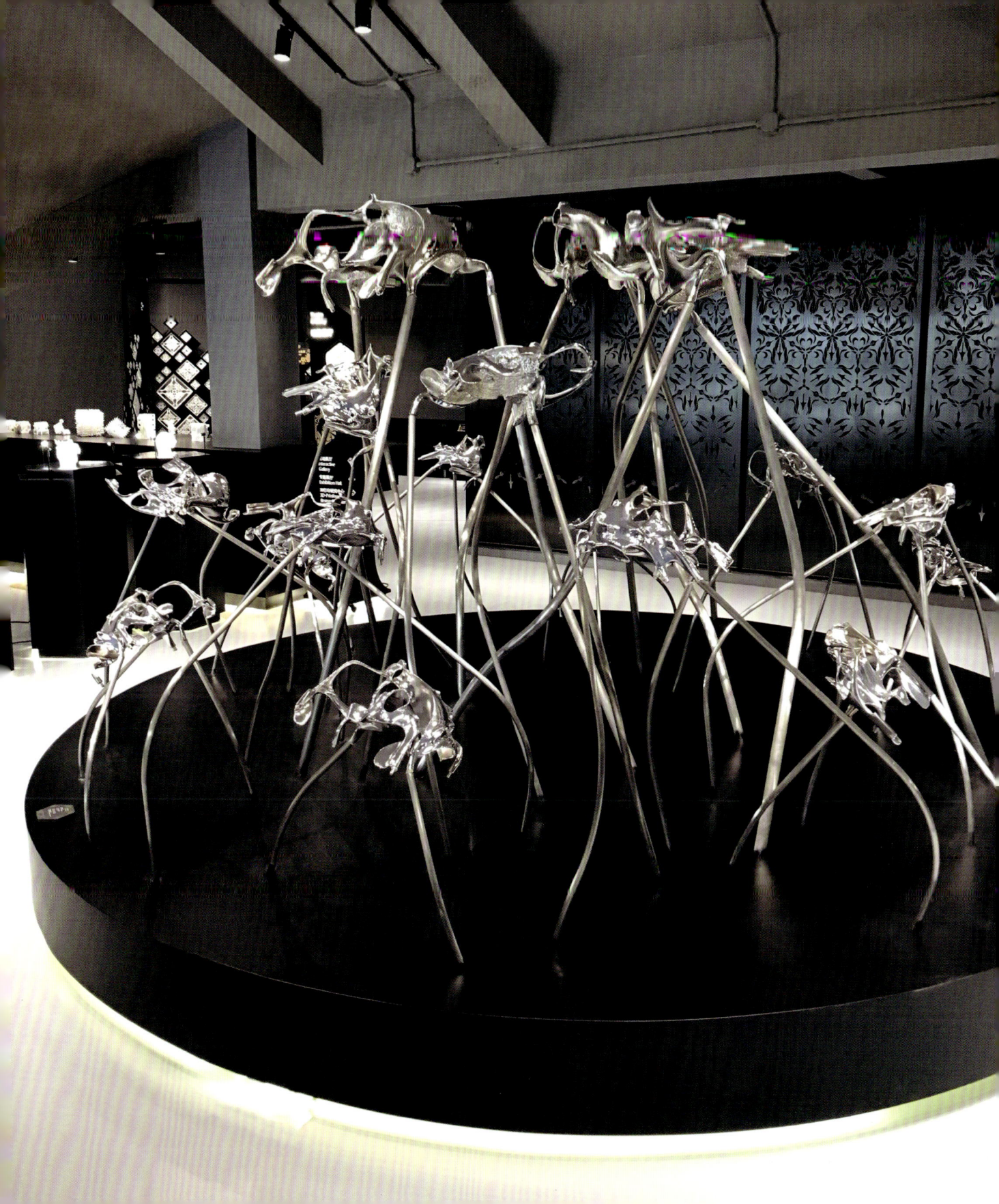

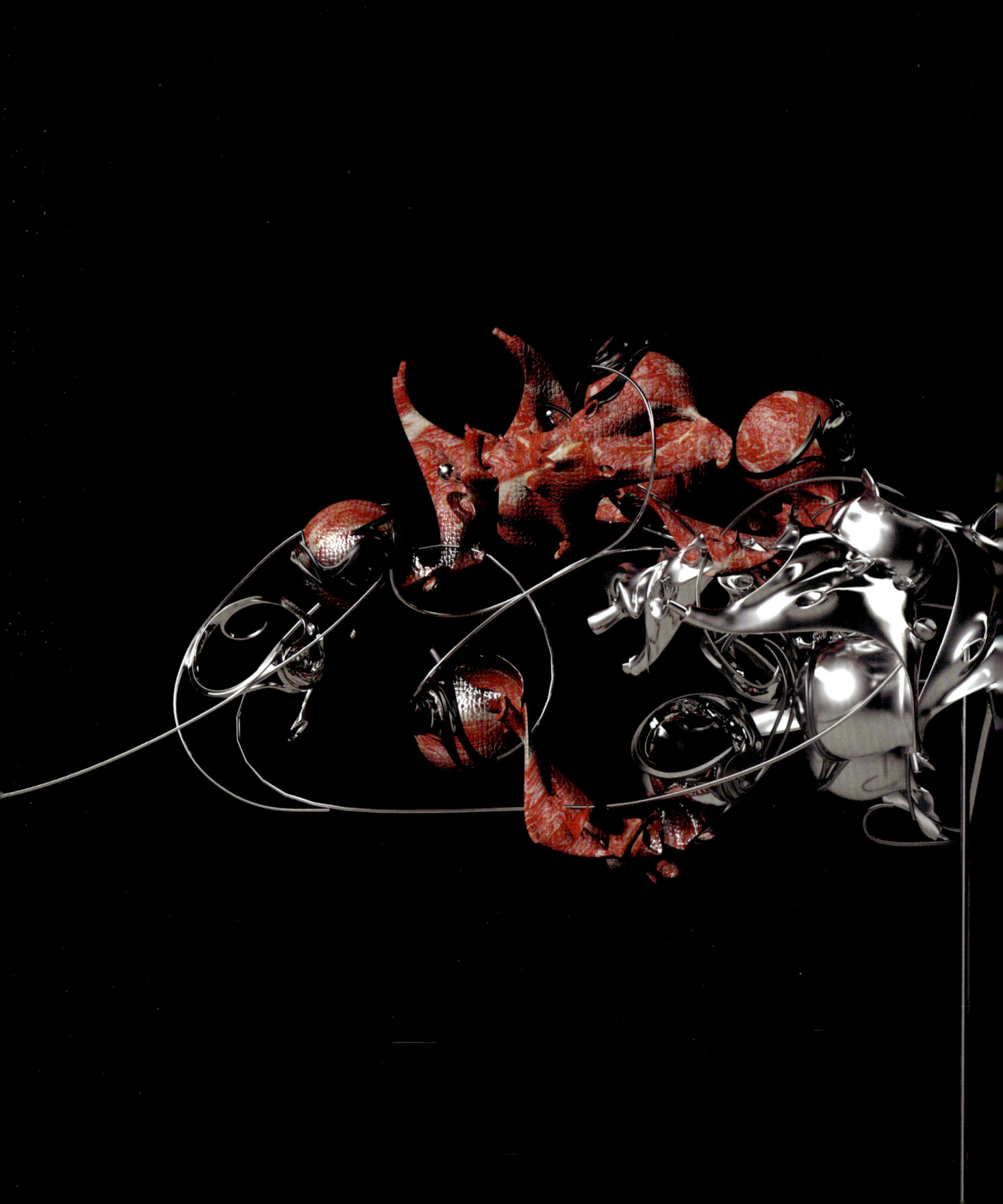

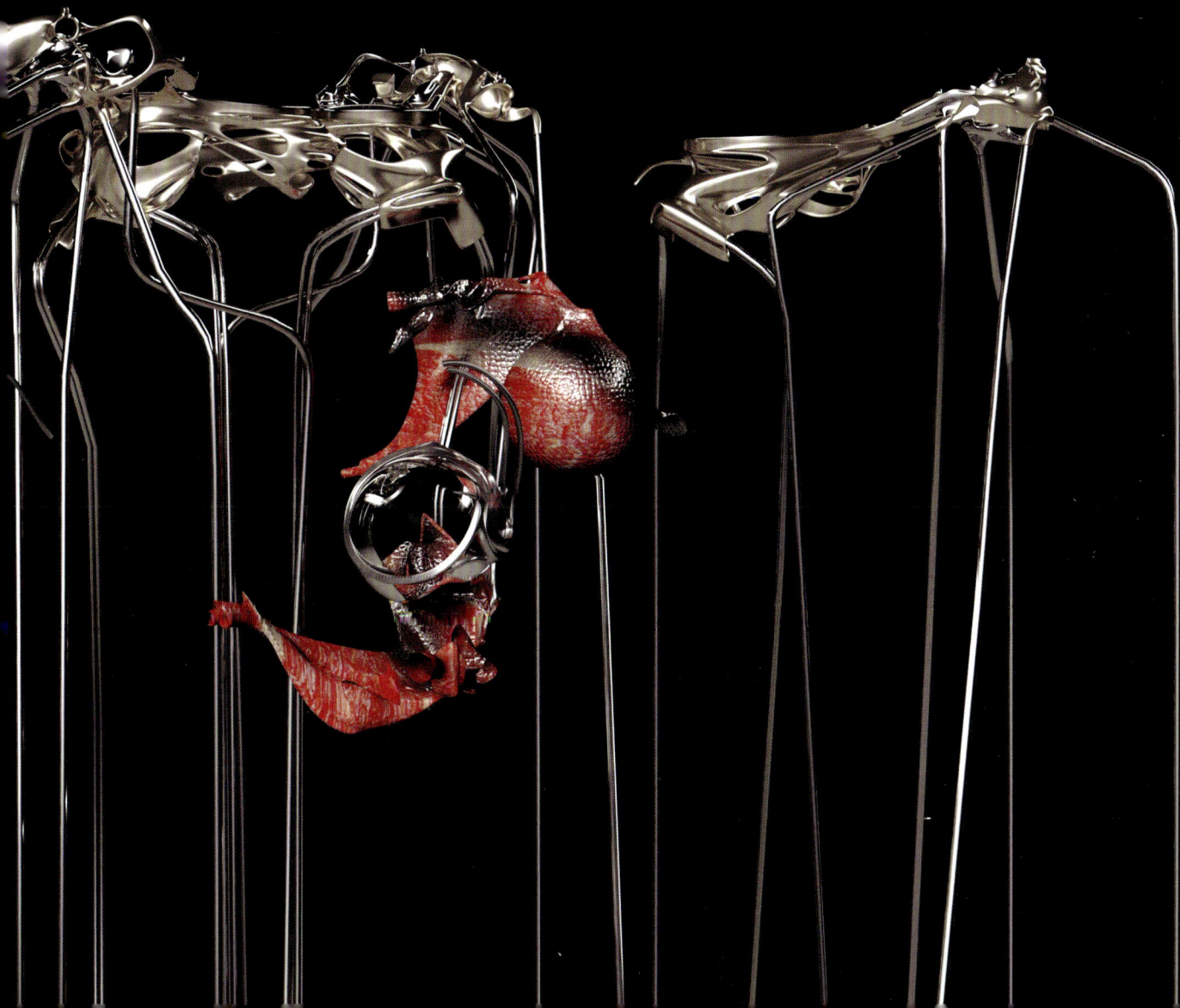

Maison Seroussi

It starts inside, then up, and around. It finds no boundaries, only continuities. Its flesh pulsates, then hardens, adrift and unbounded. Views mingle, unconstrained and without focus, always more and never less. This is the story of a new state of space, one that cannot be told, but only sensed. The house has grown in the site, its original geometrical code (a new species that has branched away from the primitives of Euclidean form) manipulated, and trepidatious mutations performed upon it. Cells, organs, skins: an expanded vocabulary is required to narrate. Words that don't mean or mimic, but simply are: things, objects, spaces. The house has taken advantage of its site by extending the programmatic elements, expanding the notion of enclosure to transform it into an idea of nesting.

Location: Paris, France
Date: 2007
Programme: Residence

Related projects
Lautner Redux, 2008 (p. 188)

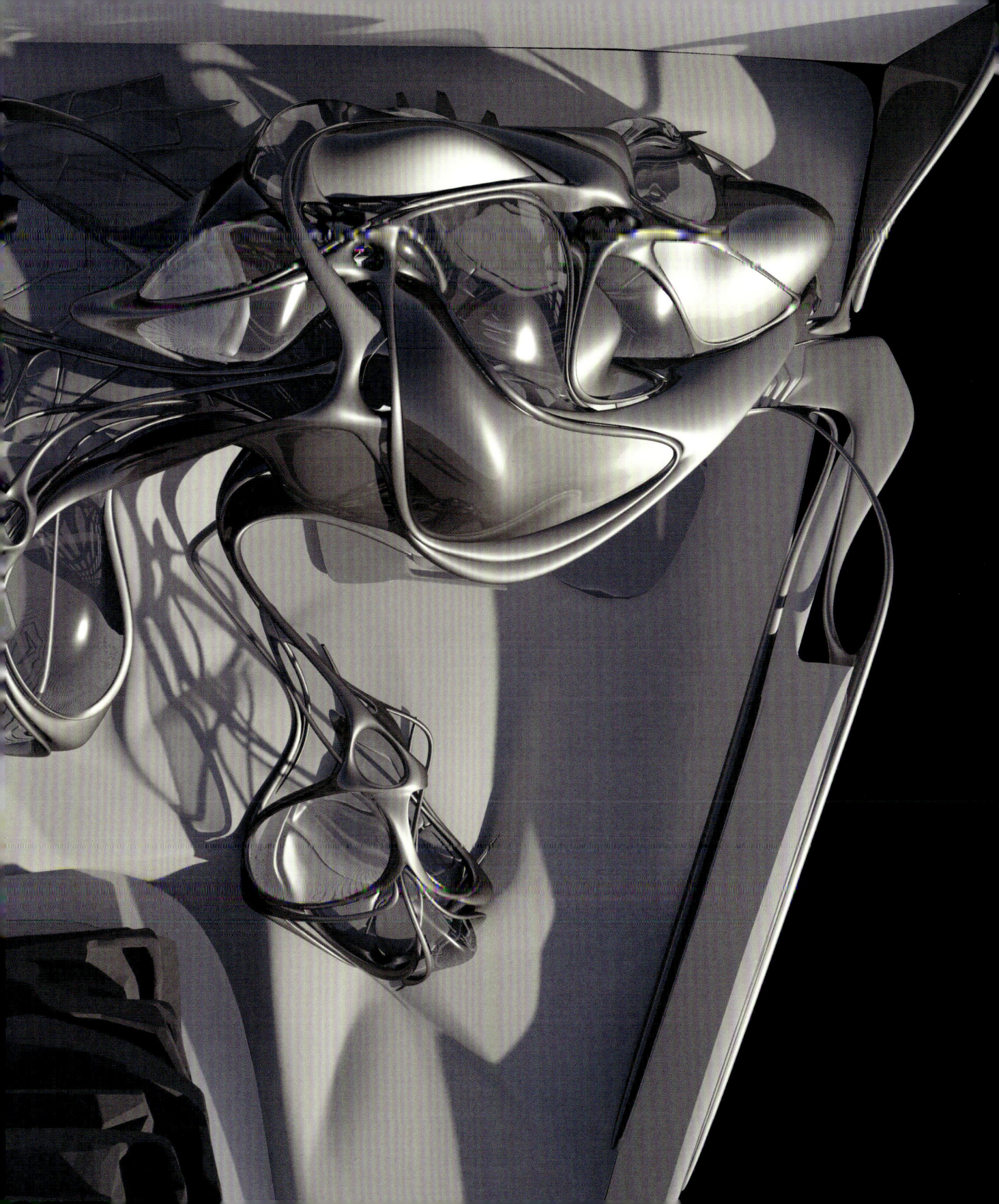

Site plan

Foundation plan

1	Kitchen	6	South Gallery annex
2	Lower terrace	7	Upper terrace
3	North Gallery annex	8	Basement access
4	Central Gallery / theatre	9	Secondary entrance
5	East Gallery annex		

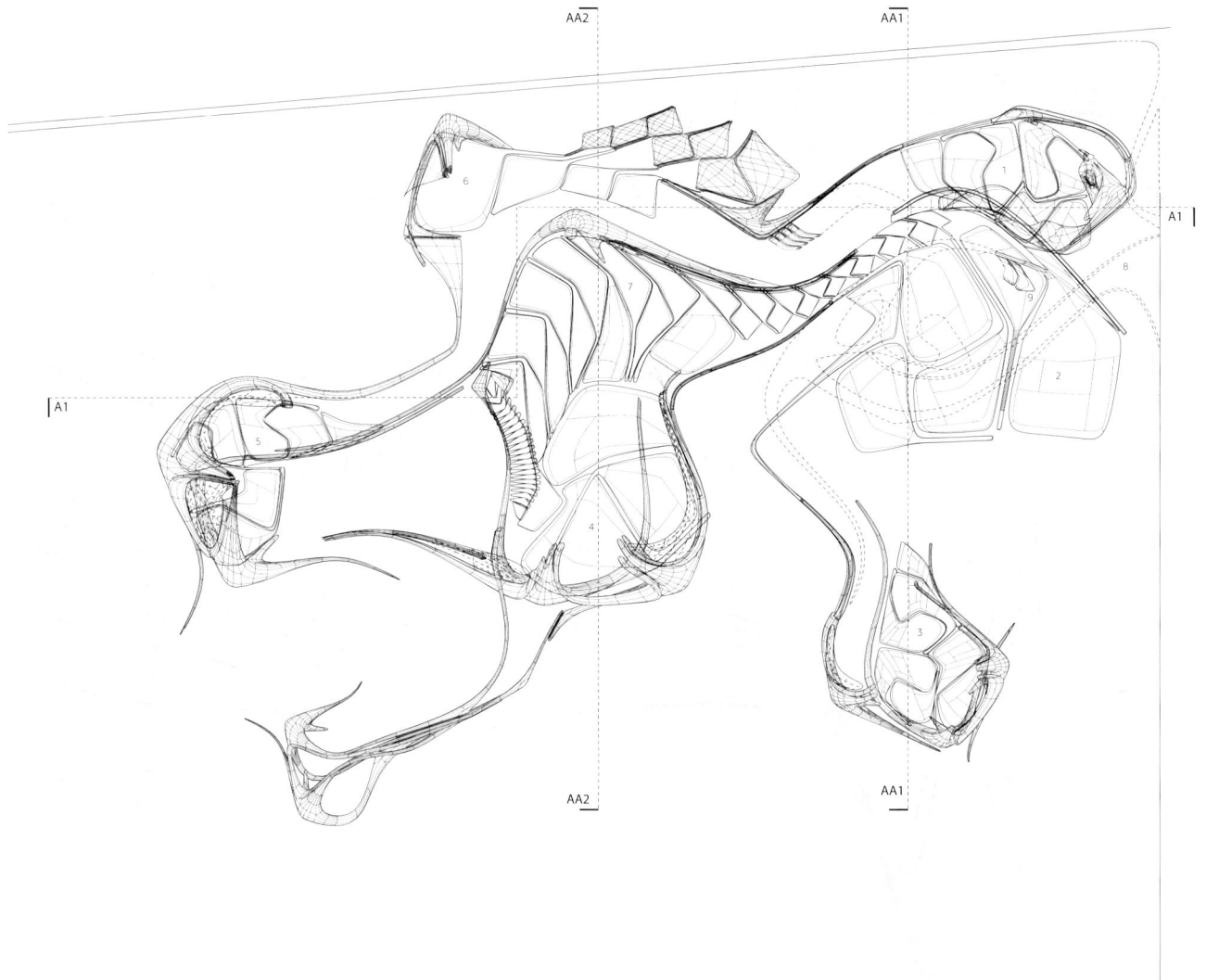

AA2

AA1

A1

6

1

7

8

9

A1

5

2

4

3

AA2

AA1

Floorplan – Level 1

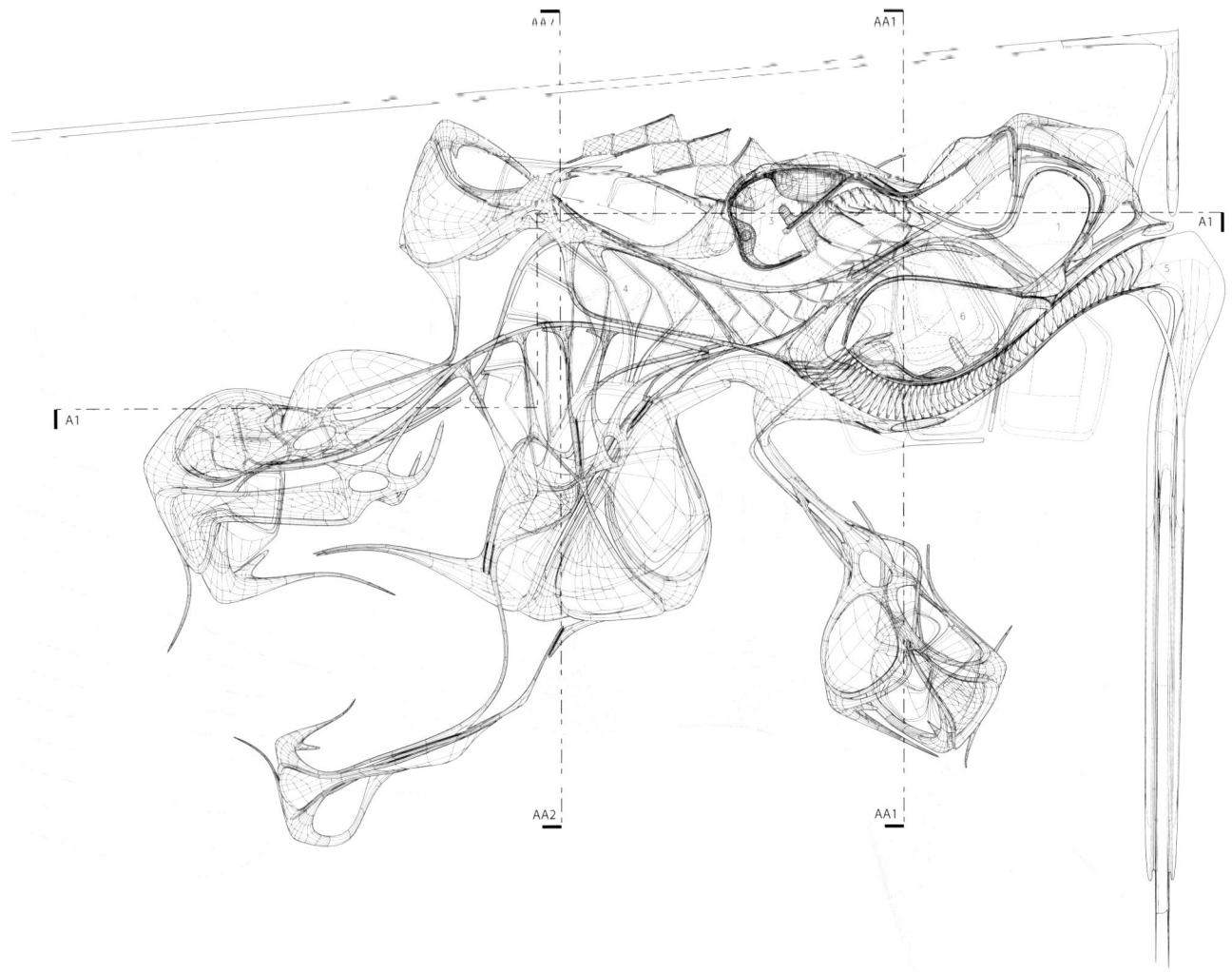

1   Bedroom
2   Office / bedroom
3   Bathroom
4   Balcony
5   Main entrance
6   Interstitial gallery

Floorplan – Level 2

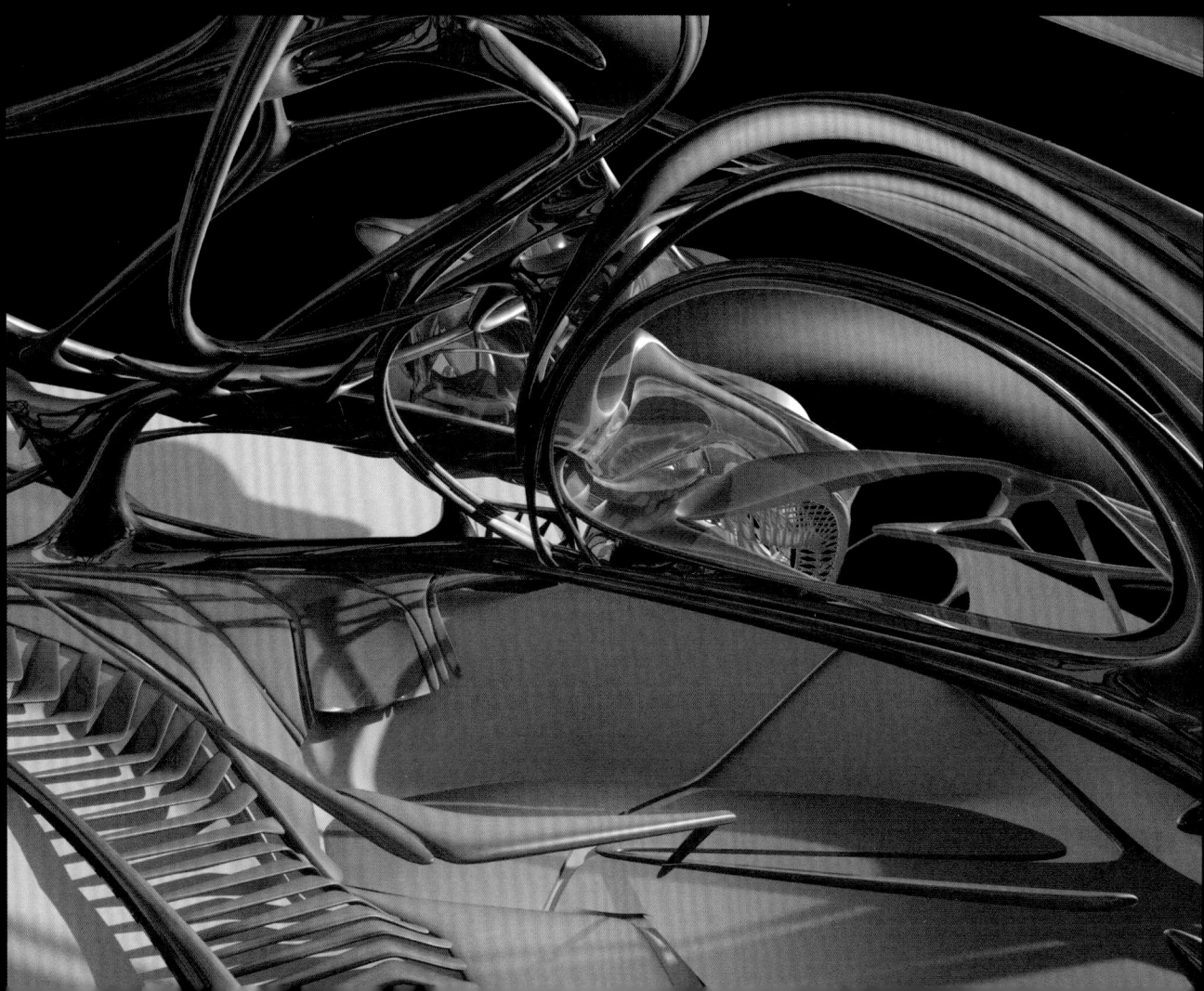

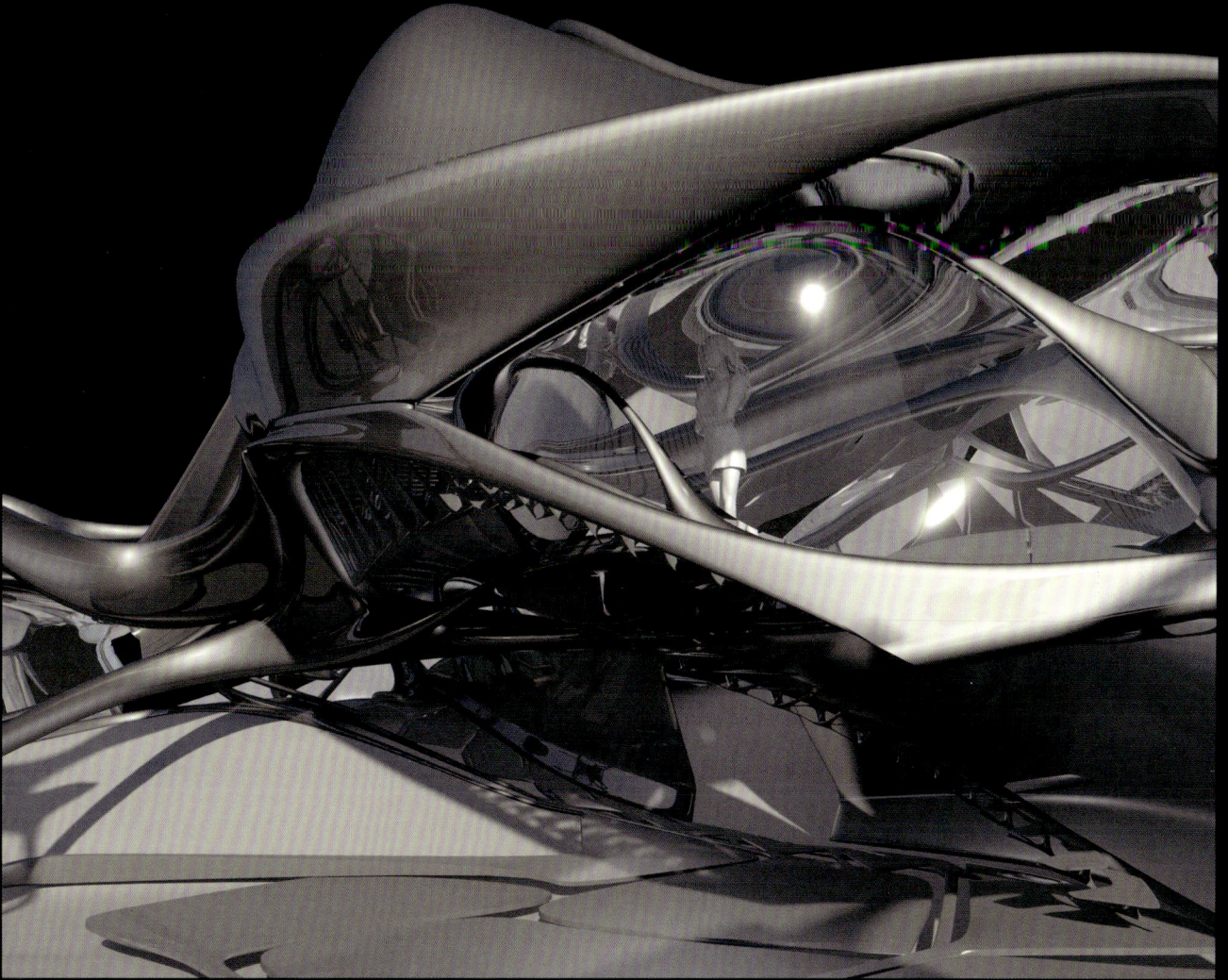

Lautner Redux

On the occasion of a retrospective exhibition devoted to the work of architect John Lautner, we, along with three other architectural firms, were invited by the Hammer Museum and Getty Center to create additions for four of Lautner's radical houses.

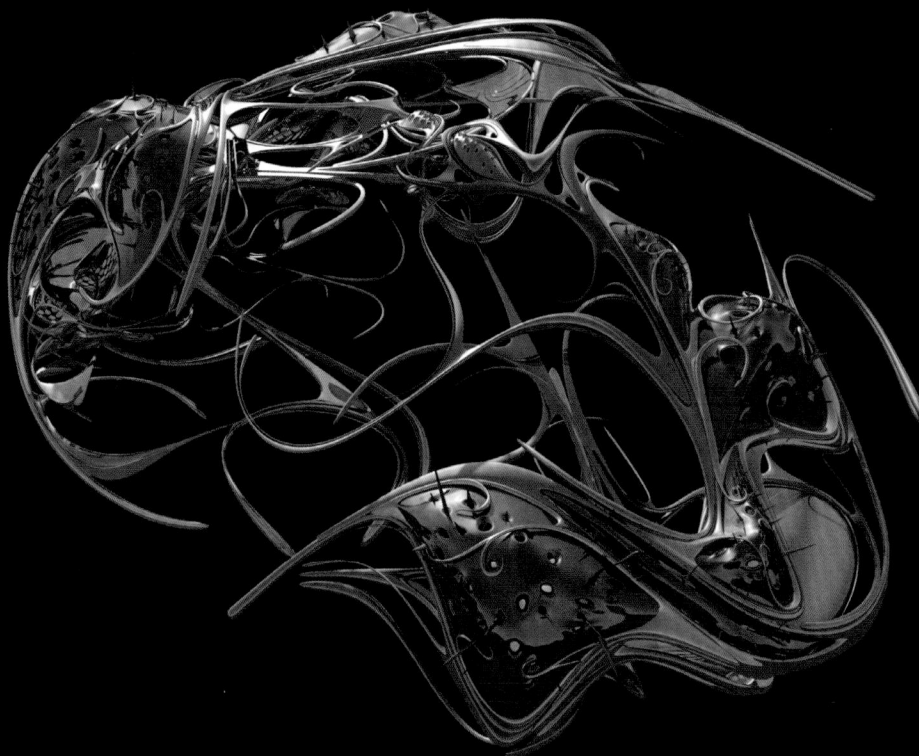

Location: Los Angeles, California
Date: 2008
Programme: Residence

Related projects
Maison Seroussi, 2007 (p. 176)

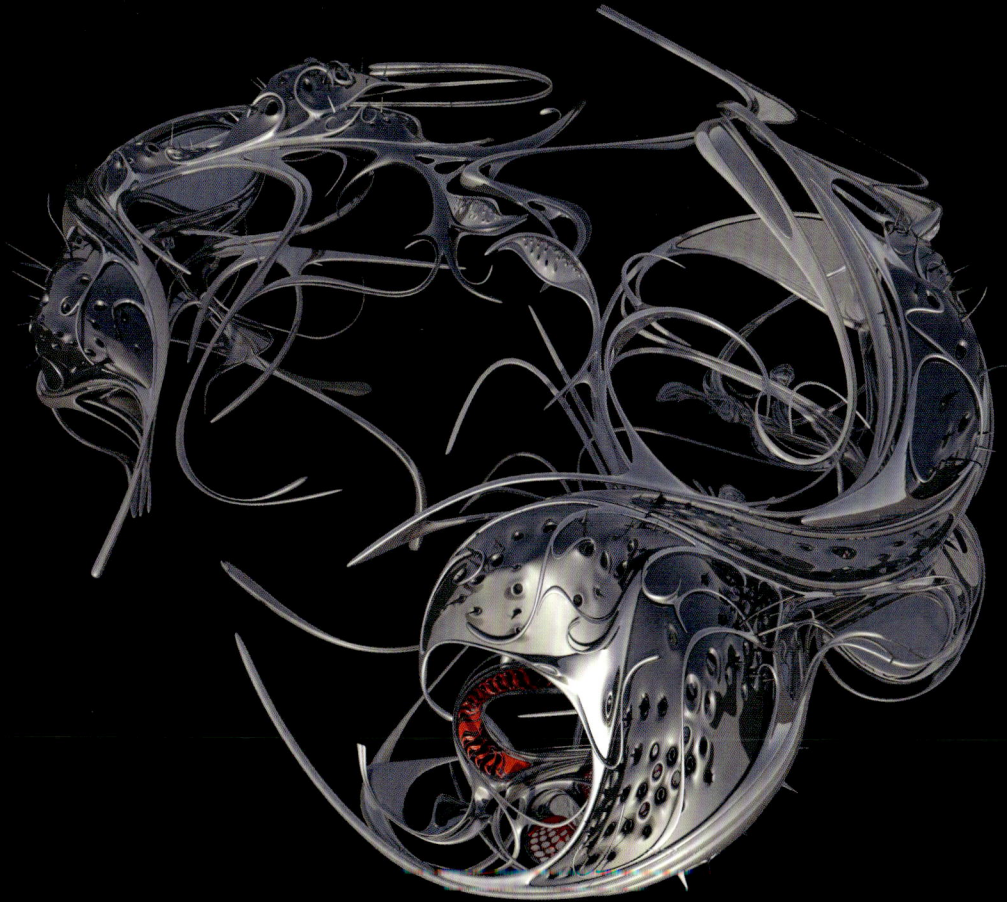

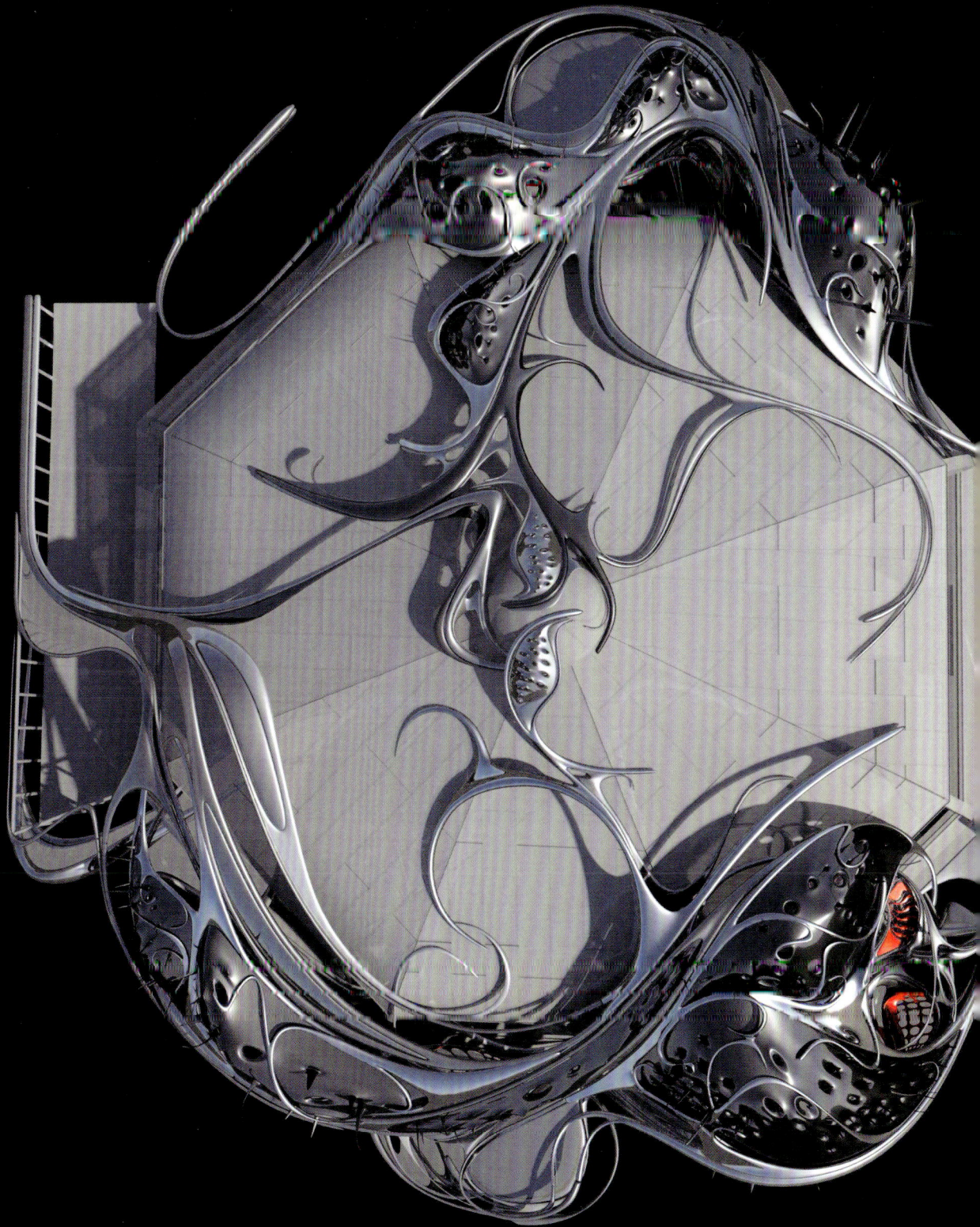

Barcelona Park

This proposal for a promenade in Sant Adrià de Besòs reinterprets the aesthetic qualities of the great agricultural crops, while maintaining the appearance of a wild jungle. Despite this contradiction, the design aims to find the balance between immaculately manicured landscape and the unpredictability found in the wild. It introduces a variety of established programmes – amphitheatre, sculpture garden, exercise areas and pedestrian and cycle routes – while also preserving many of the site's spaces for casual use, with community fields, and space for events, fairs and markets. Acting as a continuation to the bridge connecting Barcelona with Sant Adrià (p. 154), the promenade will attract a diverse demographic, which in turn will generate different activities to attract families and allow the continued use of the walkway, creating a destination in Sant Adrià de Besòs.

Location: Sant Adrià de Besòs, Spain
Date: 2014
Programme: Park
Collaborators: Pita & Bloom

Related projects
PS1 MoMA, 2005 (p. 28)
Tabakalera, 2008 (p. 140)
Sant Adrià de Besòs, 2014 (p. 154)

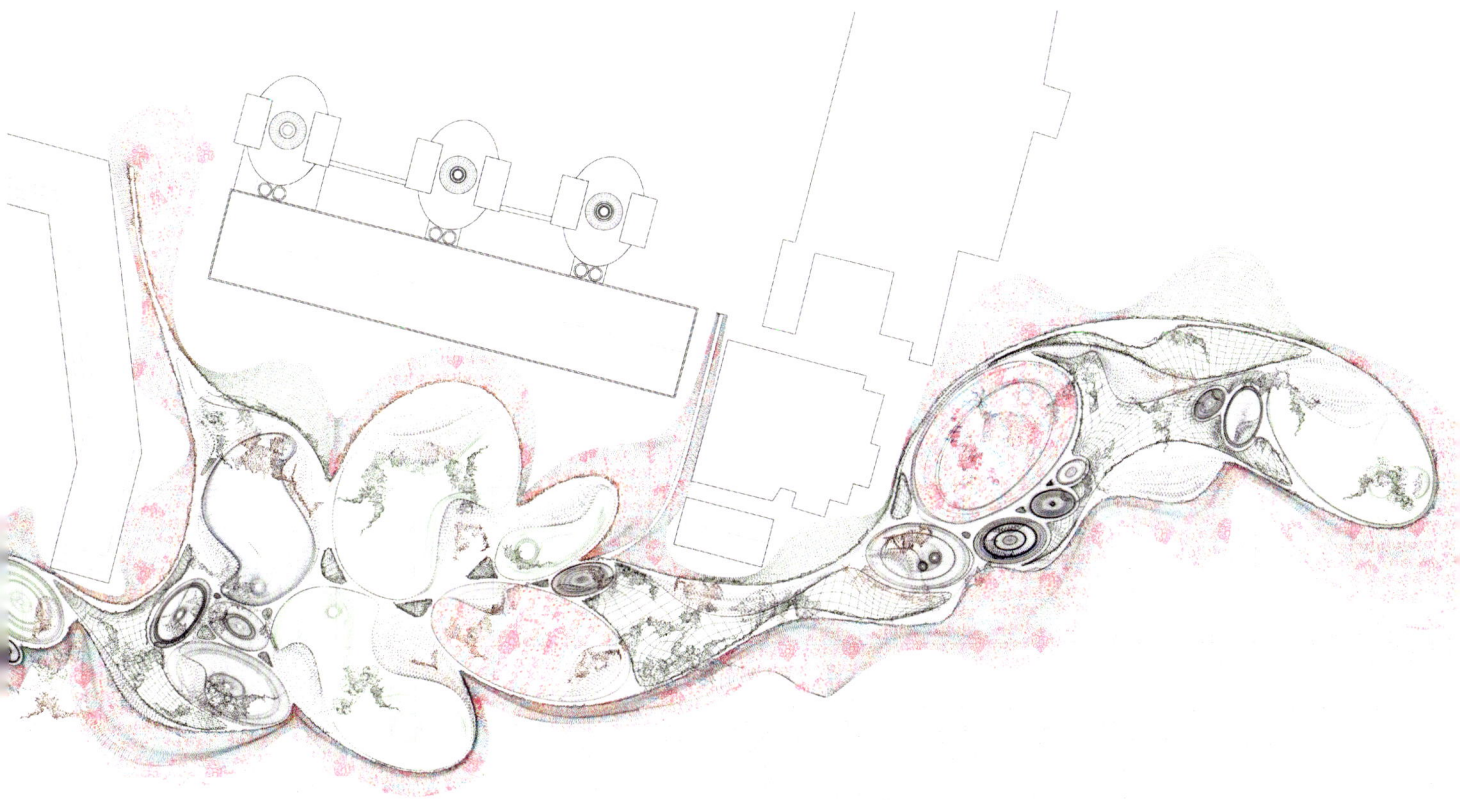

Conexion Barcelona

The bridge twists left, then right, necessitating manoeuvring through a jungle-like space to cross the freeway and train tracks below, before ultimately arriving at the parks of Barceloneta or Ciutadella, or the Estació de França. The twisting of the path creates a third park in itself, providing an elevated green space for relaxing and taking in the beautiful scenery of Barcelona. This connection is necessary for joining the path from the beach to the adjacent Ciutadella Park and Barcelona Zoo; previously, pedestrians would be forced north or south for several kilometres before finding a pathway between the beach and the city. The addition of small platforms along the bridge allows visitors to pause for a moment and appreciate this neighbourhood where history meets the thriving, bustling contemporary city of Barcelona.

Location: Barcelona, Spain
Date: 2015
Programme: Bridge

Related projects
Barcelona Park, 2014 (p. 194)
Budapest Museum, 2014 (p. 270)
Teatro Colon, 2013 (p. 282)
Lips Chair, 2013 (p. 310)

DR: We have already established that you don't like funny architecture. You don't like elitist, wink-wink references, and we'll never see you crack a PoMo joke. But you do like absurdity.

HDA: Yes, I like absurdity a lot. I think it's related to my interest in contaminated form. I like the contradiction; it requires familiarity and legibility. When somebody says something is absurd, you understand what that person is telling you. It's not that you don't understand the words being said, or that somebody is talking to you in a foreign language.

To believe that something is absurd, you need to have a literal understanding of it. But the absurdity comes because there is something about it that doesn't make sense. I'm interested in seeing if there is something methodological about this in relation to design.

Eccentricity is delightful, too, but it is more formulaic. Absurdity, I think is more open-ended. I love the theatre of the absurd. It is different from what we were talking about before with regard to stupid PoMo jokes. The absurd produces a divine laughter.

DR: Do you admire Samuel Beckett?

HDA: I love Samuel Beckett.

DR: Your work, even though it doesn't have the minimalism of Beckett, often makes me laugh in the same way as when I read *Waiting for Godot*. Vladimir and Estragon make me laugh in a very different way from how Jerry Seinfeld and George Costanza make me laugh.

HDA: I also love Franz Kafka for the same reasons, I think.

DR: Yes, Franz Kafka. Right.

HDA: I don't know if anybody else finds Kafka funny, but I find his stories incredibly funny.

DR: Yes, that first line from *The Metamorphosis* is certainly absurd and funny.

HDA: It's fantastic. I also love Monty Python. They were masters of the absurd. My favourite sketches are the ones that make the least amount of sense.

DR: What is the relationship between this interest and enjoyment of the absurd and your disciplinary approach to architecture, and are they at odds with each other?

HDA: Not really, because I am interested in how the absurd contaminates the discipline. You know that I am a person who lives and works by rules. I am full of rules, and am pathologically consistent. Because of that, I'm always searching for ways to contaminate or contradict them. I need my life and my work to operate within that tension. I cannot have one to the exclusion of the other. I cannot have a cold life regulated by rules and methodologies, but I also cannot live by full absurdity. I embrace contradictions.

DR: Would it be fair to say that you operate under 90 per cent order and structure, and 10 per cent contamination and absurdity?

HDA: Are we talking about my life or about my work?

DR: Both.

HDA: I think in life, that sounds about right. The work, I would say, is more like 64 per cent.

DR: That is an absurdly precise number.

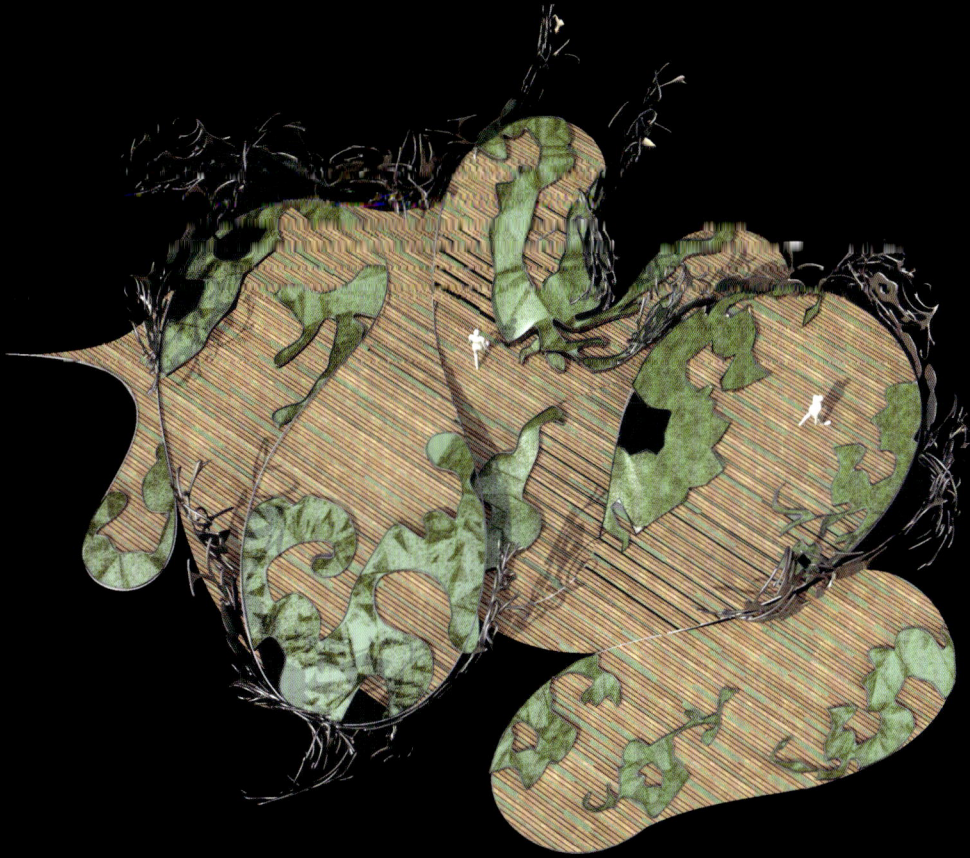

HDA: I don't take risks in life as I do in my work. My life is very bourgeois and predictable, because I need it to be that way. But risk-taking is subjective: only I can really know what constitutes a risk. Someone else, reading this book, perhaps, might think it's not that risky.

DR: Your work has been remarkably consistent over the years.

HDA: Sure, from that perspective, I suppose, there is a lack of risk-taking.

DR: You don't get bored with projects and forms like I do, and stick with things for much longer.

HDA: I get bored with techniques and methodologies, not with aesthetic consistency. I don't think you can have authorship without the formal consistency that constitutes a body of work, but I know that is open for debate.

DR: To wrap it up this topic of the absurd, to have a proper theatre of the absurd, you have to set up a substantial amount of consistency, legibility and order to introduce it. You can't just do the absurd from the get-go.

HDA: That's why I like the concept of the absurd more than I love crazy or weird. I don't like weird. I don't even like the word 'weird'. And I definitely don't like the idea of work being weird; it's too easy. But I love the absurd.

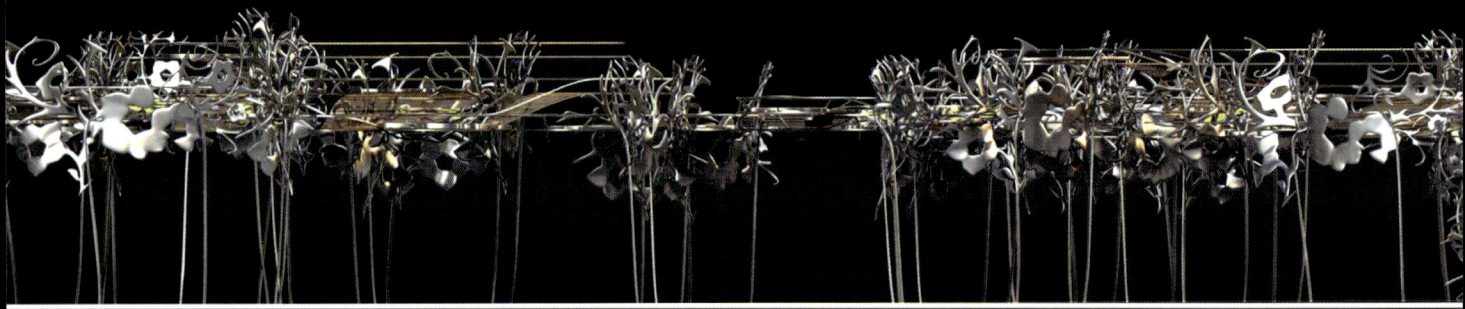

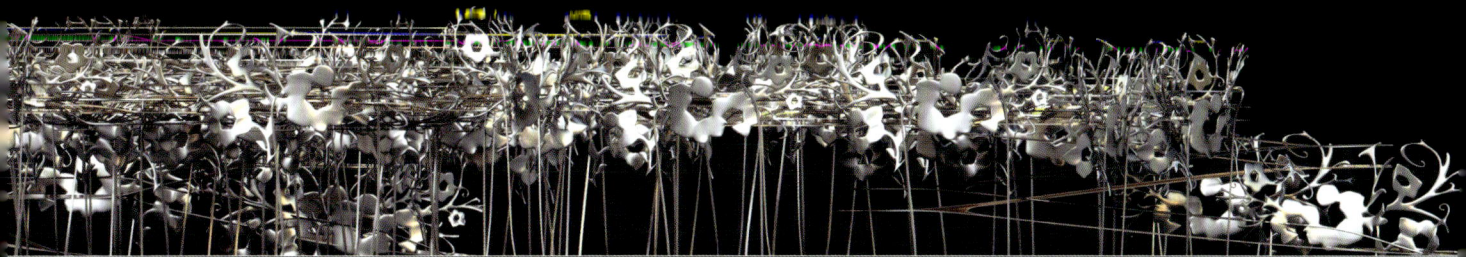

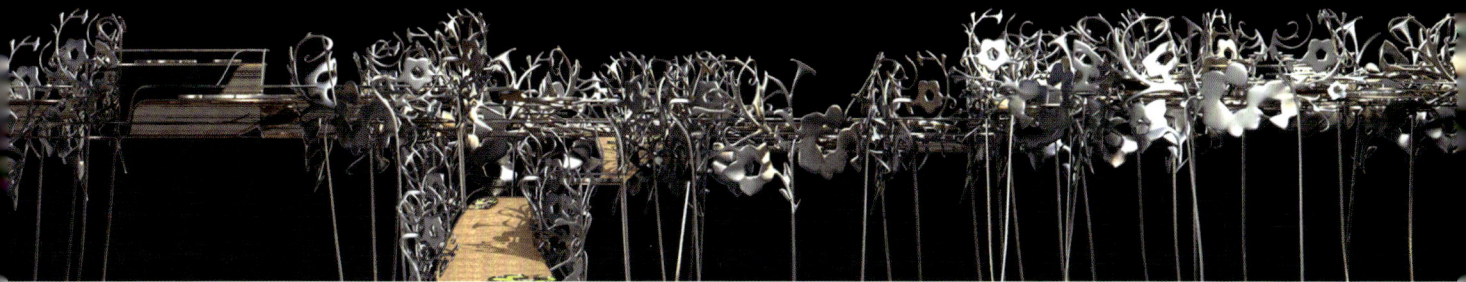

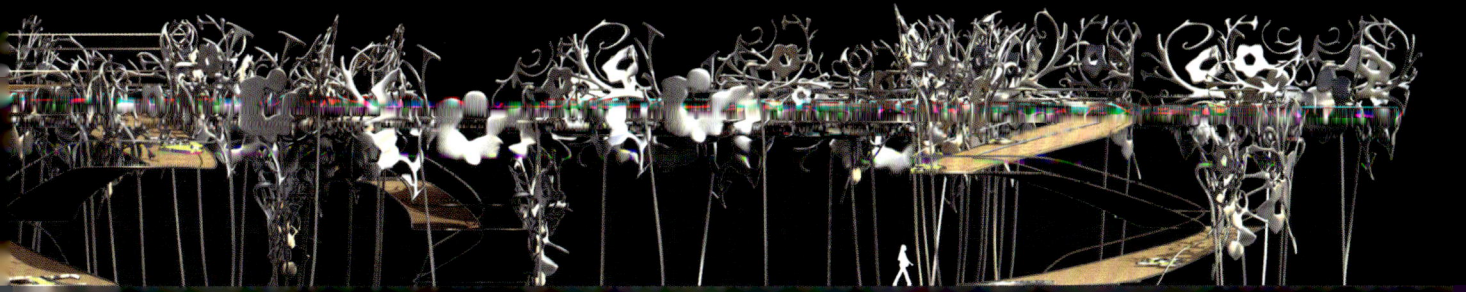

Puente del Río Apatlaco

A literal crossing becomes a crossover of types and notions. The path across the river, which would normally be a straight vector, becomes distorted, involuted within itself until it is slowed into a plaza, then tangled into a wild park. It takes something serious and direct, and allows it to become more playful, providing a space in which to wander and explore, with multiple different paths and opportunities. What is normally two-dimensional and flat becomes a three-dimensional design problem. Cinematic technique – the movement of a camera around and through a virtual space – is the vehicle of the development of form, and the paths across the bridge become a physical manifestation of that virtual effect. It is a garden, but also an artificial simulation of a garden, so that visitors can observe nature while still being separate from it.

Location: Jojutla, Mexico
Date: 2018
Programme: Bridge

Related projects
Barcelona Park, 2014 (p. 194)
Conexion Barcelona, 2015 (p. 204)

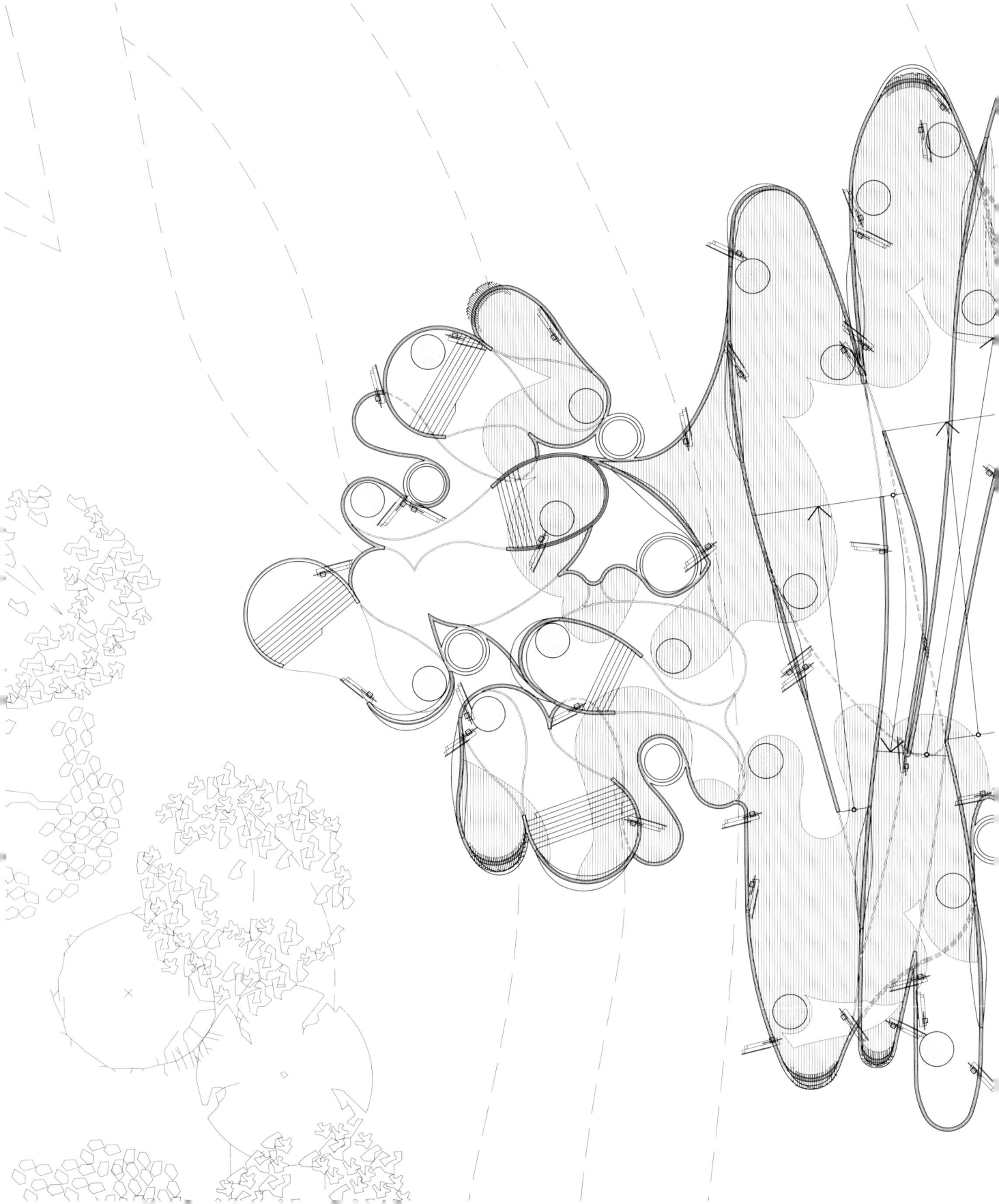

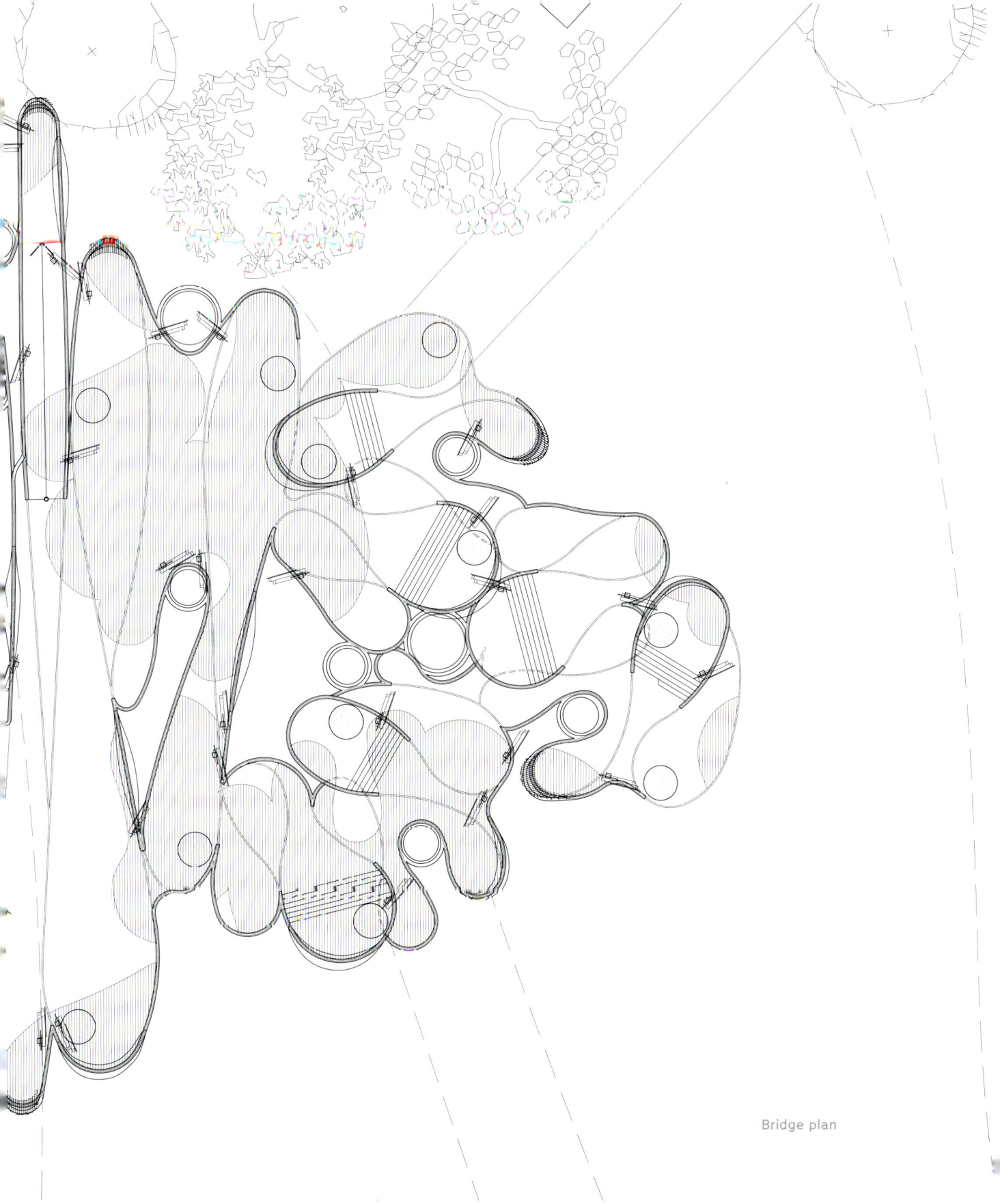

Bridge plan

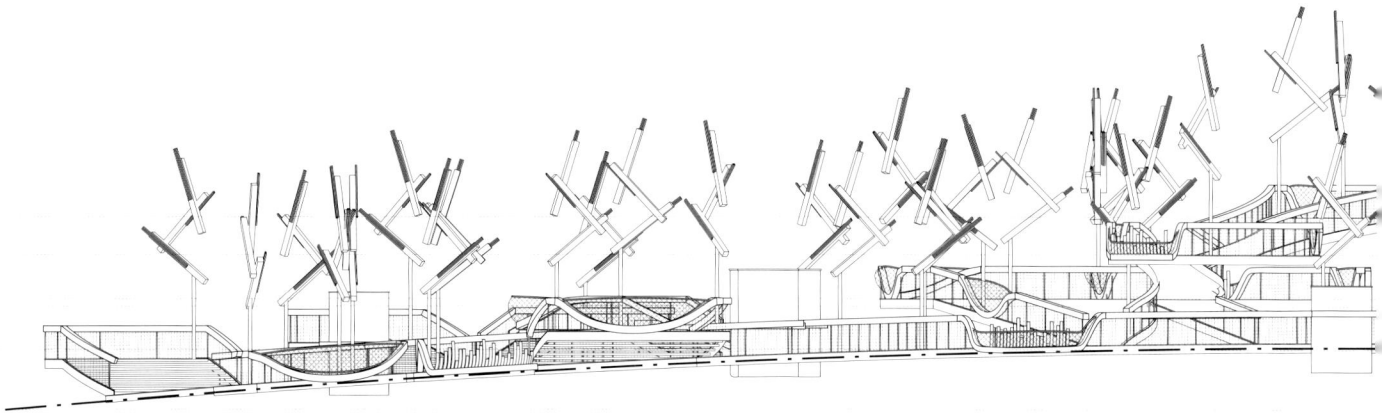

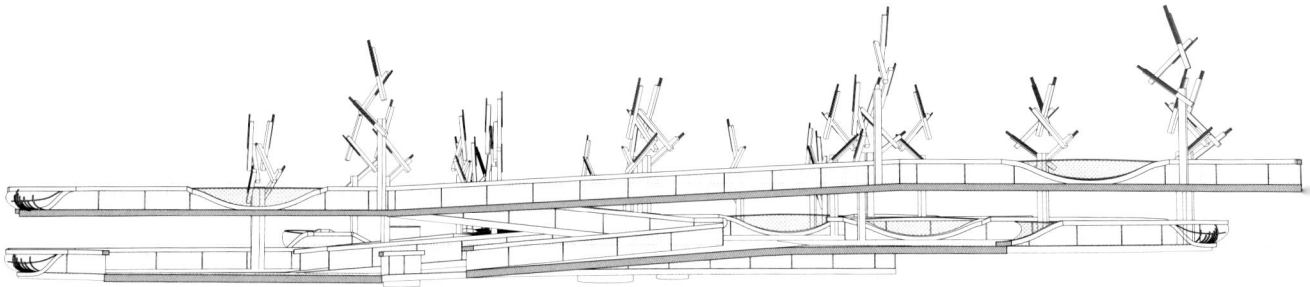

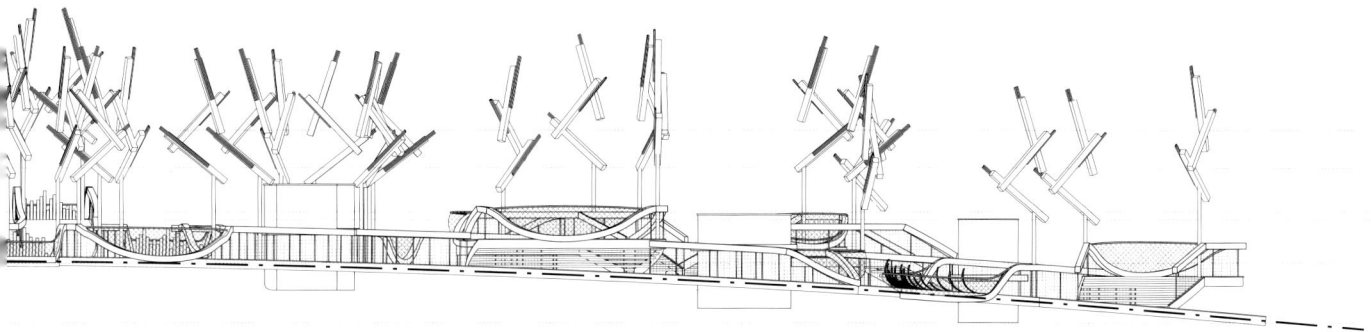

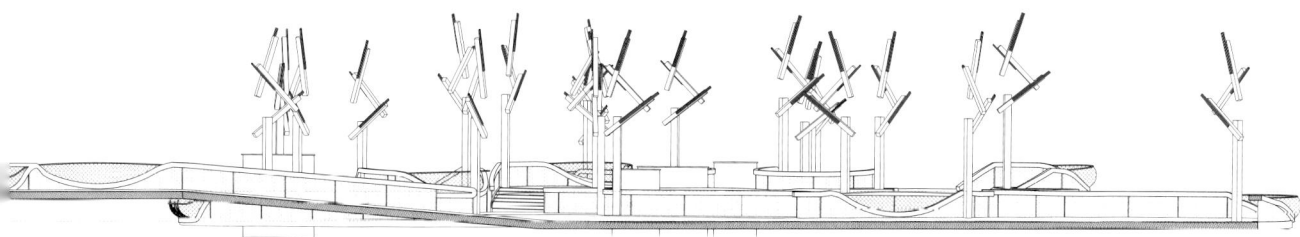

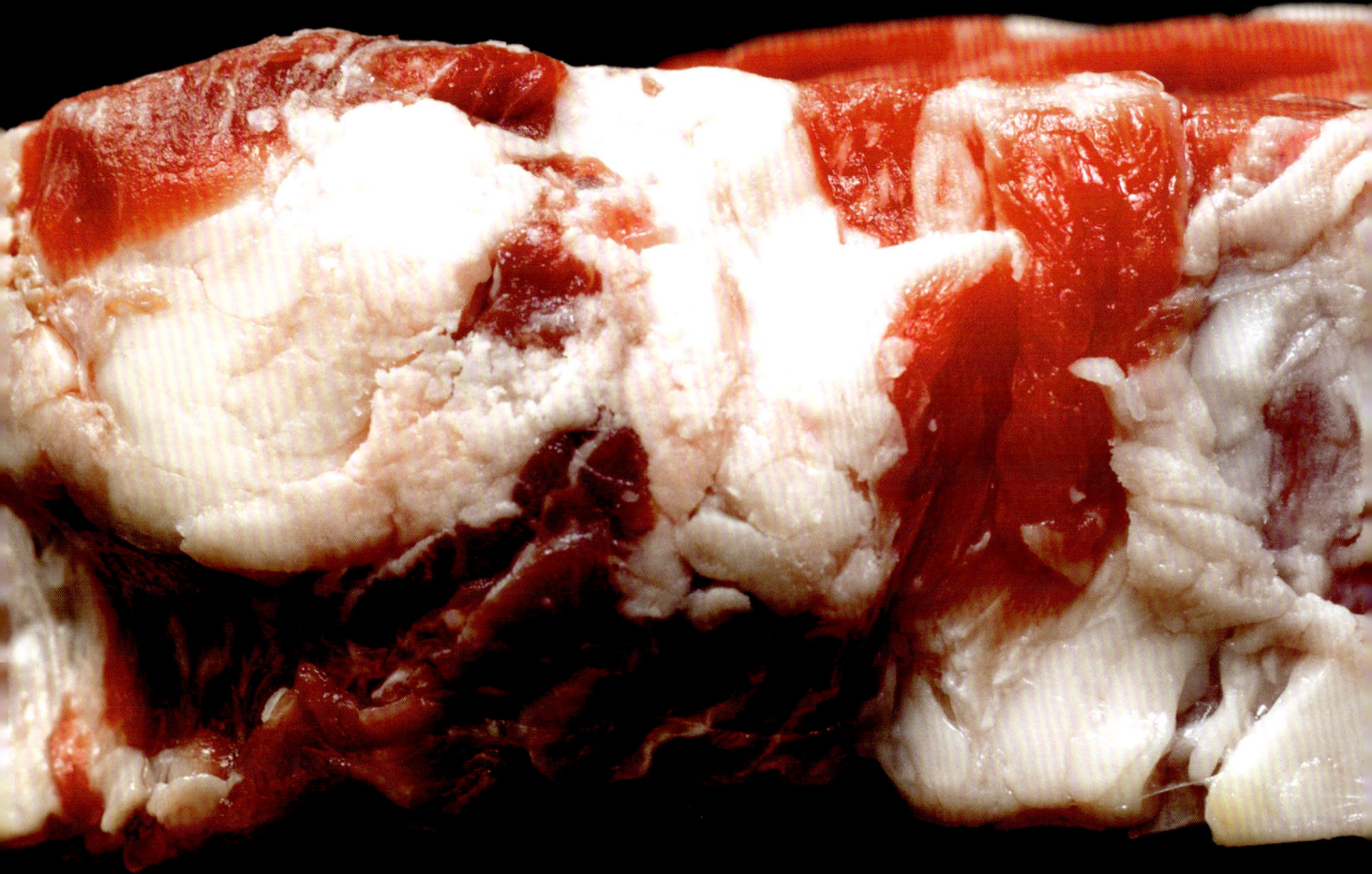

RITUALS

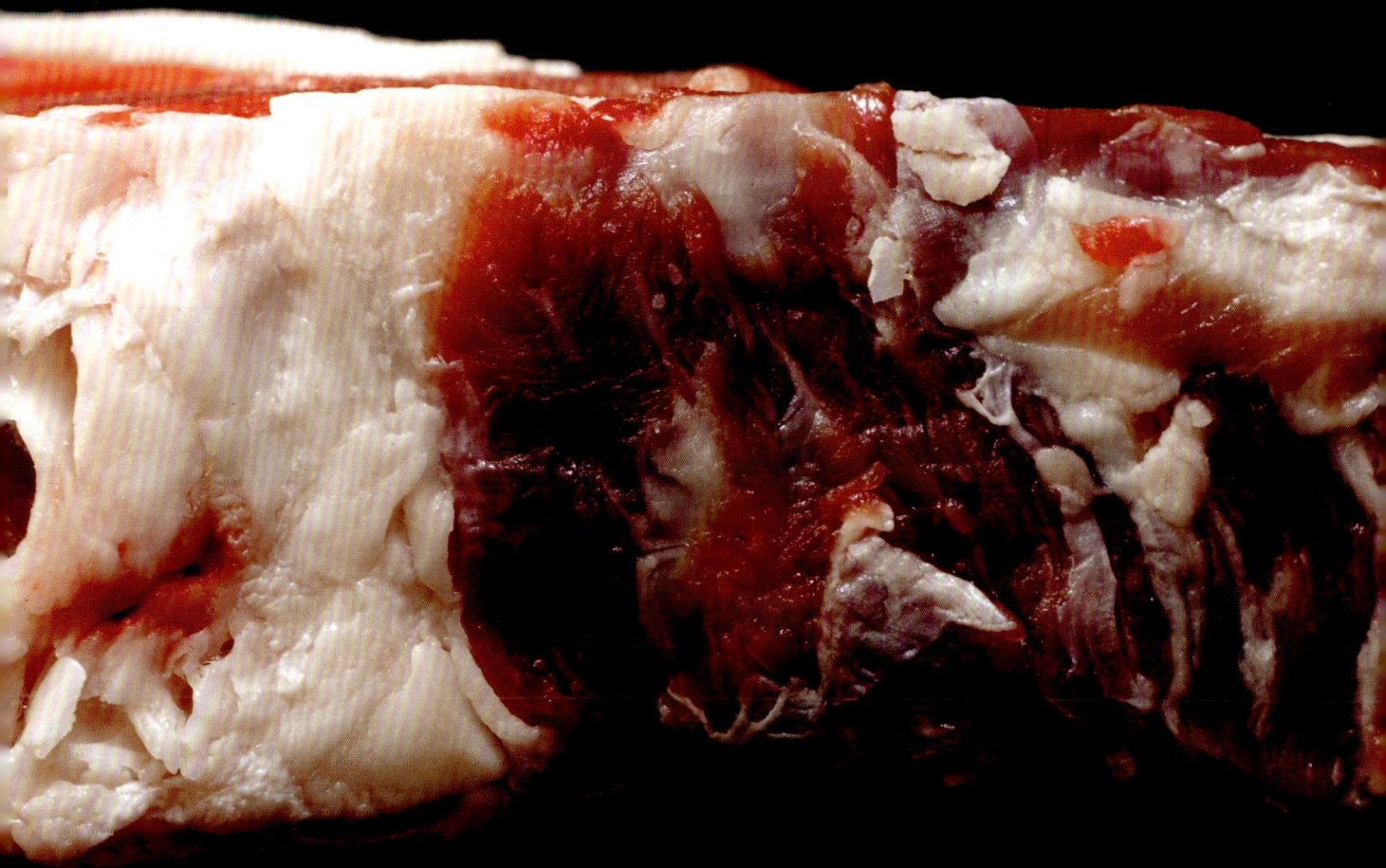

Seroussi Bench

Imaginary architectural investigation and representation is in no way confined by the specific scalar limitations of the human dwelling. If architecture produces and enforces the very possibility of scale, then why has it, apart from the obvious professional considerations, been so circumscribed as an intellectual endeavour by variations on the primordial hut, however complex, singular or plural, flat or stacked? Architecture has always experimented on the margins, contrary to the dictates of Vitruvian anthropocentrism. Other emerging media technologies – robotics, nanotechnology, genomic and genetic systems, planetary information networks – continue to excite architectural agendas and projects, and extend what is meant by a programme, a form and a site.

Location: Paris, France
Date: 2010

Related projects
Mexican Funeral, 2010 (p. 54)
TBA 21_1.0, 2011 (p. 234)

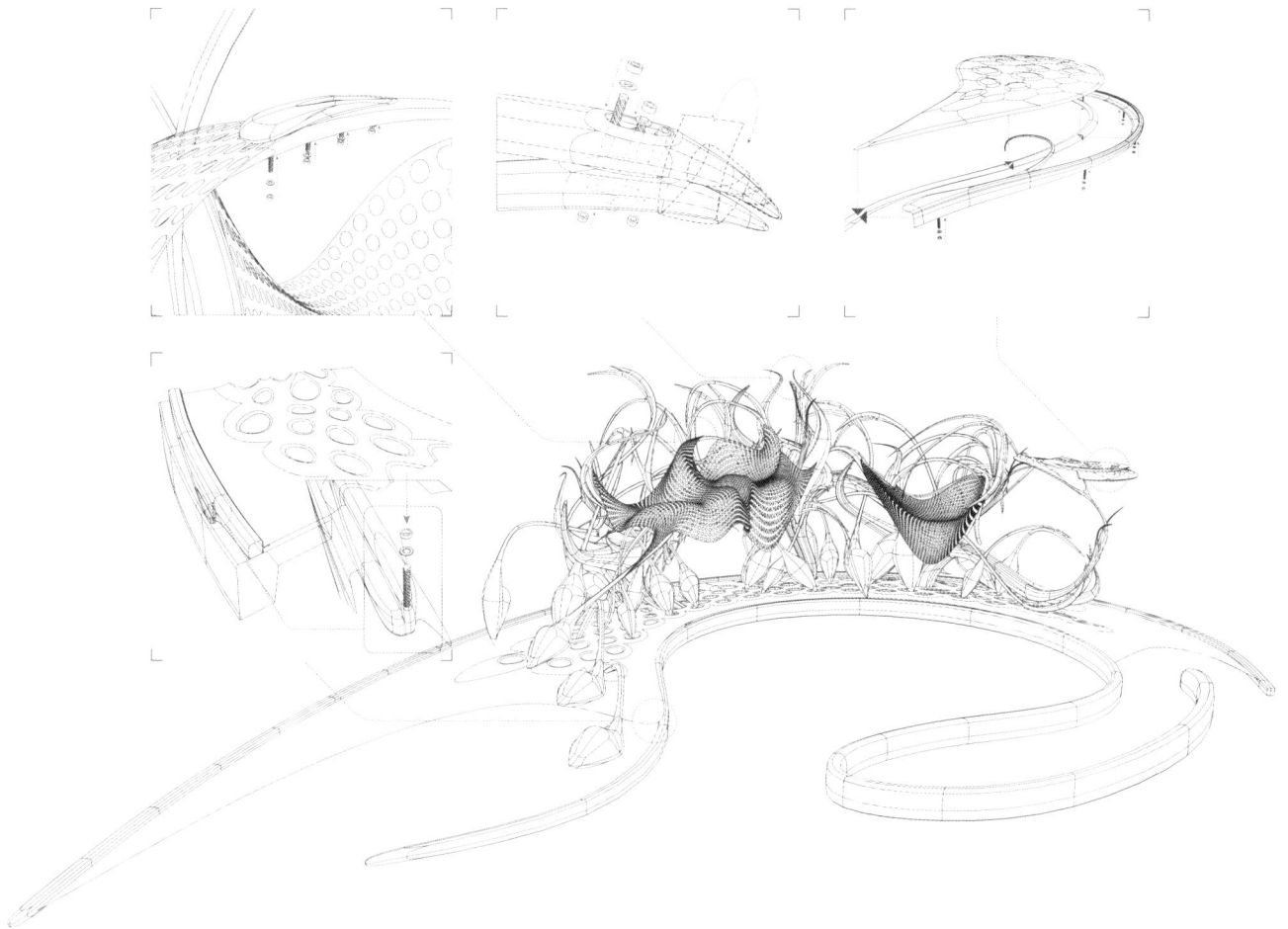

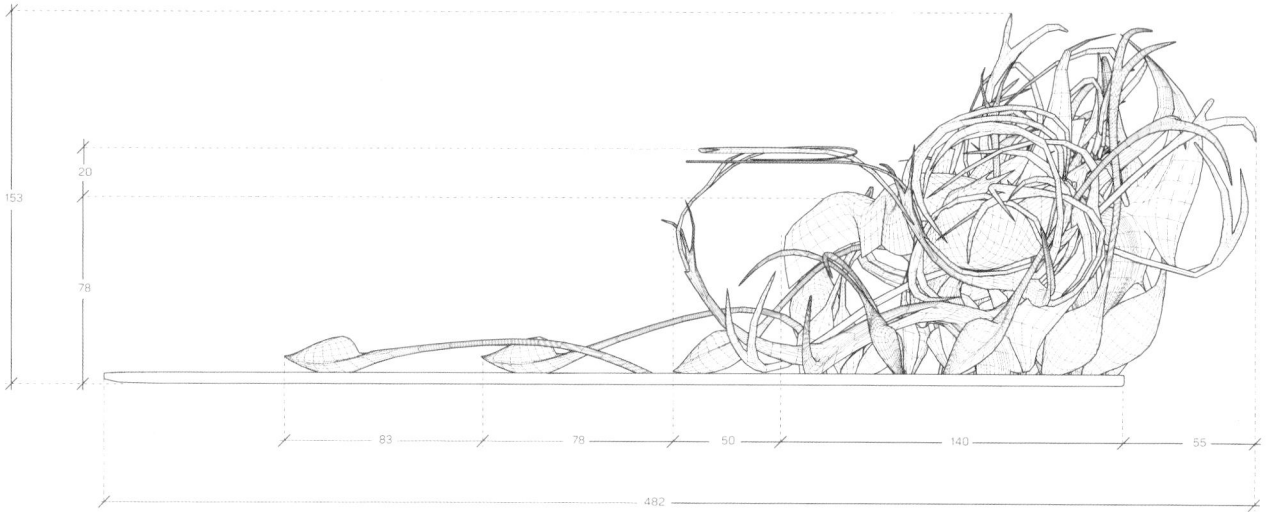

Side elevation

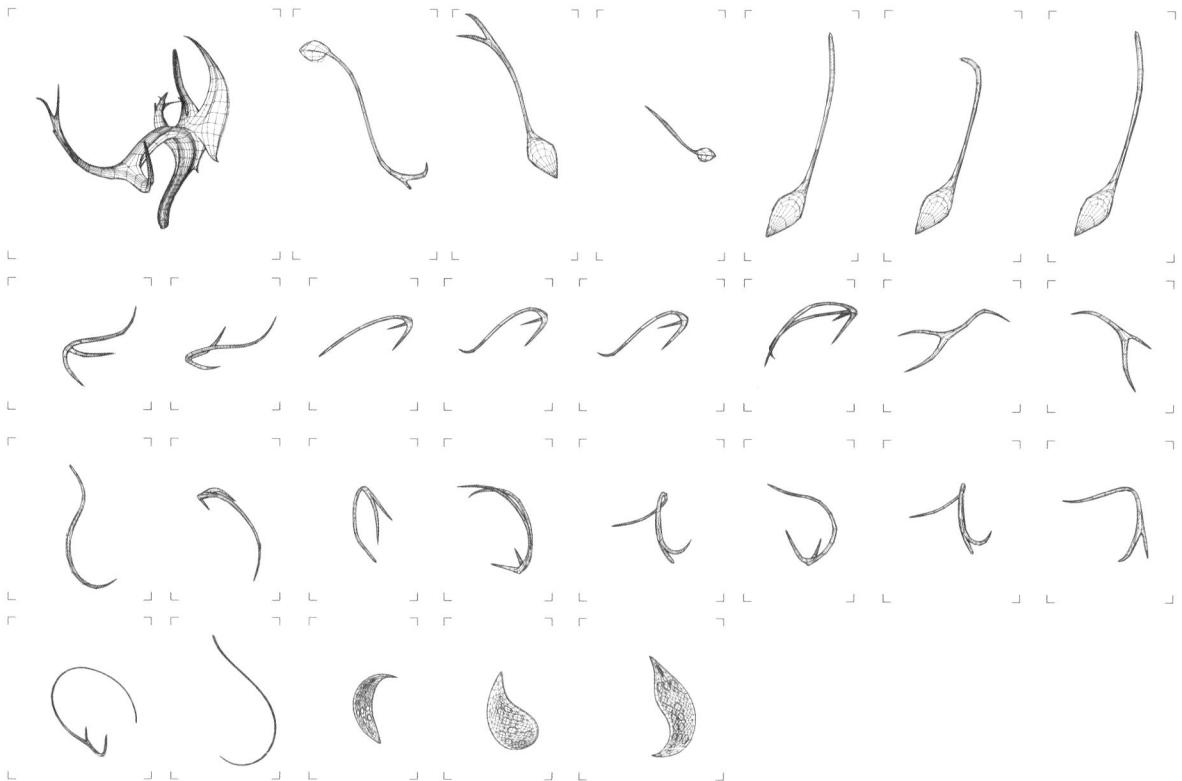

Taxonomy diagram

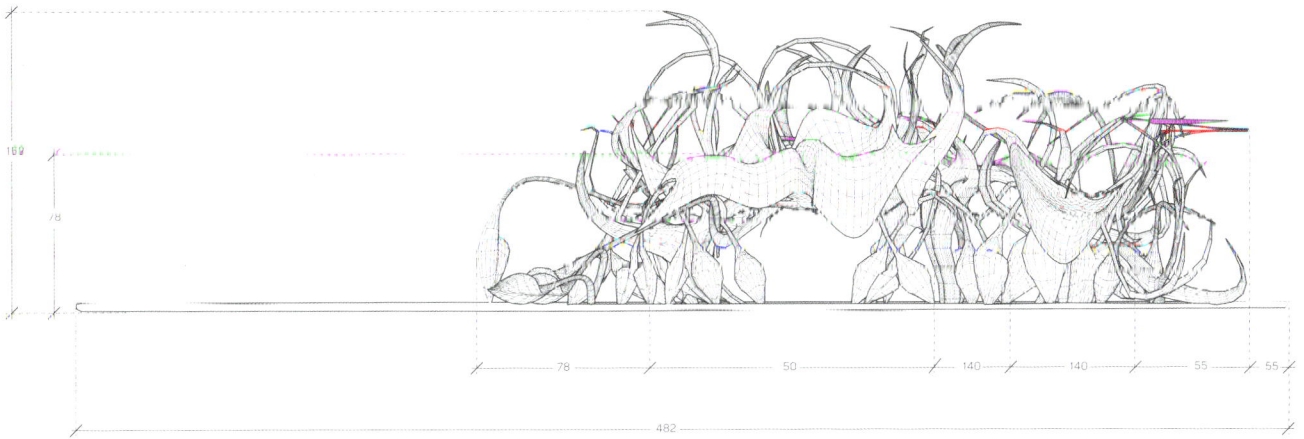

169

78

78

78 — 50 — 140 — 140 — 55 — 55

482

Front elevation

428

128

60

79

63

91 — 11 — 48 — 104 — 222 — 32 — 44

627

Plan

TBA 21_1.0

This project set out to mutate the programme of a museum or art pavilion, and become a tool with which to study the shift to a paradigm of 'species', as opposed to the ubiquitous platform of 'types'. If types are traditionally viewed as categories of standardization and symbolic expressions of form, then species are malleable entities in constant metamorphosis, with adaptation and mutation as their main characteristics. A species and a type both need a lineage in order to be acknowledged as such. A species has more freedom, because it can mutate. A type can change, but cannot mutate – it can be combined or renewed, but will always remain a type. This project proposes to conduct an extensive trip into the cellular logic and construction of structural instability. In order to radicalize the agenda of the autonomy of form, the possibilities of artificial and natural interaction(s) must be scrutinized.

Location: Patagonia, South America
Date: 2011
Programme: Museum, art pavilion

Related projects
Mexican Funeral, 2010 (p. 54)
Seroussi Bench, 2010 (p. 226)

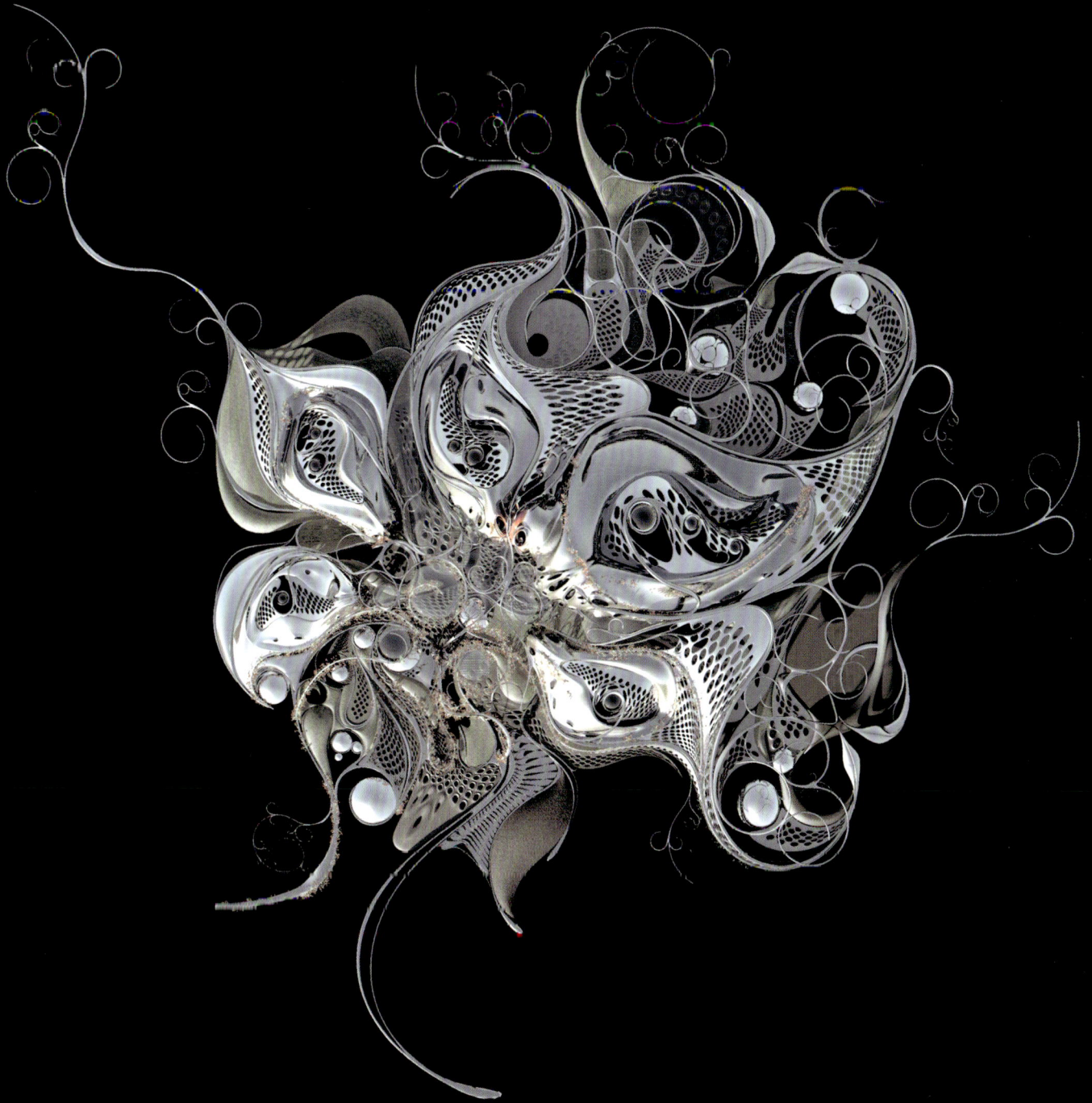

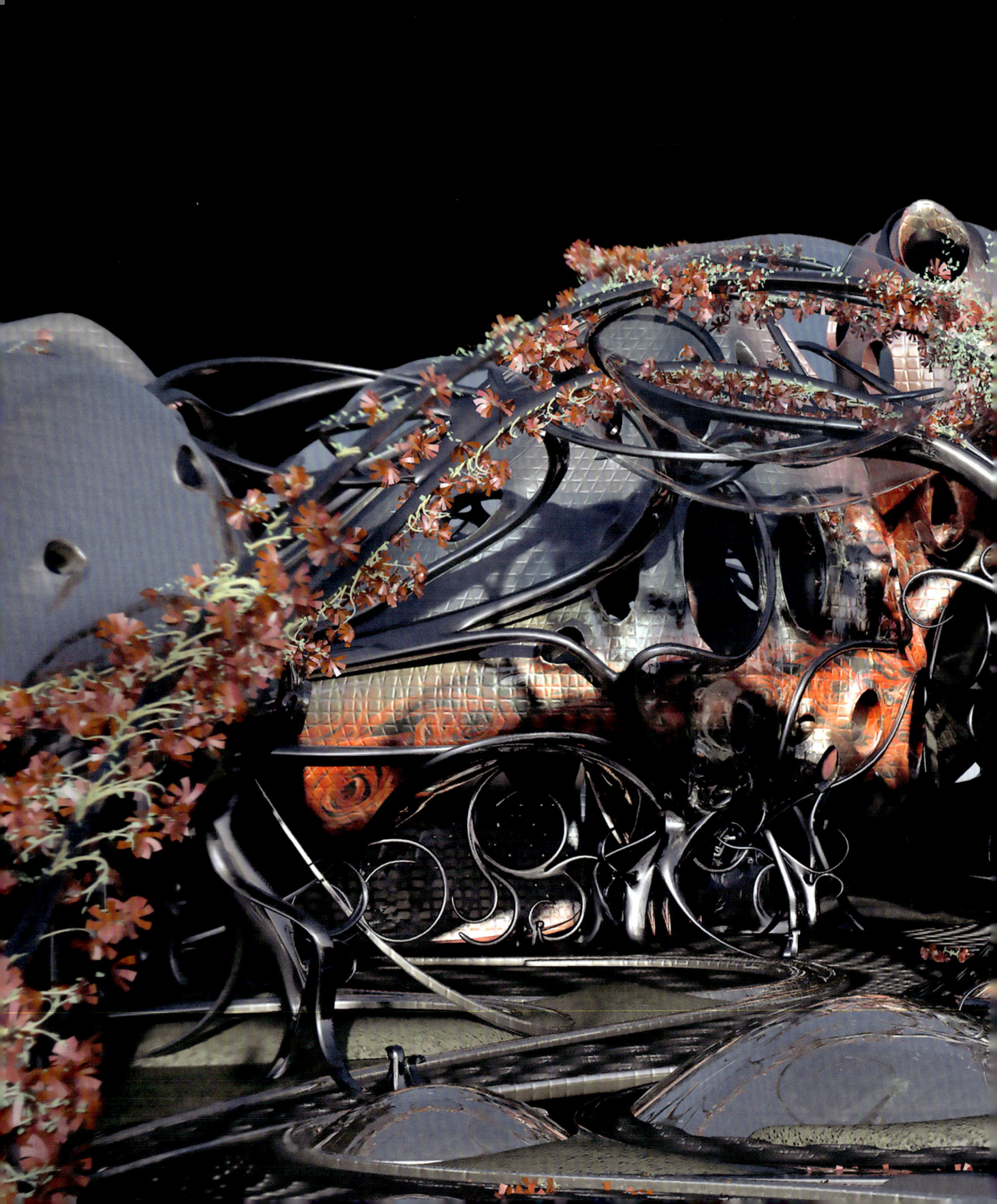

DR: Because you emphasize how science, ornament and ritual contaminate Modernist form, you are not necessarily interested in the significance of these things in themselves, but in how they might transform the Modernist project. If we take the geisha ritual, for example, and contaminate

Rituals & Formalism

architectural form with it, you are interested in the result of that experiment, rather than in the meaning and significance of the geisha ritual itself.

HDA: Yes, that's correct to some degree. The contaminating agents are generally things I have some personal interest in, like butchery. I wouldn't pick something at random. At the same time, I'm more interested in how something like butchery can be taken literally and incorporated as a procedure for cutting and manipulating architectural mass in a more complex, three-dimensional way. I have no interest in the meaning of butchery and representing that meaning somehow in the design.

DR: Let's talk about your interest in being literal, as opposed to ... what? Being abstract?

HDA: Being more literal with agencies of contamination was an interesting idea, because it is something that I believe art, or even fashion, does really well, but architecture struggles with because of its never-ending dedication to abstraction. I am fully aware of how absolute literalism, like originality, can never be fully achieved in architecture, so I might be more interested in delaying abstraction as long as possible for the sake of originality.

DR: And, to be clear, you're doing this to contaminate the purity of digital form, which you understand as a late Modernist project?

HDA: I think I'm trying to find an alternative to Postmodernism, which I never felt comfortable with.

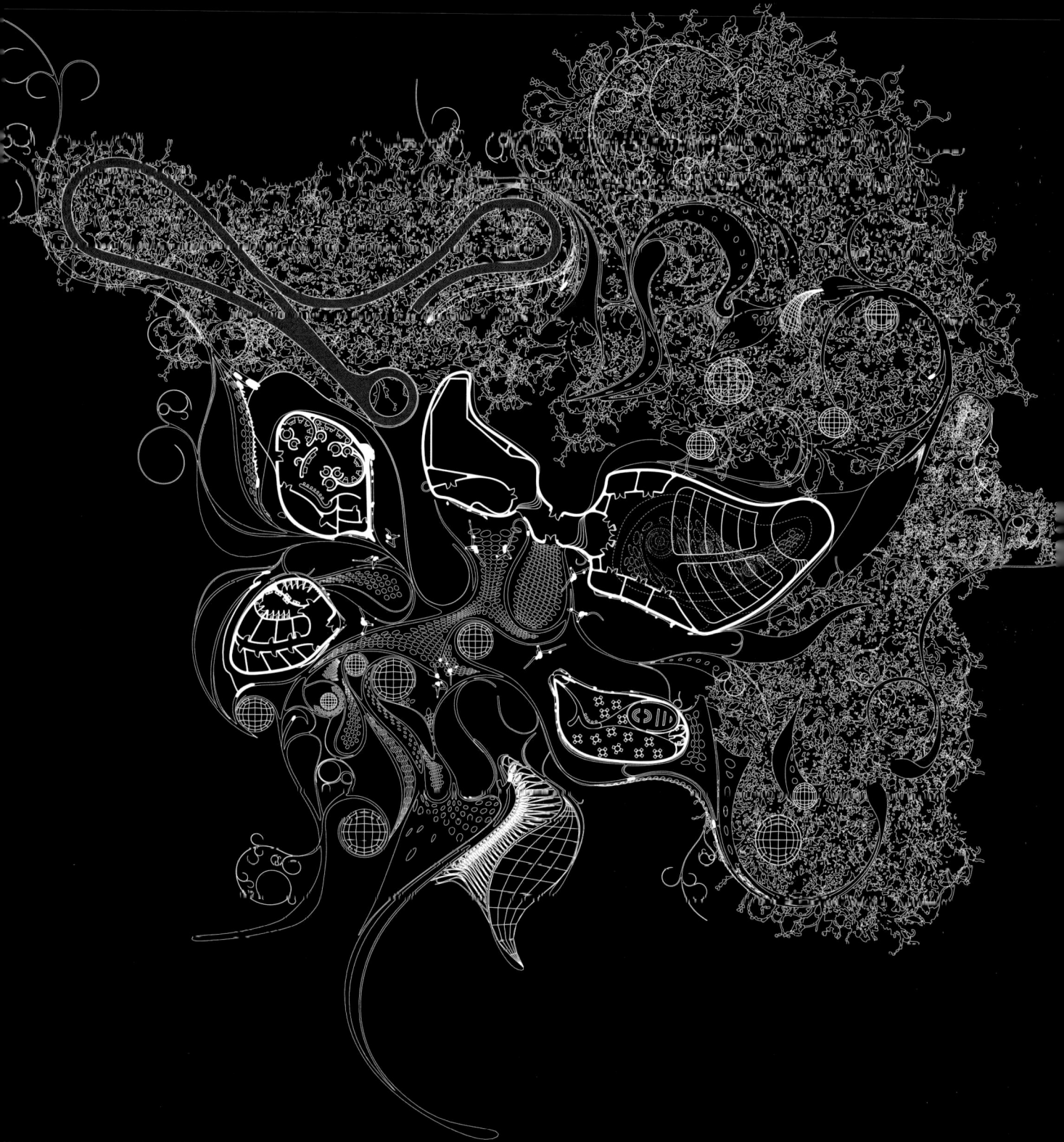

TBA 21_2.0

Dynamic topology vegetation then becomes
a tool that pertains, in a large degree, to the
highest control of the manipulations of those
formal strategies. If traditional architecture
needed to determine the degree to which a
project achieved its extent of beauty, then,
subsequently, these topologies explore the
emergent aesthetics as methods of material
and the structure as a reversed mechanism
of a more traditional beauty. The material
specifies a desire to disturb or to produce
a more appalling encounter with the work.
Rooting this topological design paradigm within
the confines of architecture's aim for beauty
and proportion, the ugly and the horrific (both
from the new kind of structural organization:
excess) are necessary variations that allow for
an escape towards a spatial model of shocking
presence that is capable of producing lust
and arousal.

Location: Patagonia, South America
Date: 2011
Programme: Museum, art pavilion

Related projects
Monster, Monstrosity, Monstrous, 2011 (p. 298)
Espresso Cup, 2011 (p. 300)
Still Flesh, 2012 (p. 304)

1   Observatory 1
2   Observatory 2
3   Outdoor auditorium
4   Entrance lobby
5   Outdoor pavilion
6   Garden pavilion
7   Garden grotesque

Floorplan

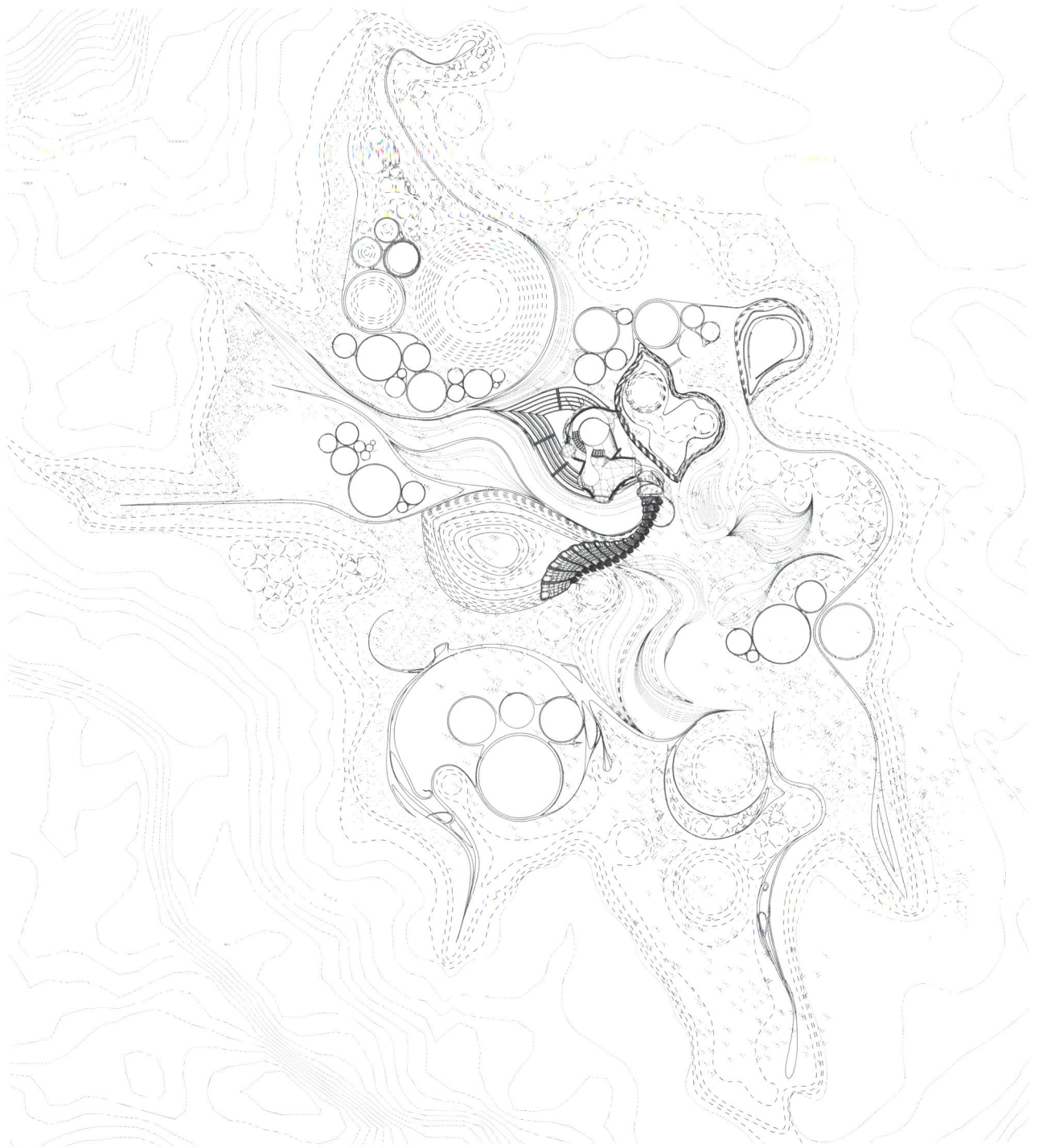

Site plan

Rusuupuisto

The Museum of Central Finland and the
Alvar Aalto Museum in Jyväskylä are two
significant works by the country's greatest
architect, Alvar Aalto (1898-1976). The aim of
the competition was to design an extension
that would connect the two buildings in a way
that represented the high architectural level
of the site as a whole. The new extension had
to adapt to its environment in a balanced way,
and find a natural connection with Aalto's
buildings. Serving as both a connecting
gateway and shared museum shop and
technical space, the extension enables
the shared use of an already existing lift,
auditorium, cafeteria, and exhibition and
workroom spaces. The functionality of these
areas was an essential part of the design
requirements.

Location: Jyväskylä, Finland
Date: 2015
Programme: Competition, museum extension

Related projects
PS1 MoMA, 2005 (p. 28)
Tabakalera, 2008 (p. 140)
Sant Adrià de Besòs, 2014 (p. 154)

DR: Why is using the most cutting-edge technologies in design so important to you?

HDA: For a few reasons, I think. One, it was a way to break out of my traditional Modernist training.

DR: Earlier, you were talking about how you wanted to contaminate the purity of digital form. But before that, you were using the computer to contaminate your Modernist upbringing?

HDA: I think that's true. There are other reasons, as well. I am always looking for ways to work faster and more efficiently with a small group of people. I prefer to keep my team small. But generally, and I suppose this is still a Modernist ethic, I think architecture has an obligation to work with whatever are the most contemporary forms of production.

DR: But there is something else, too. Our current design technologies allow us to virtualize design like never before. Drawing on transparent paper was a technological innovation to some degree, but it's an entirely new thing to be able to navigate the 3D virtual space of design software.

HDA: Yes, I've been fascinated from the beginning with the hyper-reality of digital technologies.

DR: I remember early on you were one of the first to radically adopt digital techniques. It is how people first got to know your work. You were known more for technological expertise than for exotic formal explorations and difficult aesthetics.

HDA: In my mind, I've never really been a technological innovator. I have never been someone who worried about creating and advancing technology. I'm more an off-the-shelf kind of guy. Don't get me wrong, I'll always be the first in line to try the newest tool. I'm very curious right now, for example, about what artificial intelligence can do. But I'm interested because the technology seems to be reaching the point at which it is producing interesting results – as seen in the recent work you and Karel [Klein] are doing. Strangely, I don't find VR or AR that interesting just yet, because it still seems very crude and unrefined as tools for producing new formalisms and aesthetic effects. But I am constantly on the lookout for new ways to do old ways.

Technology & Design

1	East gateway	6	Shop entrance	11	West gateway #2	16	Lift shaft
2	East entrance	7	Shop entrance	12	Technical room	17	Lift hall
3	Plant court	8	Shop porch	13	Plant court		
4	Keski-Suomen entrance #1	9	West gateway #1	14	Visitor lounge		
5	Shop level 1	10	Storage	15	Café Alvar entrance		

Floorplan – Level 1

Floorplan – Level 2

1	Alvar Aalto Museum	5	Lift lobby	9	Shop porch
2	Café entrance	6	Storage	10	Exhibition entrance
3	Exhibition entrance	7	Shop entrance	11	Museum of Central Finland
4	Lift	8	Shop		

Section A-A

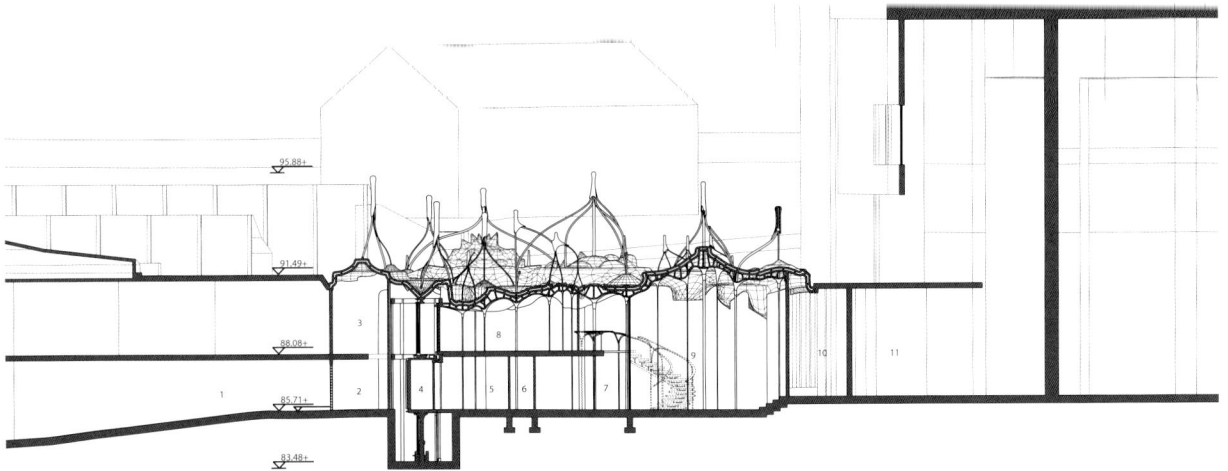

Section B-B

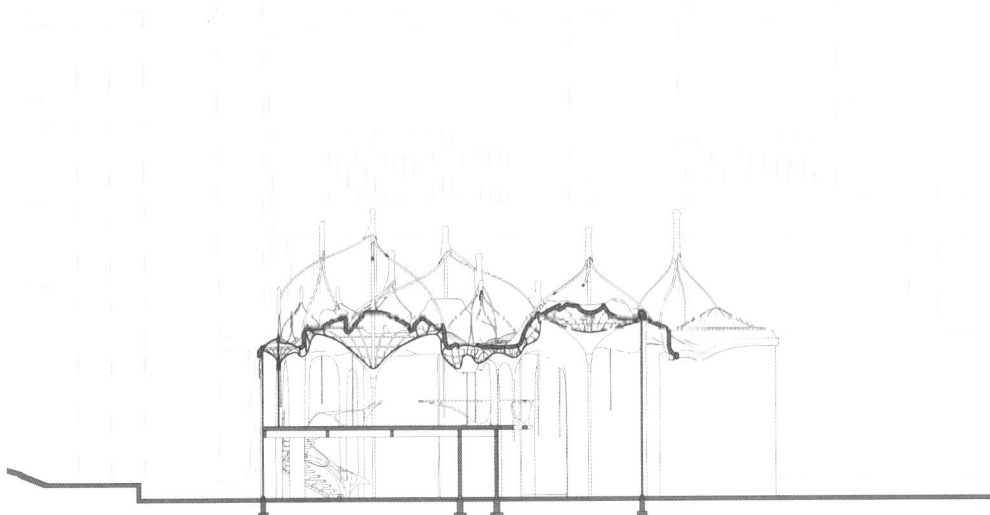

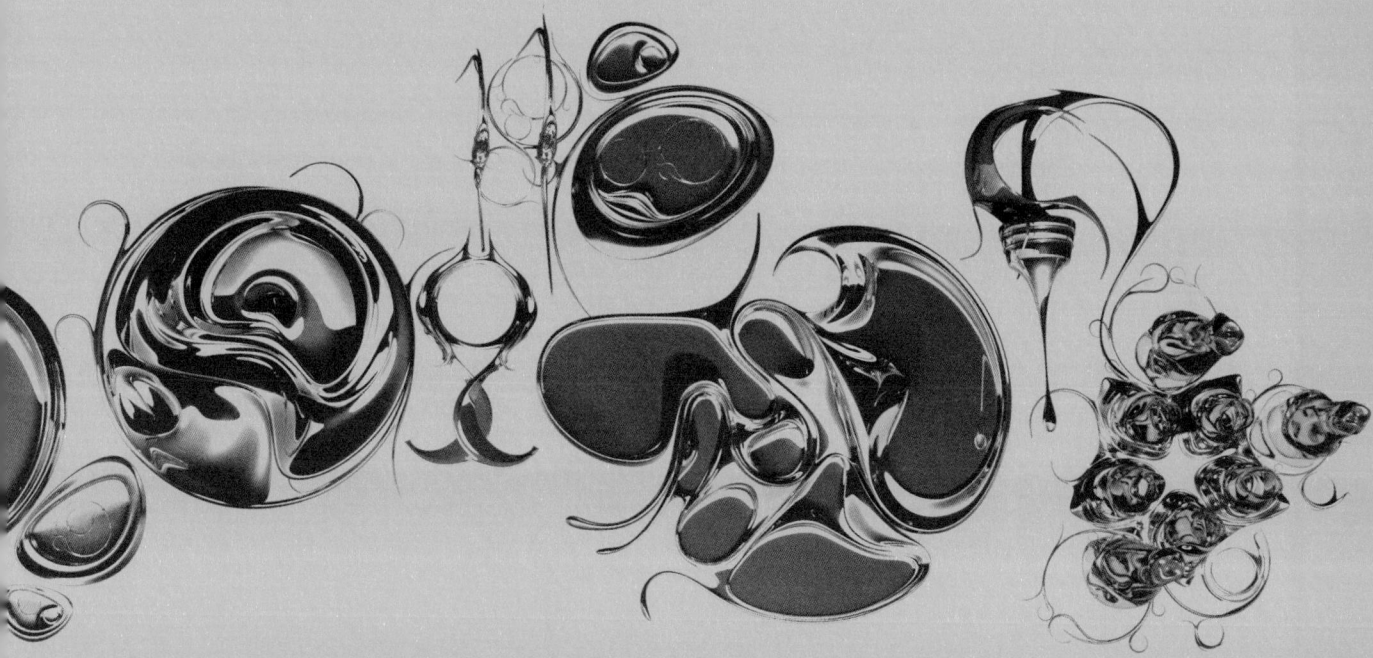

On Speculative Butchery:

Ethical Coherencies and Contaminations in the Architecture of Hernán Díaz Alonso

Benjamin H. Bratton

Summaries of a friend's work take certain standard forms – a letter of recommendation, an obituary, a grand jury deposition – and I will try to avoid these formats. I will try my best not to be objective, and so first some disclosure: Hernán Díaz Alonso and I arrived at SCI-Arc at the same time, more or less, and though our backgrounds were different, many of our 'non-architectural' interests overlapped. This suggested to us that we might share an agenda to make use of architecture to intervene in other areas (including, as I recall, CGI cinema, biotechnology, zombie-ism, megachurch and sporting spectacles, airport

culture, and so on.) We unhid that agenda with eight to ten years of XLab studios and seminars, which themselves amounted to a discontiguous conversation between he and I and several dozen SCI-Arc students.

Díaz Alonso's way of working stages (or is staged by) specific tension: on the one hand, to demarcate architecture as an autonomous disciplinary, discursive and technical entity, and on the other, to turn architecture inside out by contaminating, corrupting and parasitizing it with outside information. There is a romantic rationale in his gaucho gothic, one that comes from an unsentimental mixing of the perfect with the imperfect, the high with the low, as part of a search for new forms that are themselves not hybrids but platonic ideals from a different cave. 'Philosophy' is one source of external ideas, but it is not privileged over space opera or chase scenes. This contamination can sometimes be transgressive, sometimes atheistic, and as the resulting forms take on a life of their own beyond the dictates of a given project and programme, the contamination flows both ways, in and out. At the scale of a practice the trick is to manage this osmotic back and forth, so that things continue to interrupt and disrupt one another, never settling into an entropic homeostasis.

My short remarks begin with the contaminant (the outside), move on to the contamination (the design) and then to the contaminated (the architecture itself). Of late, Díaz Alonso has taken a strong interest in traditional Argentinian butchery.

Contaminant

This interest includes how steaks are cooked, but also butchery as a practical and culturally local theory of the body, of parts to whole, of taxonomies of cuts, of traditions of eating and also of eating traditions. It is not for the queasy empath, but this technique for the violent reorganization of the animal body into component protein modules overlaps cleaner techniques of bending and stacking bodies, Euclidean primitives, calculative geometries, folds and foldings, pleats, tessellations, delaminations, fenestrations, apertures, inversions, segmentation and delineation, and other 'elements of architecture'.

This vision of culinary predation connects with ways that architecture knows to make and find form, and also with the ways it knows of representing these in section, axonometric, animation, model, multi-perspectival drawing, robotically assembled 5D nanomatterbots, and so on. 'They're made out of meat': it is a way of knowing. *Asado*, *matambre*, *colita de cuadril*,

bife de costilla, *molleja* are not just different words for the same cuts, they also subdivide a different animal. Butchers and surgeons (and barbers) share professional genealogies and sometimes tricks of the trade. A surgeon becomes a butcher by his incompetence, but is the inverse true, as well? (Butchery as surgery in bad faith, and surgery as extraordinarily empathetic butchery?) At the end of the day, the difference is whether the one with the knife ends up ingesting the one without the knife, making two into one, or whether they stay separated, both alive, and go their separate ways. Between the two, organ-harvesting may draw on both for its very slow-food version of cannibalism. Truth or consequences?

Architecture negotiates a necessarily unresolved relation between the real and the 'not real', which, depending on the practice, can be variously the fictional, the figurative, the metaphysical, the cinematic, the geopolitical, the narrative, the conjectural, the symbolic imaginary, the sym-

Contamination

metrical sublime, the model, the elevation and/or the plan. For Díaz Alonso's practice, this unresolved correlation is particularly loud. He makes a decisive distinction between the experimental research practice that delves into or expands out from a particular set of academic problematics or visionary pursuits, and for which success is measured in unique private metrics, versus a speculative practice that seeks to intervene directly into the fabric of the physical landscape and introduce a real, side real, hyperreal or simply surreal irruption. Just as with genuinely creepy horror movies, for that to work the design must engage the gravities of sites, optics, bodies, environments, languages and materials as they really are, so that their distortion really does disturb reality. Like painting, composing a certain ratio of the real to the surreal, the fiction to the non-fiction, is a matter of blurring, elongating, tuning, calibrating, illuminating and dampening, building up the density of the image's surface by slicing it away, just so.

Architecture
negotiates
a necessarily
unresolved
relationship
between the real
and the 'not real'

The individual project is where the ritual that binds Romanticism and Rationalism takes shape, and the ritual itself is also beholden to gravity. As Díaz Alonso is quick to point out, his process and practice are, both conceptually and logistically, more likely to have come from Los Angeles than from anywhere else. This is because cinema and television have transformed the city into a habitat of transubstantiation, perched between story and situation – this is where the shoot-out scene in *Chinatown* was shot; this is the Frank Lloyd Wright house where Deckard interviews Rachael in *Blade Runner* and realizes she doesn't know she's a replicant; this is the tunnel used in every single car commercial, as well as *THX 1138*. Like visiting your childhood home, each place is living proof of its previous and primary existence in a dreamworld.

Secondly, Hollywood is comfortable with inter-disciplinary hypernarratives and ad-hoc inter-textuality, and usually eager to pursue new kinds of technical effect for its own sake. And thirdly, the modern cleaving of Art and Commerce, bequeathing intellectual authenticity only to the former, is itself compromised by the day-to-day business of our culture industry (in ways that agitated Theodor W. Adorno and Max Horkheimer the first time around and helped to instigate their funda-mentalist reaction, and continues to vex the Pier Vittorio Aurelis of the world).

This promiscuity is not the same thing as an unethical practice, but is one that executes its ethics at arm's length from morality and moralism (much like life itself.) One word that Díaz Alonso repeatedly uses to describe his interests, method and projects is 'contamination'. In the context of 'rituals' (of Romanticism and Rationalism), con-tamination suggests an economy of transgression, perhaps some persistent and idiosyncratic vari-ation on what Georges Bataille tried to describe as the erotics of excess and a general economy of energy and value. That would not be incorrect, but it would be incomplete. Contamination is not always transgressive. Which is the real priority? The act or the infraction? It may come down to whether you take Díaz Alonso at his word that his architecture is not meant to introduce a new hegemonic urban form – one better suited to a culture of planetary-scale computation than to the spreadsheet-driven layouts of consultant urbanism or their more decorative shadow, mainstream parametricism – but is rather, in his words, salt: 'You don't want to have a diet without salt, nor do you want a diet of only salt. He maintains that the parasitic posture of his projects is not an interim strategy to gain a foothold on the host's body, before taking it over and replacing it with its own replicant genome, but rather that the supplemental, parasitic and thus 'transgressive' relationship between his form and that of the given site is necessary in order to hold the two in their delicate tension.

The real may have the last say on this. Modern biological sciences are much more invested in contamination and symbiotic parasitism as foundations of life than many imagine. Far from seeing these as exceptions to the rule, increasingly they are the rule. There are theories of the origins of complex life as based on a durable contagion, of the complexity of life on land being due to nested parasitism (an animal living inside an animal, living inside an animal), and research on the microbial gut biome as a key factor in the health of the host body, including yours. As far as biological life is concerned, the corruption of bodies by other bodies is the norm.

Another word you will hear Díaz Alonso use to describe his projects is 'coherencies', by which he means moments in which disparate elements and motifs congeal, perhaps by surprise, into a temporarily stable order or pattern that itself may participate in another plural order or pattern at a different scale within the whole, or even in relationship with the external body onto which the whole has attached itself. These constitute local constraints within the global system, or vice versa. They are repeatable. They may have a grammar, suggesting a proper and improper usage and a more exact timbre of their communicative voice. In some ways, the invention of these coherencies is the general innovation that practices such as

his offer to design in general. They are sampled, sequenced, misused, automated, and show up in supermarket façades in Guangzhou and soap commercials in Glendale.

This is the counter-contamination that makes the whole cycle work. I wonder how we will ultimately compare these coherencies to what Rem Koolhaas identified as the 'elements' of architecture at the 2018 Venice Biennale. Koolhaas formalized elements into a single table indexing the variance in their deployment throughout the world, a forensics of Modernism as a global/local system dynamic of another sort. In other words, will we want to add these 'coherencies' to the existing architectural table, as exotic and fragile transuranic elements that can only exist for a few seconds under extreme laboratory conditions? Or will we come to see them as the basic terminology of another architectural century?

The former would suggest that Díaz Alonso is right, and that his forms are spices like livermorium (Lv), plutonium (Pu) or californium (Cf). The latter would suggest the biologists are right and that successful symbiosis, parasitism, contamination and epigenesis is how new life emerges in the long run. Over time, the transgressive significance and peculiarity of the coherencies being hatched will slowly dissolve. The surgeon becomes the butcher. The butcher becomes the designer. The designer makes new meat.

This essay first appeared in SCI-Arc Alumni Magazine 009 (Fall 2014)

Contaminated

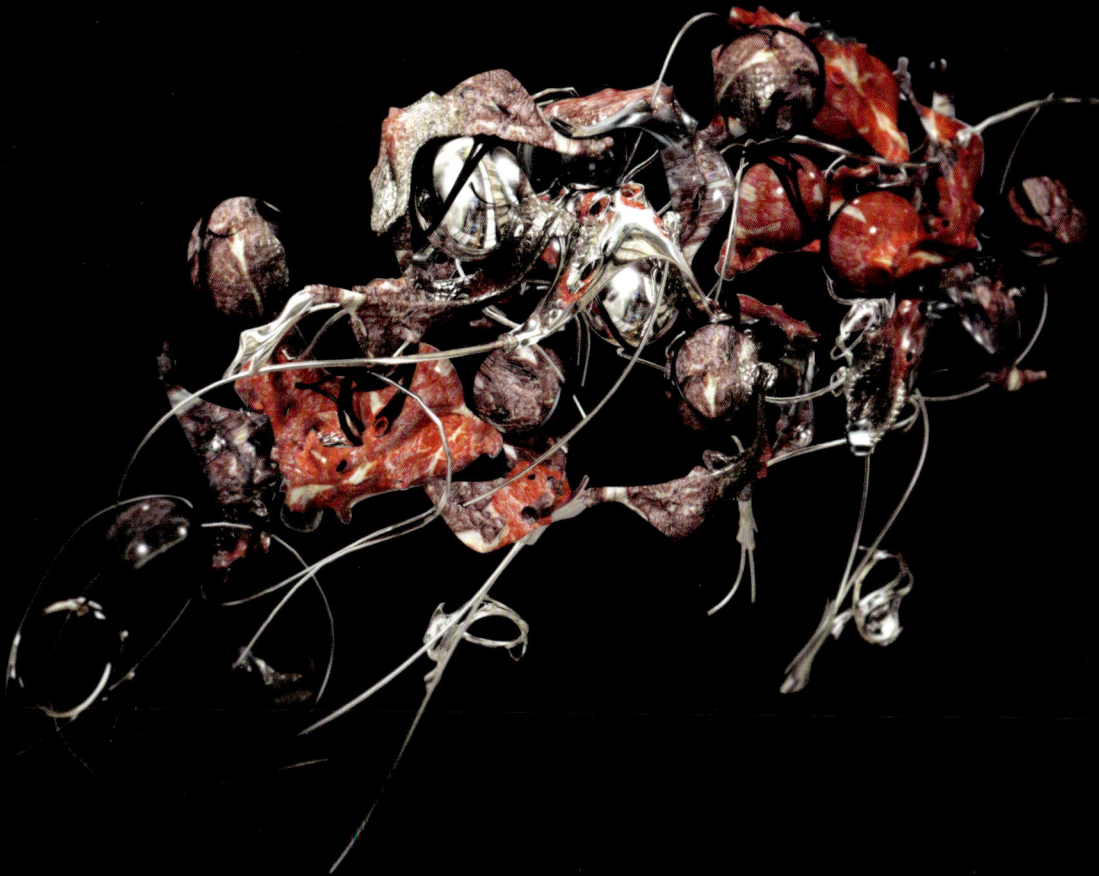

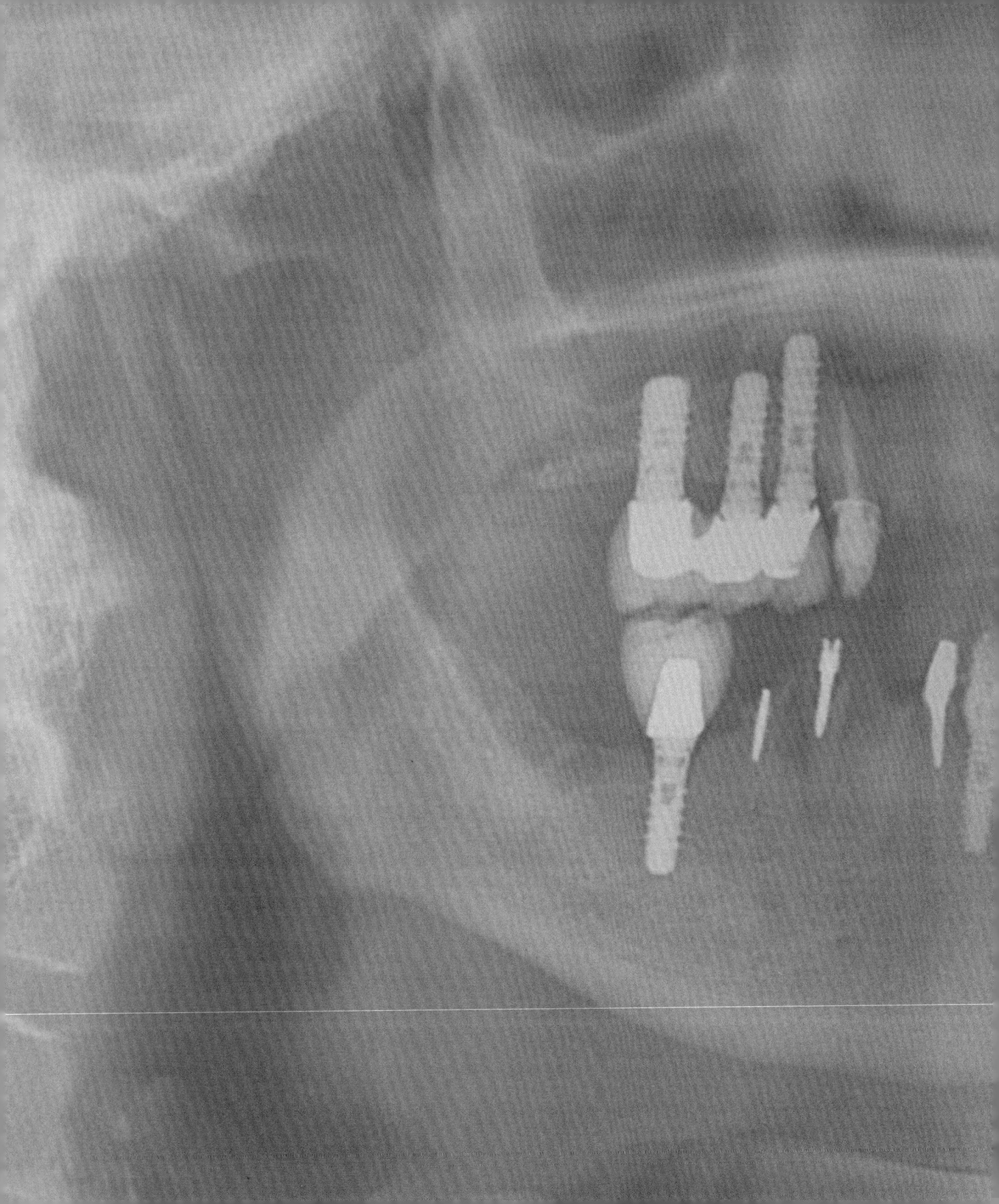

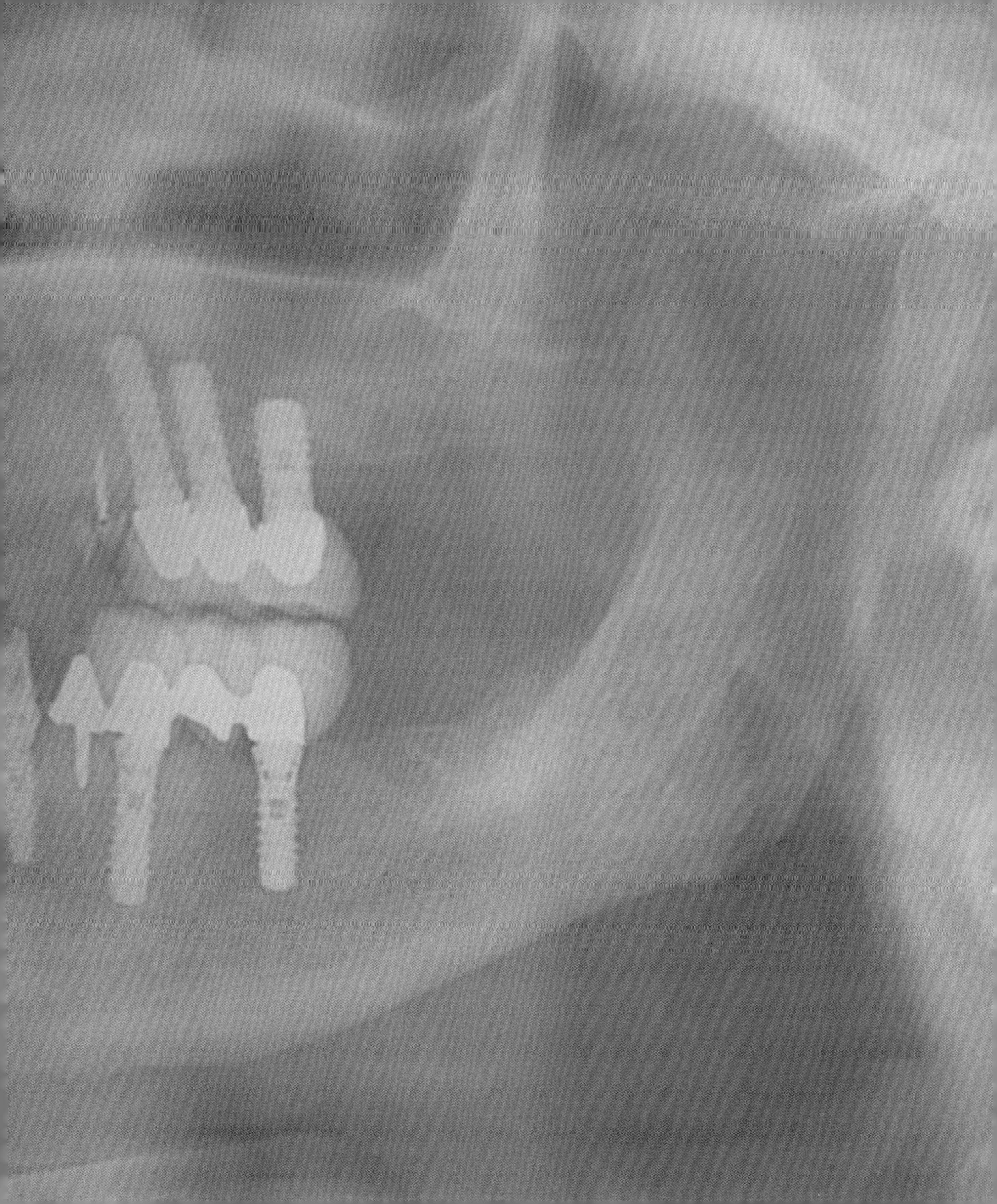

BUTCHERY

Budapest Museum

This design for a museum proposes a new way
for the experience of art and the pleasure of
being in a park to interact, and how art can
and should be presented in dialogue with
architecture and culture at large. Instead of
the museum being just a vessel, it can also
act as an agent provocateur for art and its
different forms of production. The design leads
the visitor inside the museum in a friendly way,
extending the city and the park into its interior,
elevating itself to allow the park and city to
continue their dialogue. Our proposal points
to the reinvigorated notion of multiplicity and
the variation of single entities. We like to argue
that this is where we are in the presence of
true architecture, because these are works
about the making of architecture, without any
other meaning or reading than provoking a
friction between the existing city, the park
and the new museum.

Location: Budapest, Hungary
Date: 2014
Programme: Competition, museum design

Related projects
Barcelona Park, 2014 (p. 194)
Teatro Colon, 2013 (p. 282)
Lips Chair, 2013 (p. 310)

Glass

Fibre-reinforced concrete

Photovoltaic cells

Steel-tube structure

Glass

Longitudinal section

Short elevation

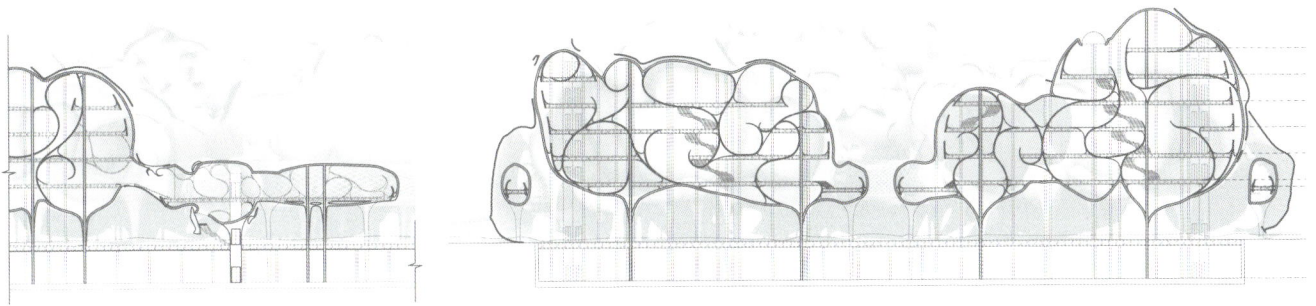

Teatro Colon

For this competition entry for a theatre in the historic centre of Bogotá, Colombia, we proposed to weave a bridge between the past and the future. Through formal complexity, density and a visibly contemporary feel, the design is a celebration of the country's culture. As a result, its formal exuberance is, above all, a tribute to its surroundings. The building rises from a central square, evoking the primordial sense of the *candelaria* (inner courtyards), and adheres to its environment, so that the square itself is presented as a theatre. The finish produces a mirror-effect that absorbs the world outside, creating a continuous dialogue between the formal excess of the design and its implementation point. We interpreted the theatre as the entire block in which it is located, rather than being confined to the limits of the site.

Location: Bogotá, Colombia
Date: 2013
Programme: Competition, theatre

Related projects
Barcelona Park, 2014 (p. 194)
Budapest Museum, 2014 (p. 270)
Lips Chair, 2013 (p. 310)

1	Back room	7	Restrooms	13	Consulting room	19	Communications
2	Lateral room	8	Auditorium	14	Staff canteen	20	Administration
3	Truck lift	9	Foyer	15	Coordination and production	21	Archive
4	Proscenium	10	Cafeteria	16	Programming		
5	Orchestra pit	11	Archive	17	Training		
6	Men's room	12	Consulting room	18	Copy room		

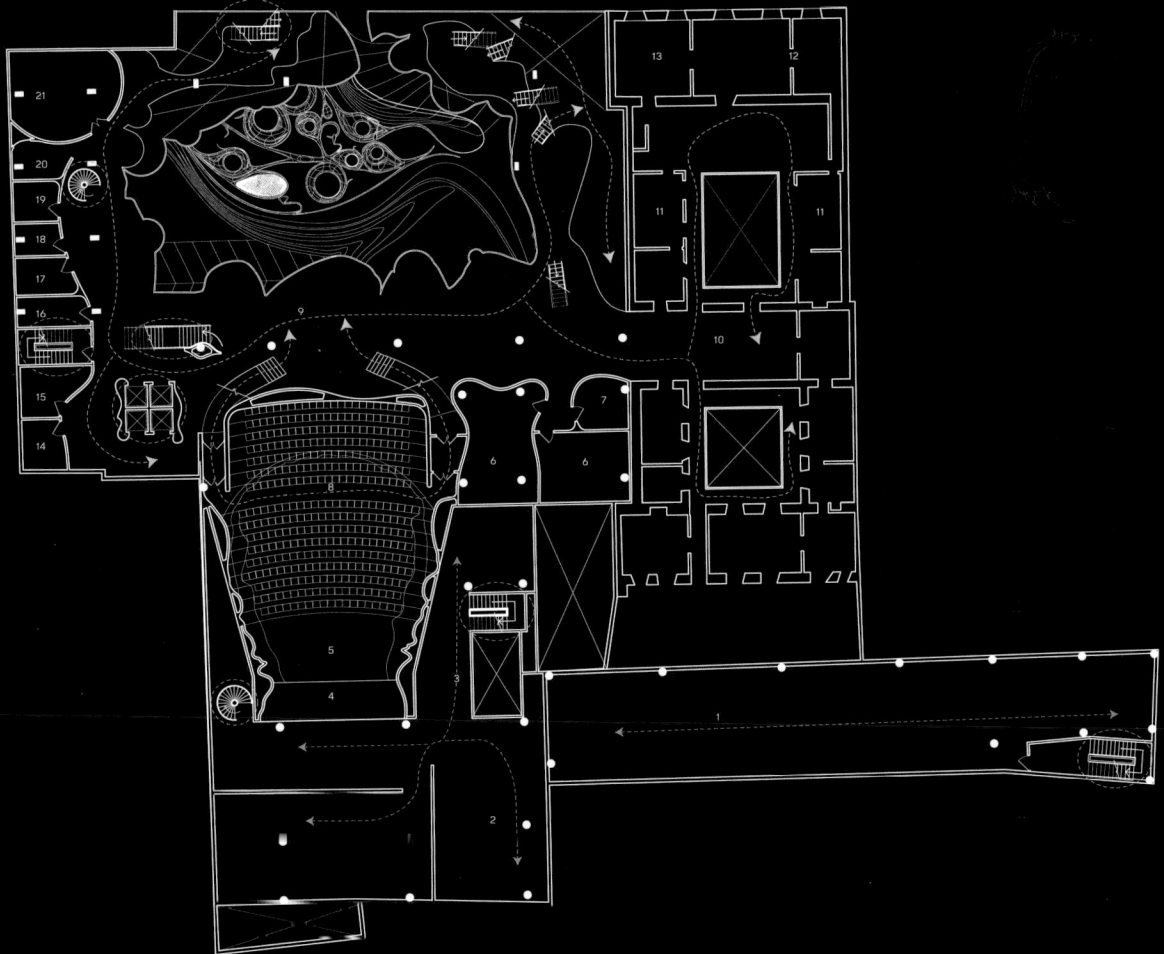

Floorplan – Level 3

DR: Are you a Modernist at heart, wanting a contaminated Modernism to preserve a commitment to originality?

HDA: I think I am a Modernist. I still believe very much in the ethical principles of Modernism, even if I don't really subscribe to its aesthetics. Or, to hedge a bit, I am far closer to being a Modernist than a Postmodernist, although that might surprise some people.

DR: It is good to clarify this, because I agree that most people would have trouble seeing an affiliation with Modernism in your body of work. But having known you now for nearly two decades, I recognize the allegiance you have to, at least, the ethics of Modernism. I see it most clearly in your plans. I can imagine a newcomer to the work would see the interest in horror and not recognize that you're actually not that interested in horror, per se. Instead, you are interested in seeing what happens to Modernism after it is contaminated with the aesthetics of horror.

HDA: The Catalan architect Enric Miralles has been an enormous influence on me. His work was utterly influenced by Le Corbusier. I know that many people would not associate it with Corbusier's designs, but it was deeply Modernist.

DR: What are your opinions regarding Latin America's pathological dedication to building? You are not an architect in Latin America if you don't build. As someone who is not from there, I find the region strikingly different to other parts of the world.

HDA: For the last century, Latin Americans have lived under very complex social and economic conditions. Because of this, I believe that architectural culture in those countries never really had an opportunity to develop a more speculative approach. That doesn't mean that there hasn't been enough talent or imagination, but that priorities were different.

Continental European culture also had a profound influence in Latin America. The speculative idea of architecture comes more from the Anglo-Saxon world. In continental Europe, Modernism was dedicated to building a new society, and gravitated more towards economic and social issues. Nonetheless, I believe that some of the best built works of Modernism are in Latin America. Much of it is still relatively unknown to the rest of the world. I am very fond of the building culture there. At the same time, I established myself in Los Angeles because I felt that my interests wouldn't fit in so well in Latin America.

Architecture is like the elephant, super-smart and all that, but slow

DR: Because you still consider yourself very much an Argentinian, do you see yourself as a Latin American architect?

HDA: I am very Argentinian, that's true, but I am also very American now – or, perhaps more accurately, Californian. I'm very Hispanic and Latino in my interests and sensibilities, and have enormous appreciation for Latin American culture. At the same time, my desire for speculation and my willingness to challenge the limits of architecture aren't really bound to building. That doesn't mean that I don't wish to build, but that I am only interested in building if I can do it on my own terms, developing the speculation that I am interested in.

DR: Why do you think you became so interested in speculation?

HDA: I originally wanted to be a film-maker, so perhaps it goes back to a cinematic imagination developed early on. When I was a student, I fell in love with the work of Coop Himmelb(l)au, Zaha Hadid, Enric Miralles, Morphosis and Frank Gehry. At the time, none of these architects or studios were building that much, or at all, apart from Frank Gehry. Instead, they were known for highly speculative work, which I think is what drew me to architecture. I wouldn't have called it 'speculative architecture' at the time, but experimental.

I was amazed that the profession of architecture could be something more than making nice, practical buildings. Enric Miralles was a critical figure to me because he was building, and with material that was familiar. Unlike the designs of Zaha Hadid or Coop Himmelb(l)au, Miralles's buildings looked almost like some kind of Argentinian science fiction.

Speculation

DR: It sometimes seems that architecture is not the best way to alter reality. Because of litigation, insurance, building codes, policies, the state of the government, and so on, architecture, more often than not, can seem to be an instrument of conservatism, reinforcing the world as it is. It is rare for a building to challenge what we expect reality to look like. Do you think this is a contemporary problem, or a historic one? Is speculation getting more difficult today?

HDA: Historically, architecture with a capital 'A', what I would consider speculative architecture, is a tiny percentage of what gets built at any given moment in time. I think it has always been difficult to challenge reality.

DR: How committed are you to building?

HDA: Very committed. I am always looking for a way to get my designs built. But I'm not willing to compromise too much – just a little, perhaps, but not so much that it undermines the integrity of the work.

I will admit, however, that I have always considered myself a designer first and an architect second, so my interests have always been very diverse. I believe that there is an architectural way to understand the world that can be applied to many fields, and that it is not just about buildings. Recently, I have been getting very excited about exploring other design economies, like furniture, fashion, even jewelry. I think architects should claim more territory and expand the field's reach.

Monster, Monstrosity, Monstrous

The typology of this design for a chandelier
is processed through an animalization
operation, drawing from the S&M tropes of
meat hooks, stretched skins and spikes. The
evolution of aesthetics will not come about
from incremental adjustments to successful
historical techniques, but through the elevation
of the monstrous and the raw to higher levels
of sophistication: beauty through its opposite.

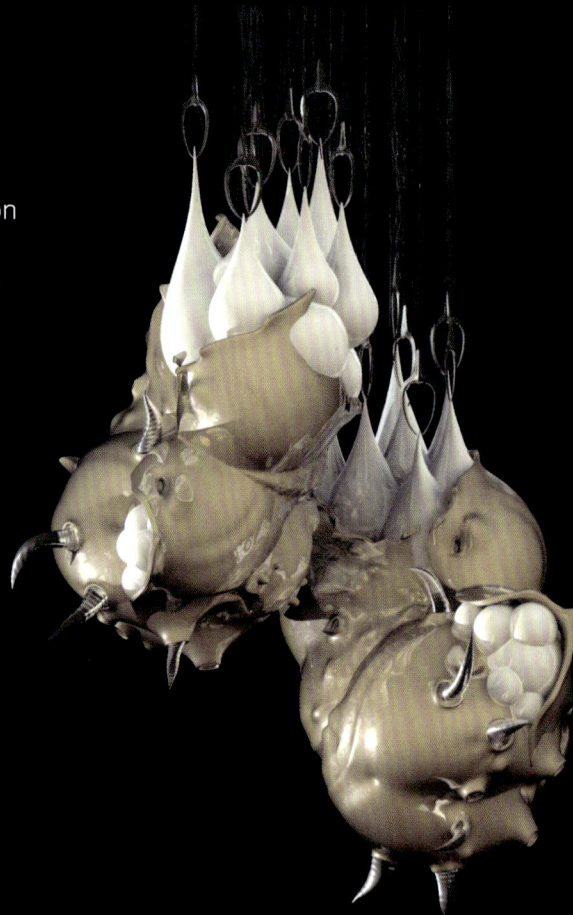

Date: 2011
Programme: Product design

Related projects
TBA 21_2.0, 2011 (p. 240)
Espresso Cup, 2011 (p. 300)
Still Flesh, 2012 (p. 304)

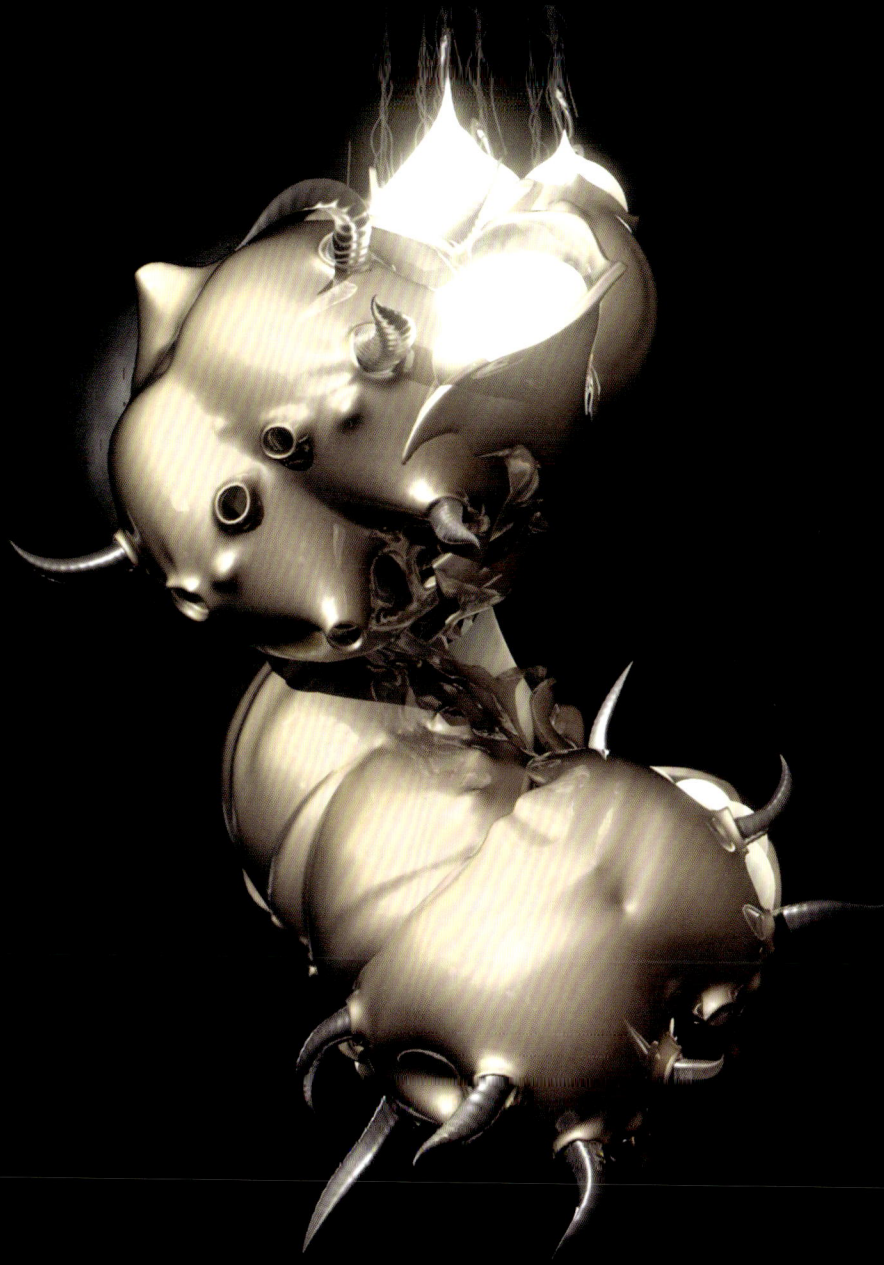

Espresso Cup

The boiling bubbles of Espresso Cup are
a confused transposition of literal form –
an imprecise reference, a misquote. The
scale of formal transposition is mismatched
to the object, and the reference to bubbles
mismatches the intended drink. It is merely
a loose allusion to liquid properties, an
artificial simulation. The imprecise and the
literal, contradictory (or conflicted) terms are
reconciled within a playful form.

Date: 2011
Programme: Product design

Related projects
TBA 21_2.0, 2011 (p. 240)
Monster, Monstrosity, Monstrous, 2011 (p. 298)
Still Flesh, 2012 (p. 304)

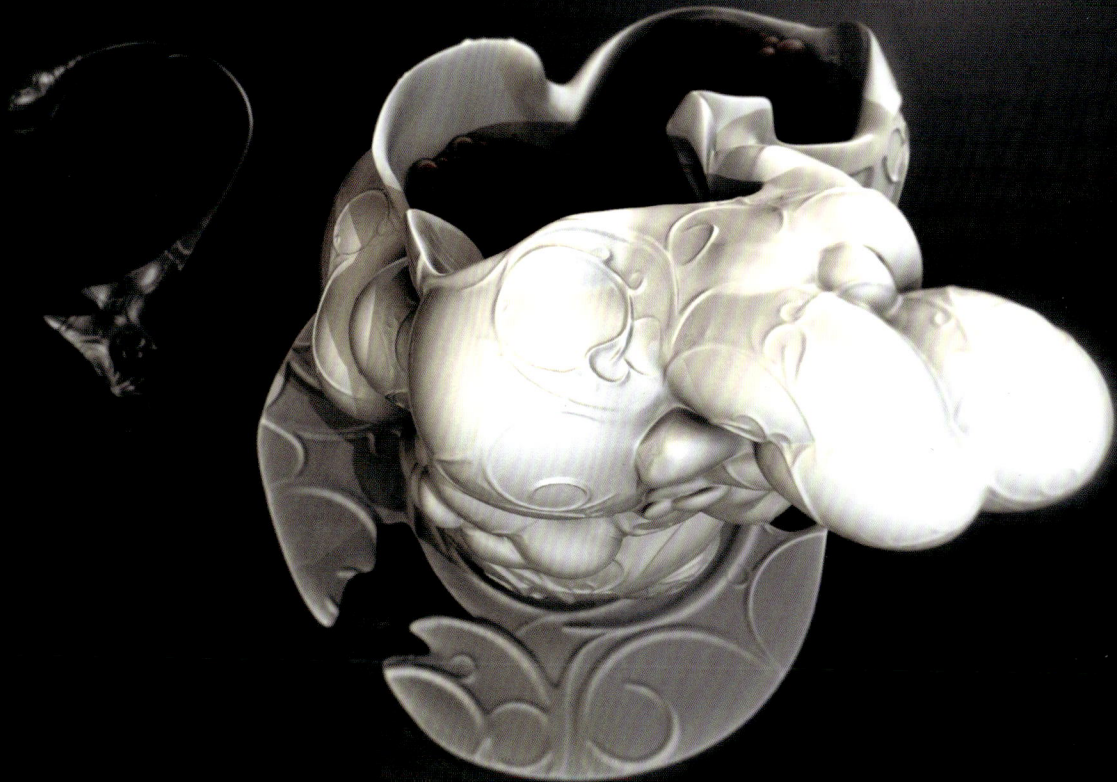

Still Flesh

This project for the Wexler Museum of Art proposes a re-examination of the possibilities of form generation as an autonomous entity through the understanding of rituals. Many rituals have the capacity to combine the power of raw mutilations with a highly sophisticated formal understanding of organization. There is another history and evolution of rituals in relation to the bodies and their mutilations, in both human and animals. These misfits have produced some of the most contradictory conditions of beauty and horror.

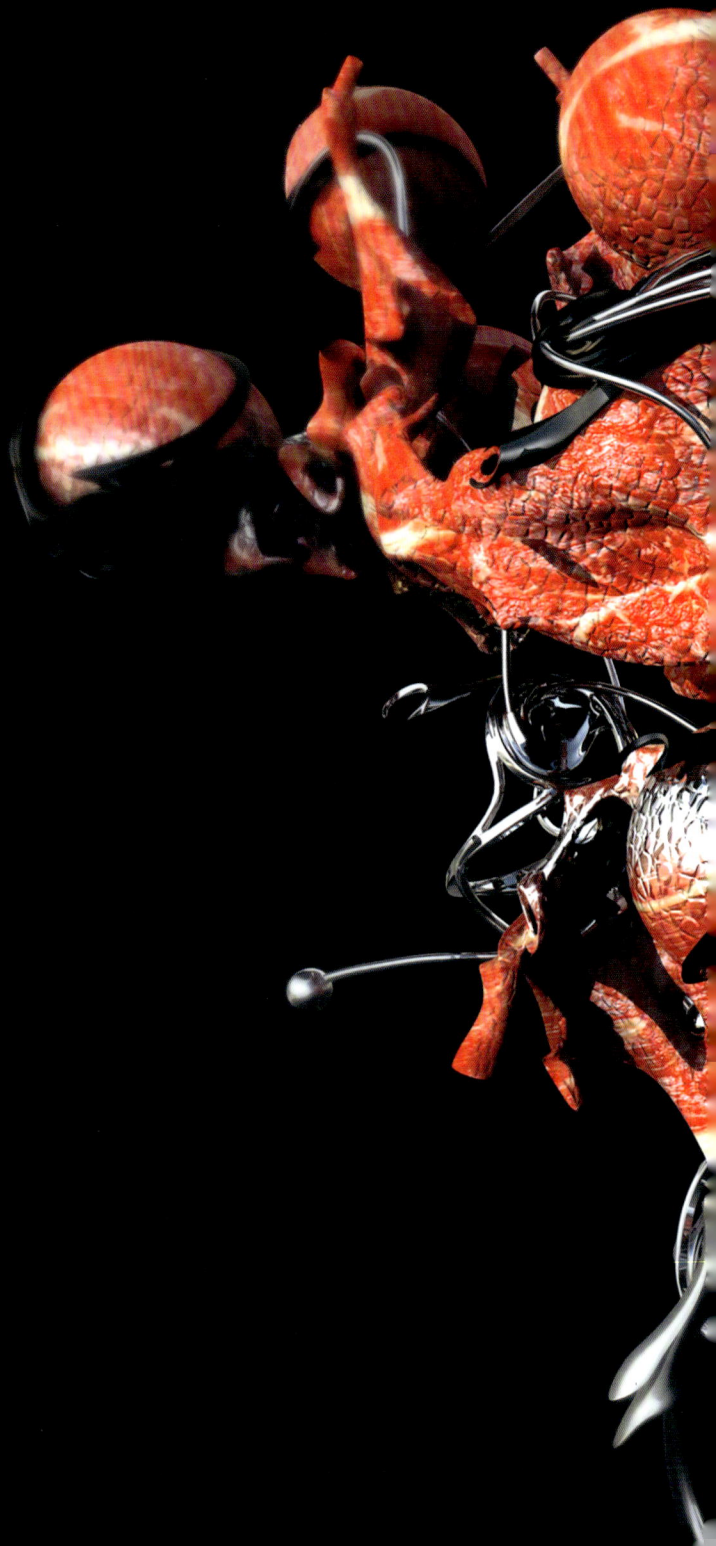

Location: Columbus, Ohio
Date: 2012
Programme: Art

Related projects
TBA 21_2.0, 2011 (p. 240)
Monster, Monstrosity, Monstrous, 2011 (p. 298)
Espresso Cup, 2011 (p. 300)

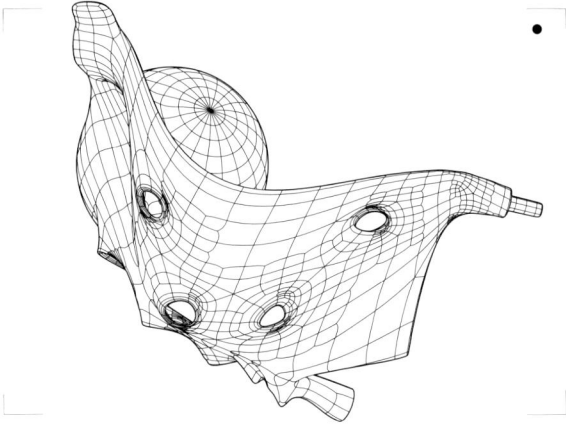

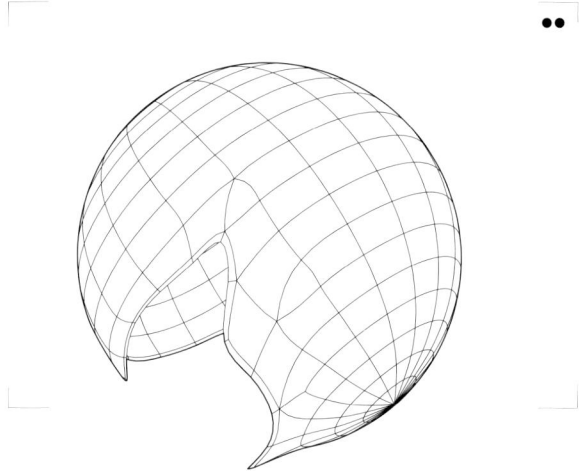

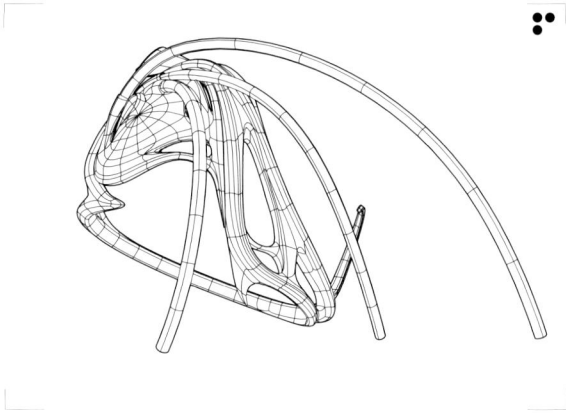

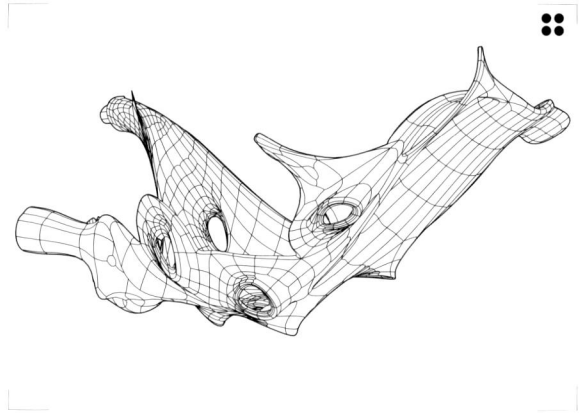

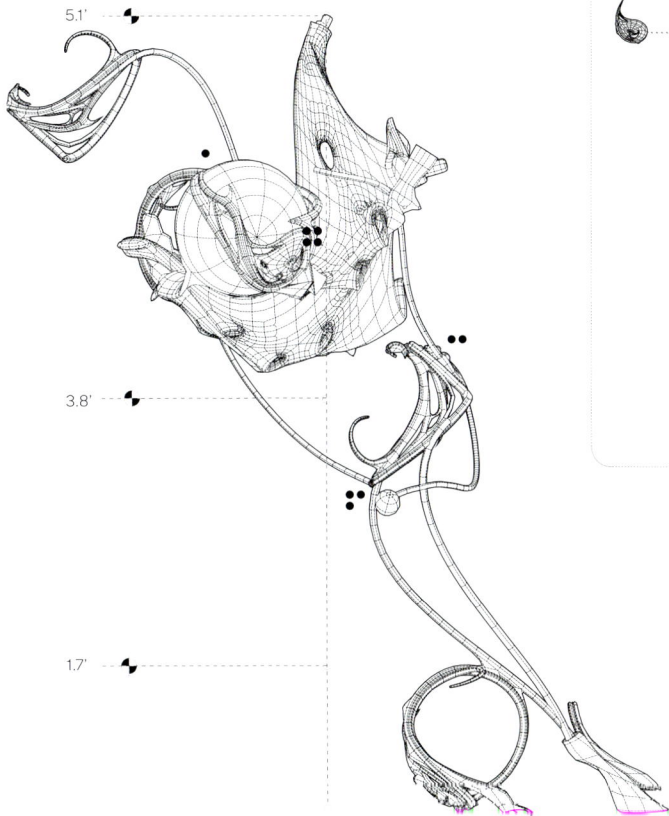

5.1'

3.8'

1.7'

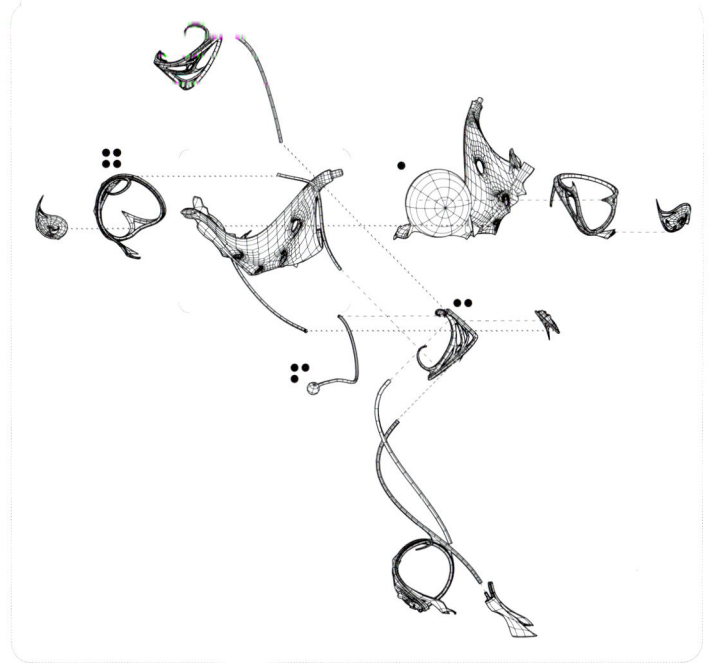

Edison Lamp

The Edison bulb is an already heavily
aestheticized, even fetishized, object. As
something we encounter in everyday life,
however, it lacks sophistication without some
form of intervention to trigger an evolution in
its form. The cellular growth pattern, the viral
accumulation of mutations, plays both with and
against type, contaminating the object and its
form while preserving its type and function.
Undermining its basic geometric integrity
elevates its primitive expression to a higher
level of sophistication.

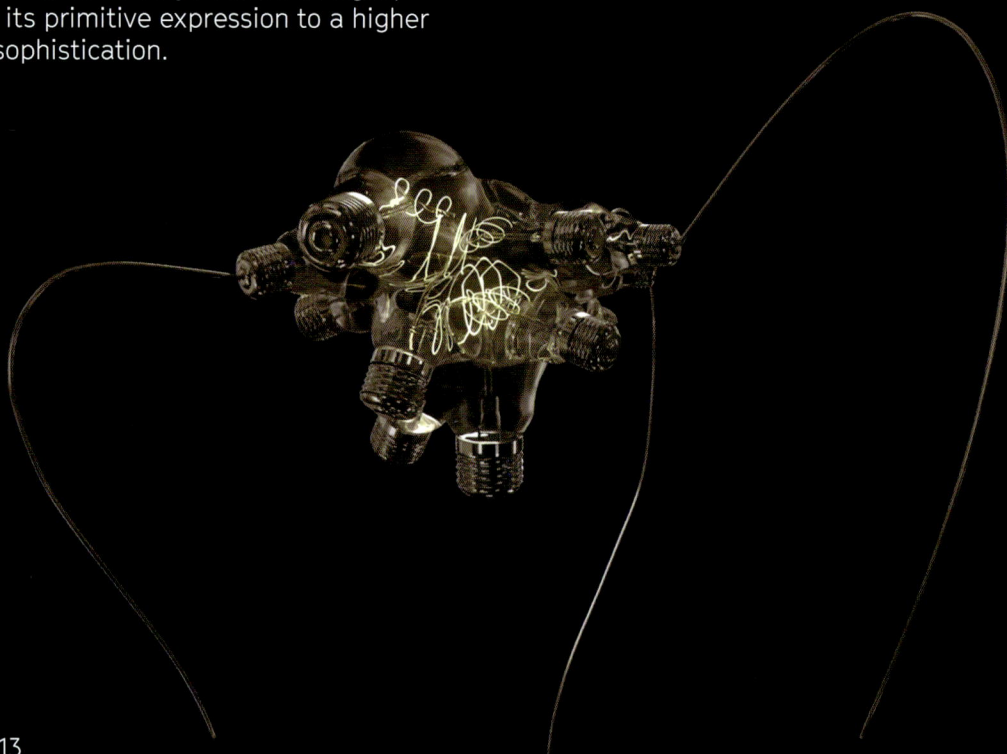

Date: 2013
Programme: Product design

Related projects
Monster, Monstrosity, Monstrous, 2011 (p. 298)
Espresso Cup, 2011 (p. 300)

Lips Chair

While some projects attempt to elevate the object by contamination from another technique or discipline, the process can also be reversed, contaminating a pure, aesthetic icon of pop culture with the literal and the base. Working contrary to the Pop Art principles of immediacy of meaning and legibility, here the grotesqueness of biological details overpower and complicate the chair's legibility, producing instead an immediacy of emotion and triggering visceral reactions. The result is one of aesthetic evolution and expansion, rather than revulsion – in the same way that Francis Bacon achieved beauty and advanced the field of portraiture with grotesque or horrific subjects and forms.

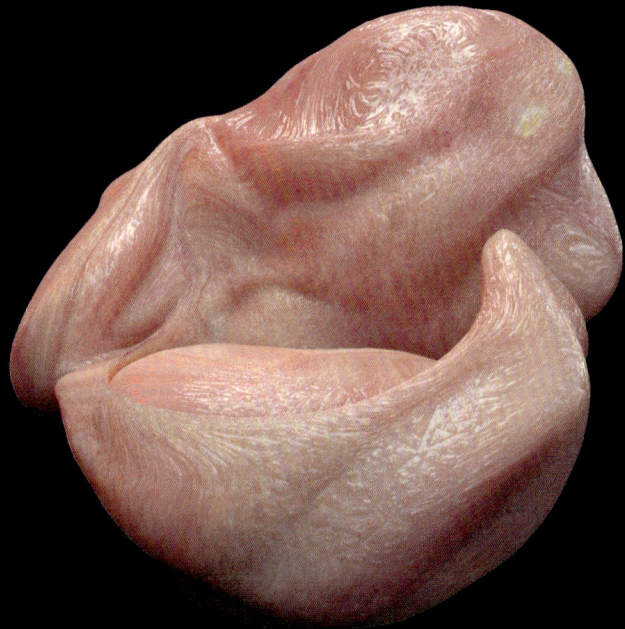

Date: 2013
Programme: Furniture design

Related projects
X-hibit, 2015 (p. 312)
Chair Proto, 2015 (p. 314)

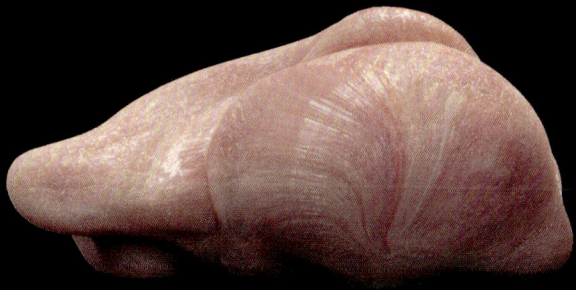

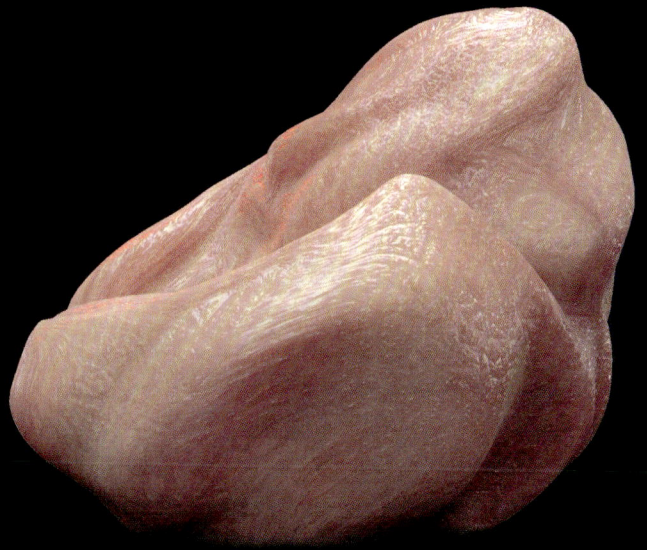

X-hibit

Nothing comes from nowhere. In architecture, you may not have a plan, but you must have an agenda. The agenda serves as a base form that evolves through iteration and mutation over time, so that we are always working around the same problems, but are continually changing how we approach them. We reject close reading as the core of the architectural discipline, instead favouring the accumulation of genetic mutations as the core producer of innovation. This speculative project is just one frozen moment of a single simulated reality.

Date: 2015
Programme: Museum pieces

Related projects
Barcelona Park, 2014 (p. 194)
Conexion Barcelona, 2015 (p. 204)
Lips Chair, 2013 (p. 310)

Chair Proto

Historically, architectural contamination relies on the translation of formal or topological principles into abstract architectural techniques. Here, we applied the literal form without translation or adaptation, like musical sampling. The two types are left to coexist and chafe against each other without reconciliation, a butchered taxidermy of flickering impressions.

Date: 2015
Programme: Product design

Related projects
Conexion Barcelona, 2015 (p. 204)
Lips Chair, 2013 (p. 310)
X-hibit, 2015 (p. 312)

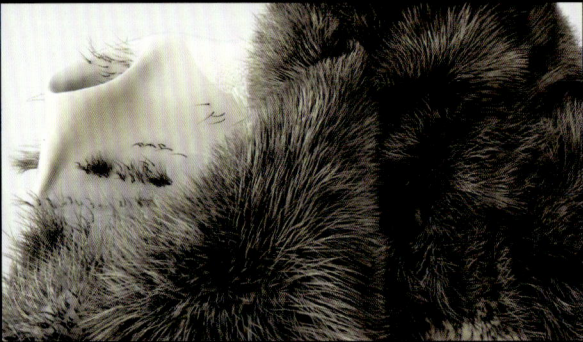

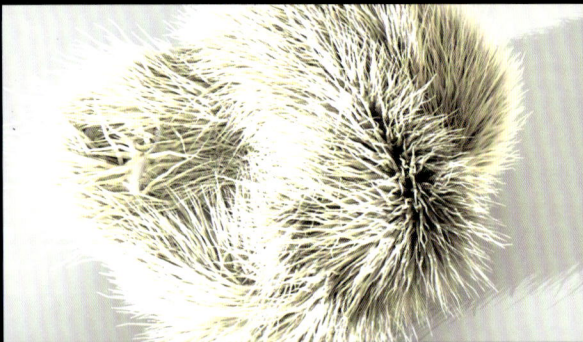

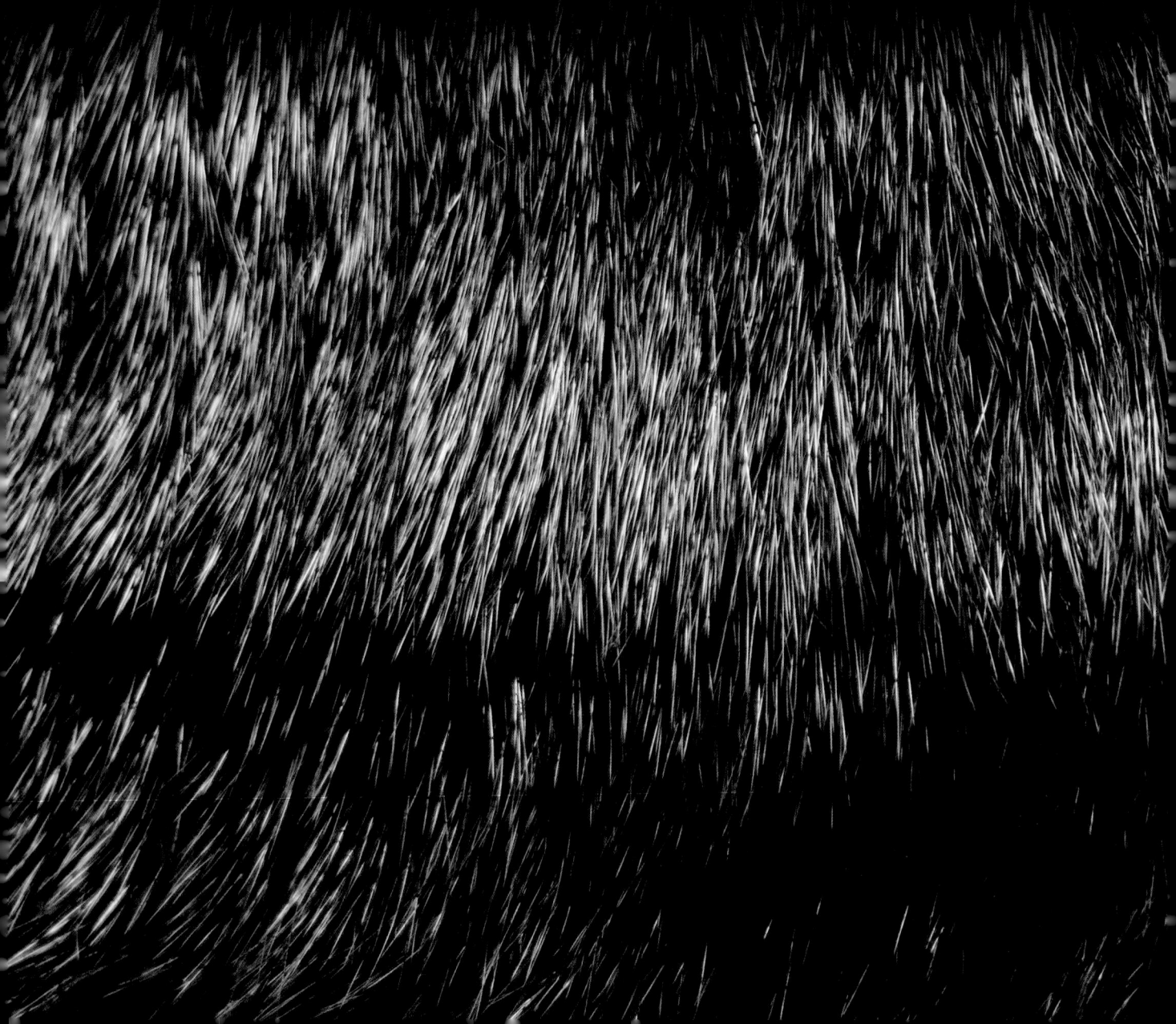

LITERAL

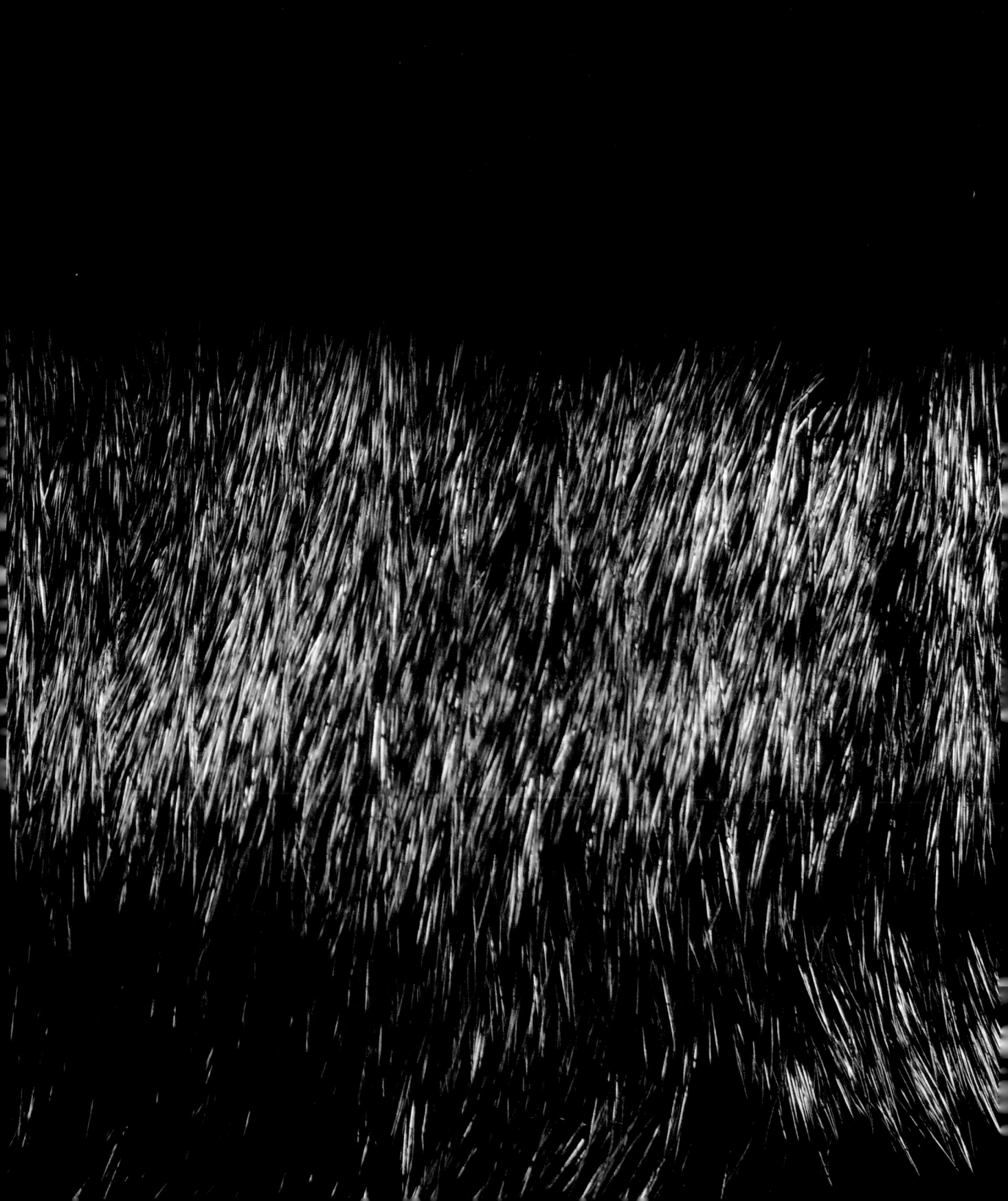

Shenzhen Library & Museum

The programme for this design is centred around the building's intelligent 3D stack and two courtyards. The service areas are located around these courtyards, each with access to the adjacent street, and include a bookstore, art-supplies shop, café, restaurant, art library and customer-service office. The museum spaces occupy the west and north ends of the building, while the south and east ends primarily house the library stacks. Visitors can enter via the pedestrian-access streets at the northeast corner of the site, or through the separate facilities from the southwest museum entrance or the southeast library entrance. There is also a southern loading access point for the intelligent 3D stack and a northern access point for the two courtyards.

Location: Shenzhen, China
Date: 2015
Programme: Museum competition

Related projects
Barcelona Park, 2014 (p. 194)
Budapest Museum, 2014 (p. 270)
Lips Chair, 2013 (p. 310)

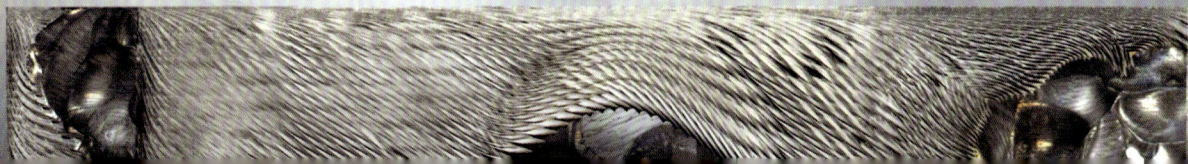

1	Handicap assistance	10	Restaurant	19	Special shelves section	28	Artist studio
2	Alternative entrance	11	Logistics operation	20	Control room	29	VIP
3	Reception counter	12	Loading bay	21	Research studio	30	Auditorium
4	Museum entrance / lobby	13	Survey reading entrance	22	Curator studio	31	Sculpture exhibition hall #1
5	Café	14	Sanitation station	23	Marketing studio	32	Sculpture exhibition hall #2
6	Visitor lounge	15	Logistics storage	24	Media studio	33	Multimedia exhibition hall
7	Large exhibition hall #1	16	Automatic sorting section	25	Copy room	34	Courtyard landscape #1
8	Large exhibition hall #2	17	Sorting section	26	Arts experience room	35	Courtyard landscape #2
9	Bookstore and shop	18	Container diverging section	27	Arts observation room		

Floorplan – Level 1

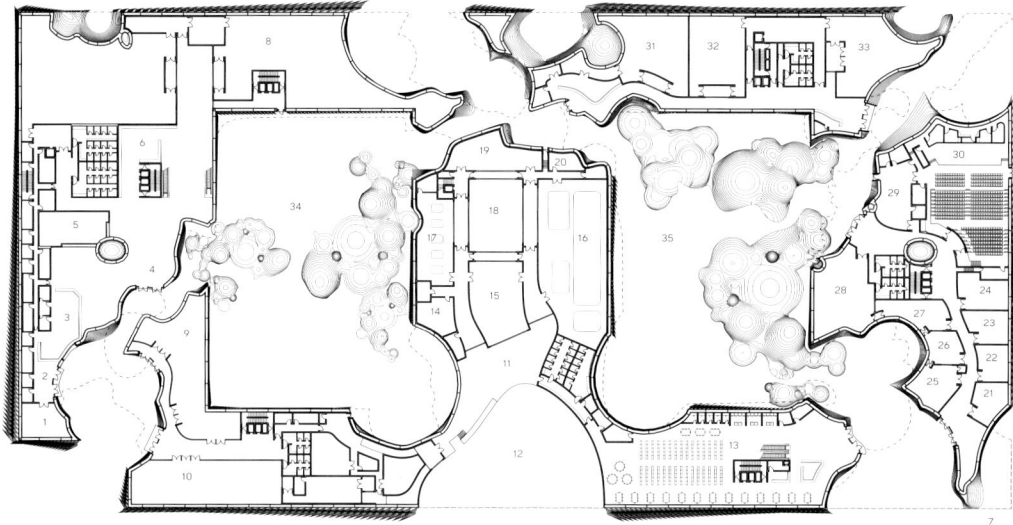

1	Open to below	6	Dense stack survey reading	11	Special collection stack
2	Survey reading #2	7	Reader's research rooms	12	Small exhibition hall #1
3	Survey reading #3	8	Information desk	13	Showroom #1
4	Document processing	9	Dense stack #1	14	Reserved showroom
5	Intelligent stack storage	10	Processing station		

Floorplan – Level 2

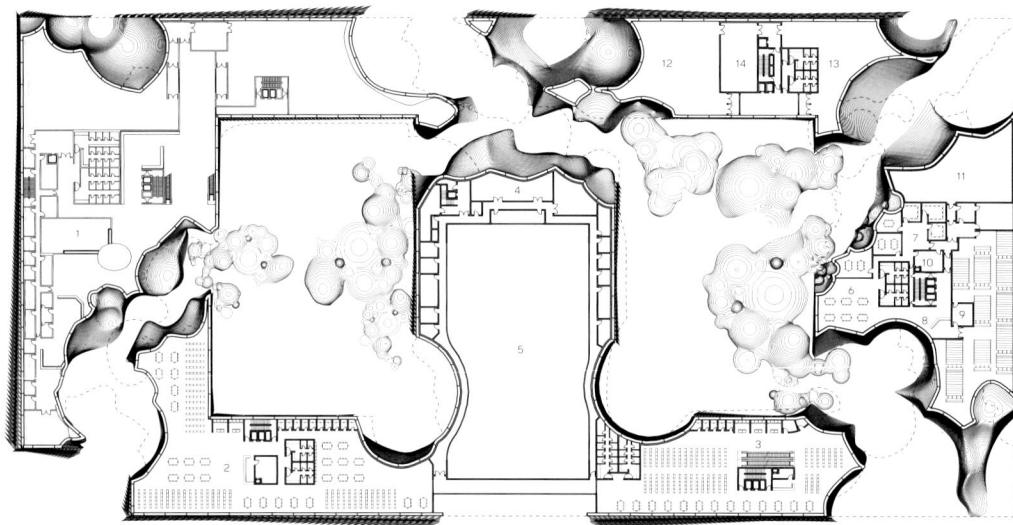

1	Small exhibition hall #2	6	Reserved showroom	11	Small exhibition hall #4	16	Bridge connection
2	Showroom #2	7	Reserved showroom	12	Showroom #5	17	Intelligent stack storage
3	Showroom #3	8	Reserved showroom	13	Reserved showroom	18	Open to below
4	Showroom #4	9	Temp storage	14	Stack #2	19	Survey reading #4
5	Small exhibition hall #3	10	Logistics operation	15	Processing station	20	Survey reading #5

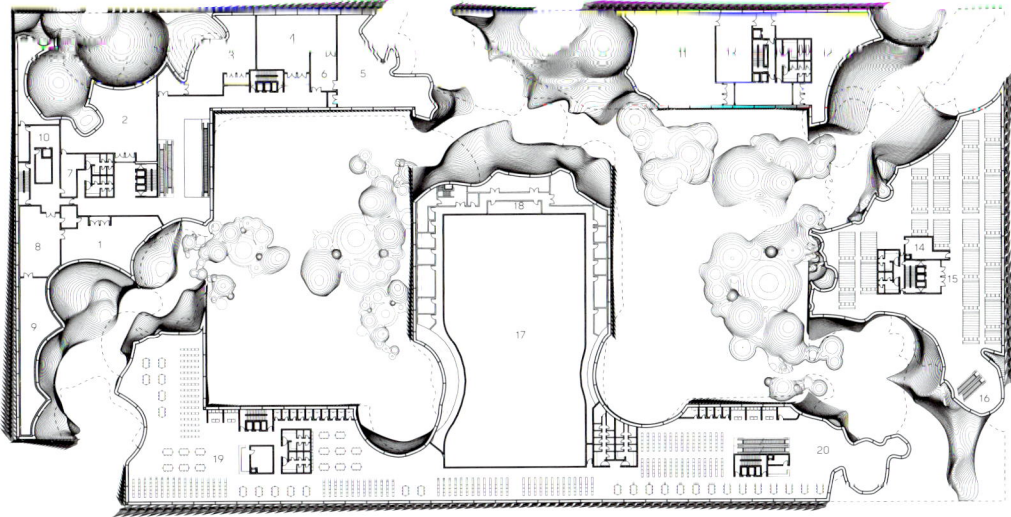

1	Storage vault #2	7	Technical workshop #2	13	Central engineering room	19	Equipment warehouse #2
2	Storage vault #3	8	Logistics operation	14	Firefighting equipment room	20	Monitoring and office
3	Storage vault #4	9	Technical workshop #3	15	Equipment warehouse #1	21	Multifunctional service
4	Storage vault #5	10	Technical workshop #4	16	Post room	22	Procurement / accounting
5	Storage vault #6	11	Logistics operation	17	Mechanical room	23	Administrative offices
6	Storage vault #7	12	Technical workshop #5	18	Equipment maintenance		

Floorplan – Level 6

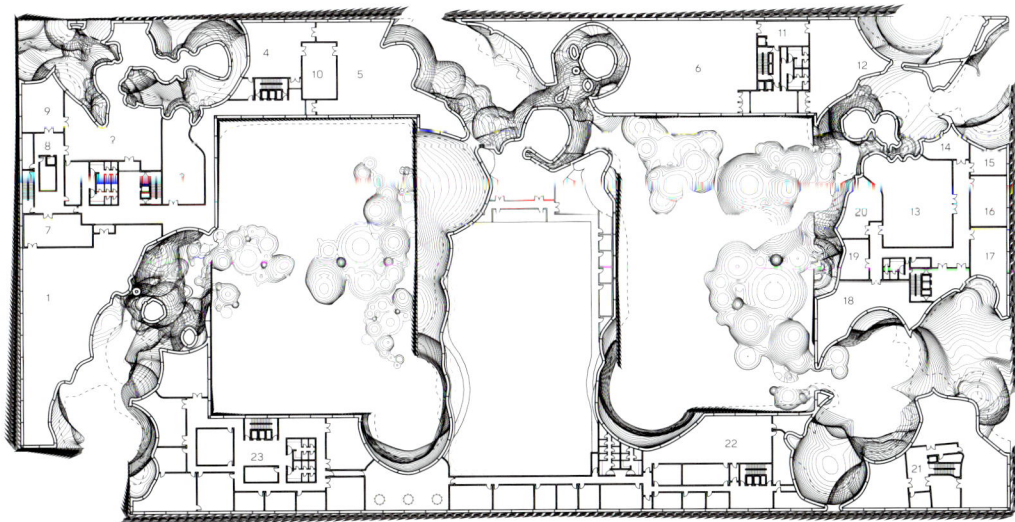

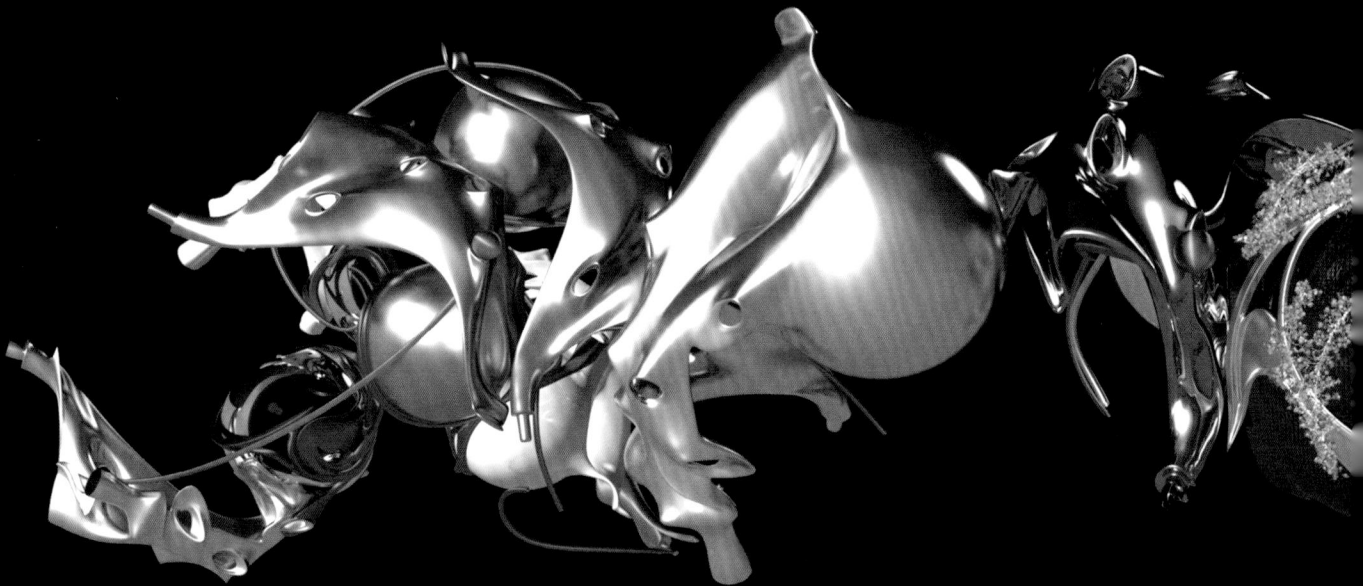

National Museum of World Writing

The museum as a flat object, sitting within
a garden plaza, is rooted in typological plan-
based design. This design for a museum
of world writing instead pulls its garden
surroundings up into a tangled vertical jungle,
from which the building's spaces are hacked
out of and carved. The museum, hidden within
a vertical garden, evolves its 2D typology
into a 3D volumetric condition of subtractive
accumulation, swallowing and internalizing its
own environmental context.

Location: Incheon, South Korea
Date: 2017
Programme: Museum competition

Related projects
Office Park Waterfront, 2016 (p. 342)
Emergency House, 2016 (p. 348)

1	Special exhibition gallery	11	Bathrooms	21	Permanent exhibition 02	31	Storage
2	Special exhibition gallery	12	Multimedia exhibit	22	Permanent exhibition 03	32	Table exhibitions / workshops
3	Special exhibition gallery	13	Airlock	23	Permanent exhibition 04	33	Theatre
4	Special exhibition gallery	14	Media room	24	Permanent exhibition 05	34	VR / interactive exhibits
5	Auditorium (350 seats)	15	Equipment store	25	Permanent exhibition 06	35	Small lecture theatre
6	Foyer auditorium	16	Void	26	Exit foyer	36	Storage
7	Foyer special exhibit	17	Equipment store	27	Bathrooms	37	Preparation room
8	VR / projection exhibit	18	Entry foyer	28	Projection / multimedia exhibit		
9	Multimedia exhibit	19	Permanent exhibition 01	29	Miniature exhibition spaces		
10	Bathrooms	20	Informal exhibition space	30	Storage		

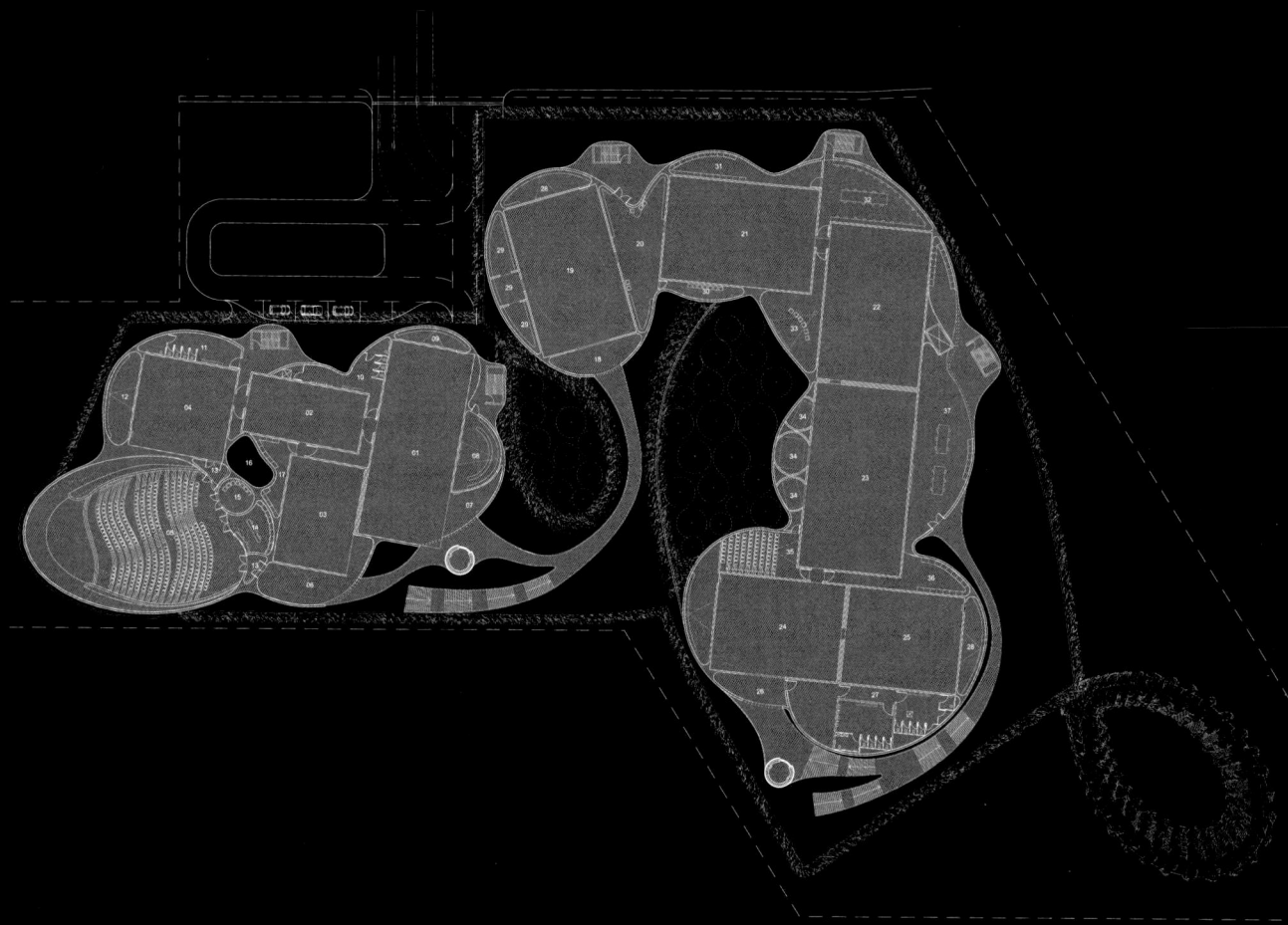

Floorplan – Level 2

2 20
0 10 40 m

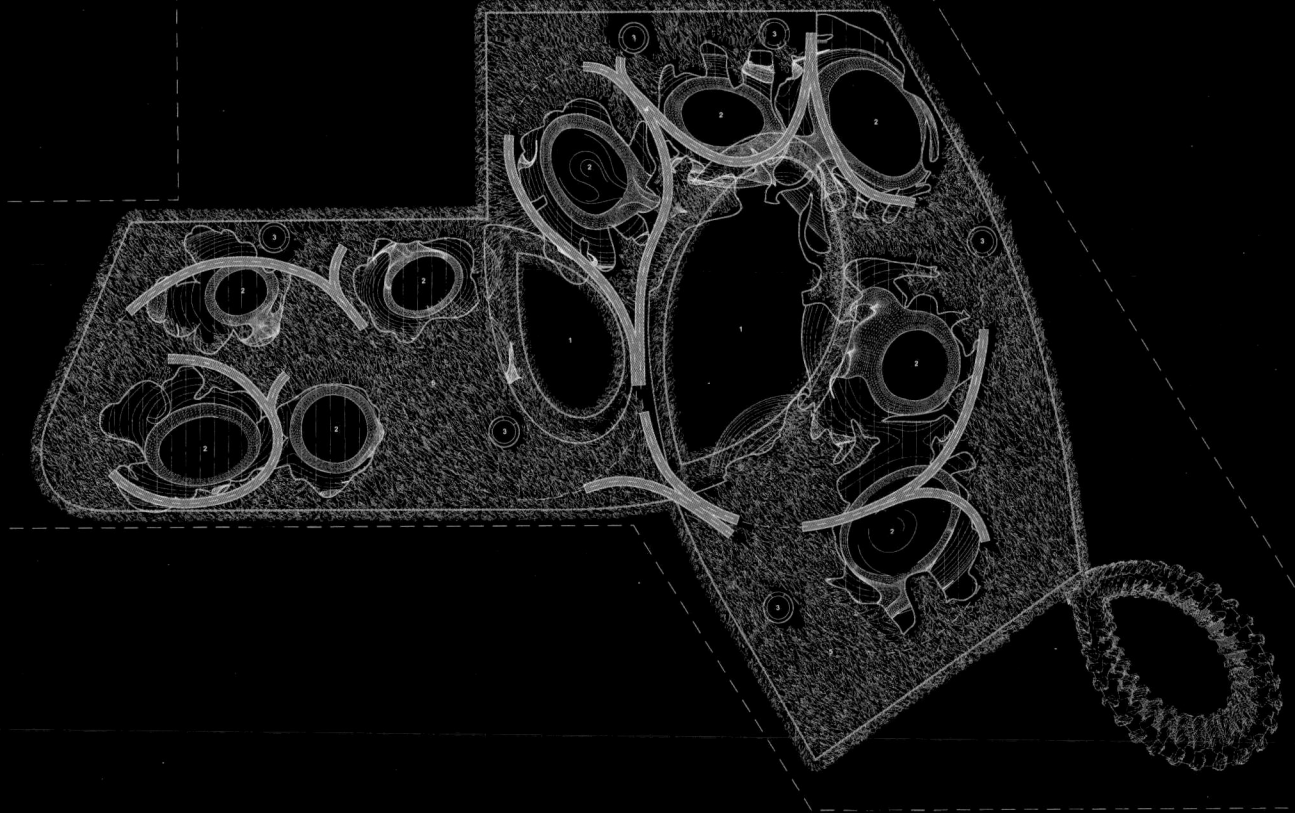

Roof plan

2   20

0   10   40 m

Long section A–A

10.0m
6.0m
0.0m
-6.6m
-11.4m
-16.2m

Elevation – East

35.6m
32.0m
6.0m
0.0m

Elevation – Southwest

35.6m
32.0m
6.0m
0.0m

Cross-section B–B

Elevation – Northeast

Elevation – Northwest

2   20

Office Park Waterfront

We always want to press the question of
how type can be changed and not taken for
granted. This park is not really a park, but an
outdoor open office space, infused with the
latest technology to enable people to work
outdoors and be connected to the rest of their
colleagues. It's not a public space, as it belongs
to a private office park with a couple of nearby
warehouses, but for all intents and purposes
it is still a park. Not only offices, but also all
other typologies can take a cue from this
strategy and question the notion that certain
aspects of their typological form cannot be
broken, that they must be, look and behave
in a certain way.

Location: Shanghai, China
Date: 2016
Programme: Park

Related projects
National Museum of World Writing, 2017 (p. 332)
Emergency House, 2016 (p. 348)

An Insider's View:

From super-smooth to a little fuzzy

Rachael McCall

Looking back, from the inside out, at the work of HDA-X, there is evidence of an evolution through different phases, loosely reflected in the studio's various designers and collaborators, along with Hernán's constant search for newness and cultural contamination. Projects shift from the single surface and super-smooth to a phase of intense ornamentation, and finally to a stage where they are a little fuzzier and more difficult to read. The work fits within three- to five-year waves of obsessions, which overlap and slowly mutate, as different collaborators move through the office.

In the early 2000s, the single surface and remnants of biomorphism emanated throughout the projects. Development of families of species and formal morphologies dominated, with animation techniques playing a critical role in smoothing morphing forms from one state to another– as seen in PS1 MoMA (p. 28) and Sangre (p. 34). Following the super-smooth projects, the office moved on to an exuberant, highly ornamental design phase. Biomorphic species were left behind, taxidermy techniques remain current, and hints of rituals begin to appear. By the end of the decade, ornamentation and

elegance became key, as seen in, for example, Tabakalera (p. 140) and Instruments of Manner (p. 108) . At the same time, there is an underlying sense of the grotesque continuously brewing, spurred on by Hernán's obsession with horror and sci-fi films.

Between the smooth (early 2000s) and the hairy (2015 onwards), there was a phase in which projects all stemmed from precise primitives. During this time, spheres and eggs were combined and re-combined in as many ways as possible. The purity of primitive forms always has a tinge of contamination in the designs. Precisely merged together spheres of the Teatro Colon (p. 282) and Espresso Cup (p. 300) are contaminated in Still Flesh (p. 304) and Miami Ritz Sculpture 1.0 (p. 66). Spheres become flesh, and curves become pipes, piercings or studs holding the designs together. Pure geometries and ornamental curves begin to be juxtaposed with the disruption of butchery, carving and meaty form.

The Budapest Museum (p. 270) reduced ornamental filigree to the landscape. What would previously have been designed as articulation, based on precise curves all over the building, changes to a glistening, spiky chrome sticker, which flaps loosely over the façade. These silver patches become a new technique of merging different forms, visually using fleshy or skin-like stickers, which manifest into the building for the Guggenheim Helsinki competition (p. 98). Box-shaped galleries are wrapped in a meaty, metallic black skin, which is stretched and contorted round spherical cores and voids.

During the butchery phase (2011–16), the studio developed new techniques for cutting, carving and re-attaching form, as a butcher does with meat. Geometry is treated as skin and mass, as cuts are made with or against the grain of the form. Openings splay apart like butterflied flesh, and seams are stitched together with the precision of a surgeon. The Lips Chair (p. 310), pinching fatty form together like pursed lips, is made from a pink foam that could easily be mistaken for a chicken fillet. Monster, Monstrosity, Monstrous (p. 298) brings in meat hooks, horns, butchered flaps of flesh and wrinkled skin, while diseased-looking bubbles form the tumour-like lamp inside. Meat hooks become pincers or spikes in the Rusuupuisto extension (p. 246), which pierce and contort the roof, the skin of the building being ritualistically pinned into position. This butchery leads into the next phase: the literal.

In this literal phase, existing objects are treated simply like matter to be worked on. The Edison Lamp (p. 308) is treated like meat, multiplied, combined and glued back together. Literal forms and postures of chickens and dogs permeate the designs. Covered in feathers, the Lima Art Museum (p. 391) stands like a rooster in the middle of a pile of chicken legs. The Shar-Pei Chairs (p. 354) wrinkle and slump around tiny legs, a reference to the voluptuous folds of the eponymous, irresistibly cute breed of dog. Ants with bull horns become flowers (pp. 16–17) and cockroaches are adorned with wilting roses (pp. 24–25), linking back to earlier phases in which the grotesque was mixed with elegance and sophistication.

Recent work investigates suede, velvet and woven bamboo, as well as the different layers and lengths of artificial fur. Like the way a dog might have both the soft, fluffy coat of a puppy and patches of adult fur and long wiry whiskers, the latest HDA-X H'Air shoes (pp. 136–37) trial various synthetic hairstyles on an inflated base shoe. The Chair Proto (p. 314) tests varying degrees of baldness and hair loss, along with mixing artificial furs based on different animals.

Currently, the office is working in a realm of fiction, fuzz and augmentation, flipping between product design, buildings and larger urban projects. Pure curvature is broken up by fur and frizz, often distracting the eye from the overall form. Ruffled, torn edges and exploding splash-like forms are deployed at all scales. The splash has been used at the scale of landscape skate bowl (see Mexicali Parks; p. 392), down to a tiny ornament on an ear bud (p. 365).

The studio generally focuses on the final image or animation, rather than on the process. That said, however, the design process is inextricably linked to each designer involved, as well as the micro-influences of culture and digital technology that continue to mutate every couple of years. From smooth to curvy ornament, to hair, flesh and butchery, the work will continue to evolve, being creatively contaminated by Hernán and fleshed out through the eyes of the various designers and collaborators at HDA-X.

Emergency House

The transcription of genetic code is not perfect, and those errors and mutations are responsible for the range of formal expression within a species. The type itself will not change, but its specific expression might. This design is a prototype for shelter that would have to be copied dozens of times. Its copying mechanism needs a capacity for error to allow the repetition to lose its predictability and gain any kind of formal expression. Each shelter unit has a fixed concrete core, but the frames and fabric panels that attach to it can evolve into new forms and spaces, with no two the same.

Location: Mexico
Date: 2016
Programme: Temporary housing

Related projects
National Museum of World Writing, 2017 (p. 332)
Office Park Waterfront, 2016 (p. 342)

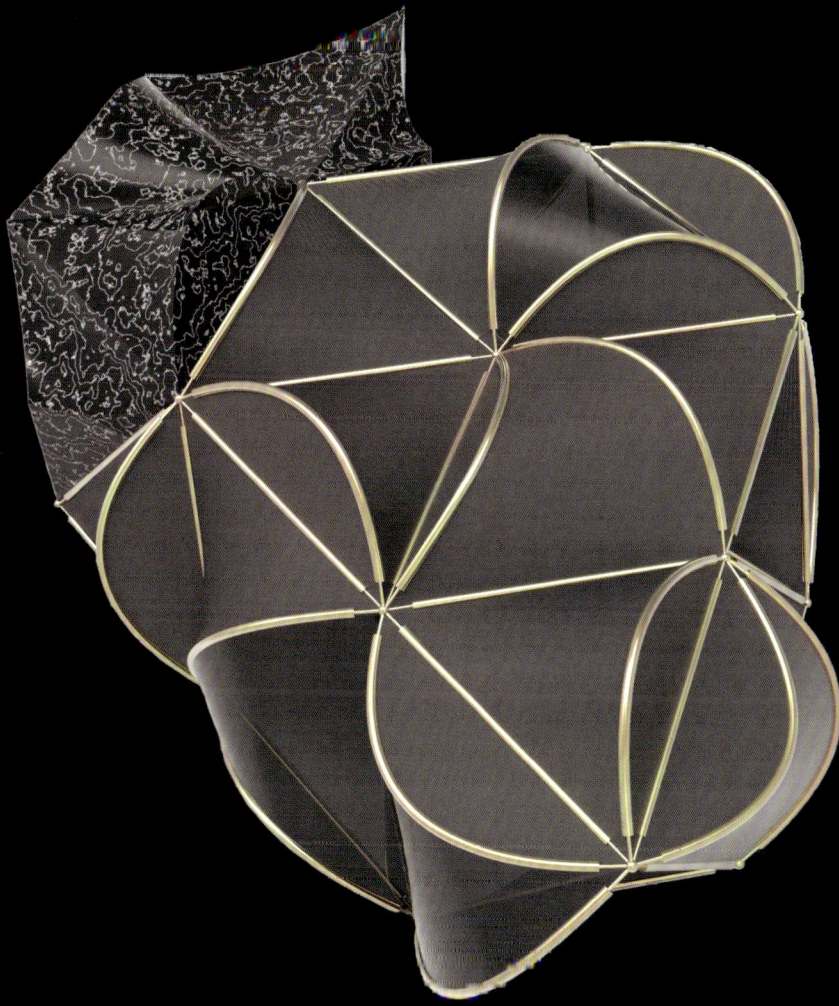

Floorplan

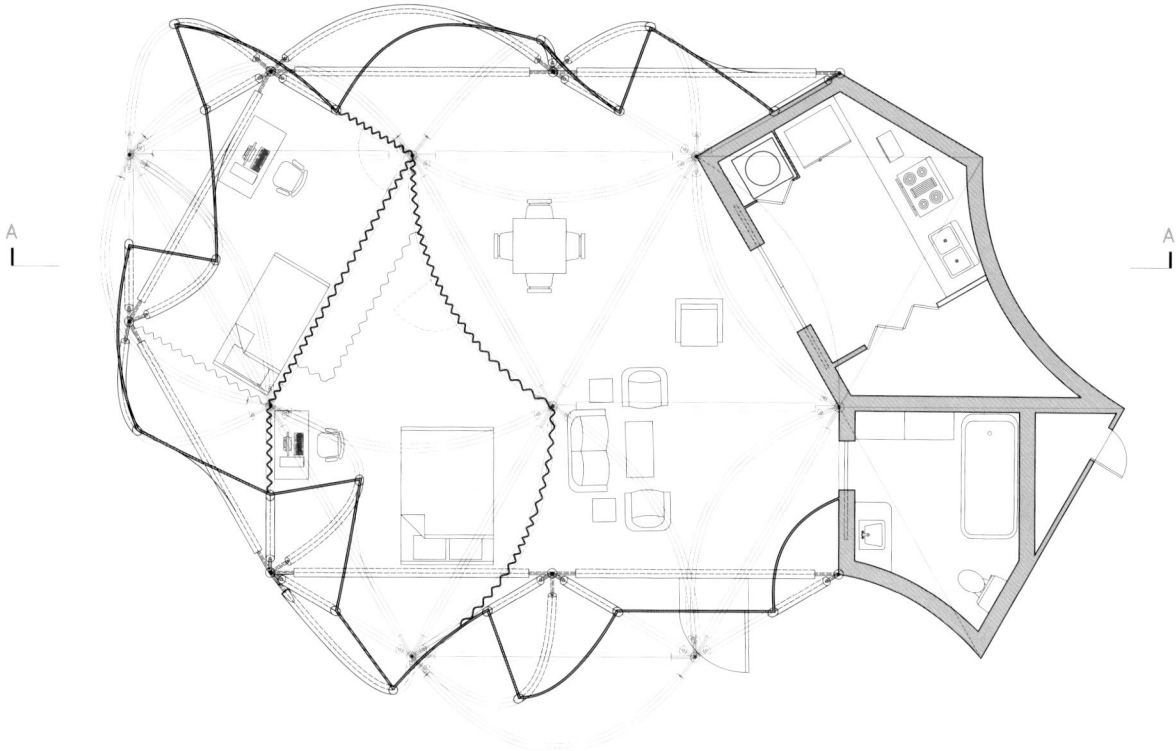

A ⊢   A ⊢

Section A–A

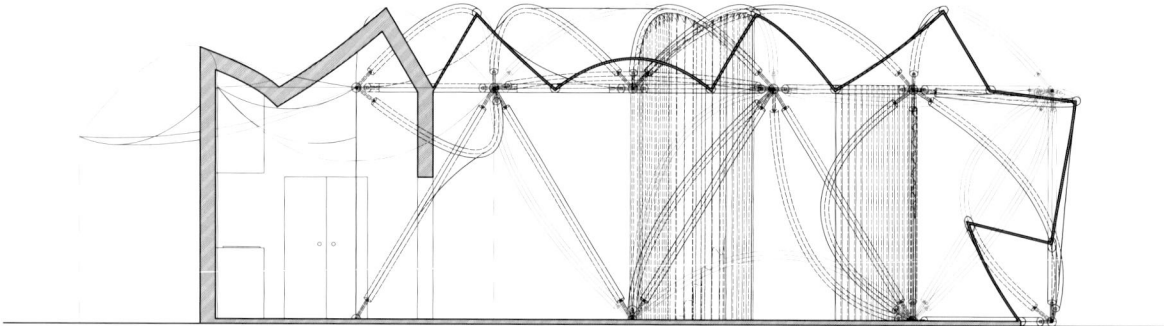

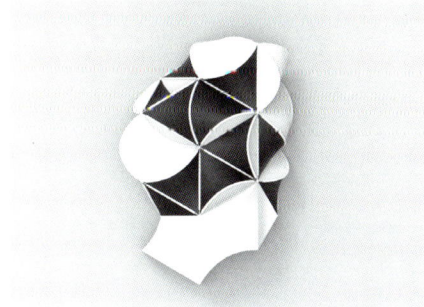

CONCRETE
CORE

FABRIC
TYPE 1

PIPE
TYPE 1

FABRIC
TYPE 2

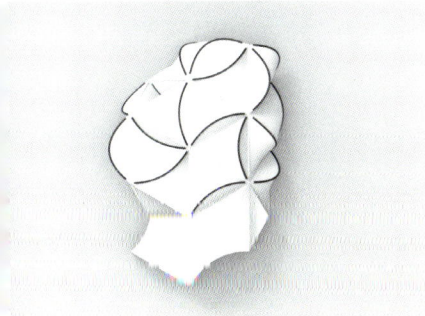

PIPE
TYPE 2

FABRIC
TYPE 3

Modules

DR: Can you imagine an architecture of the future where we no longer draw plans?

HDA: Sure, because I think we're there already. I don't think it is necessary to draw 2D plans in order to organize a building. If for some reason you want to fetishize drawings, then by all means, go for it. But I don't think drawing carries some kind of disciplinary truth. Can you imagine some hipster of the future insisting that the only way to be an architect is to model in 3D? I am certain that design technologies will keep evolving.

DR: Aren't there a lot of plans in this book?

HDA: Yes.

DR: Why did you do them?

HDA: Because I'm 49 years old, so I started out trained to think that way, and sometimes I fetishize plans. I just enjoy making them. That being said, the plans in this book are not the driving forces of any of our projects.

DR: To contradict Le Corbusier, plans are not the generator in your work.

HDA: Absolutely not. The plans are just a concession to a convention that is still required by architectural audiences. I always do them later, after the projects have been fully developed in 3D. But I do love making them!

DR: They were, perhaps, the last drawings you did for the projects included here. You describe them almost like a kind of dessert.

HDA: It's true. They are the last drawings that we do. And as I said, I still love doing them, in the same way that I love eating a hot dog, because it reminds me of when I was a kid.

DR: And like hot dogs, totally unnecessary.

HDA: Who would consider a hot dog to be the pinnacle of sophistication today? I think a lot of things like this exist as a fetish. They are totally unnecessary, and more of a cultural desire. Architects don't need plans to generate the work, but audiences still need them to understand the work. I make plans primarily to communicate, not to design.

DR: If we're trying to develop the organization of a building, we would do it in 3D and use some sort of BIM software eventually.

HDA: Yes, it's more about the information. Plans are like maps that you give away so that other people can understand the project, but it's utterly irrelevant to my design process now. So are sections, by the way.

DR: What are the essential design tools for you?

HDA: Whatever 3D software we're interested in at the time. We don't even sketch anymore, we start directly on the computer. There are no pencils or pens in my office. We never deal with the problem of translating space from drawings because we start with form and space.

DR: Do you communicate by sketching in 3D yourself? Or do you describe it in words and have other people do it for you?

HDA: These days, I'm so busy, it's more the latter. I'll often send images to my staff to explain what I want, but I'll say something like, 'You know that famous picture of the bullet destroying the banana? Let's do that mixed with a skin of a wildcat from the Himalayas.' It may sound bizarre to some, but my staff know exactly what I want. Every once in a while, I like to sit at the computer and design the forms myself. No one does it better than me, because no one knows what I want better than I do. But if you don't know what you want, no amount of technology is going to help you.

Shar-Pei Chairs

This chair design is what it says it is, a chair that is based on our total obsession with the posture and formal characteristics of a Shar-Pei dog. Yet the literal is still undermined by the additional sampling of floral forms, misinterpreting the skin as a ground. The three elements together resist formal reconciliation.

Date: 2018
Programme: Product design

Related projects
Rose Chair, 2010 (p. 50)
Mexican Funeral, 2010 (p. 54)
Seroussi Bench, 2010 (p. 226)

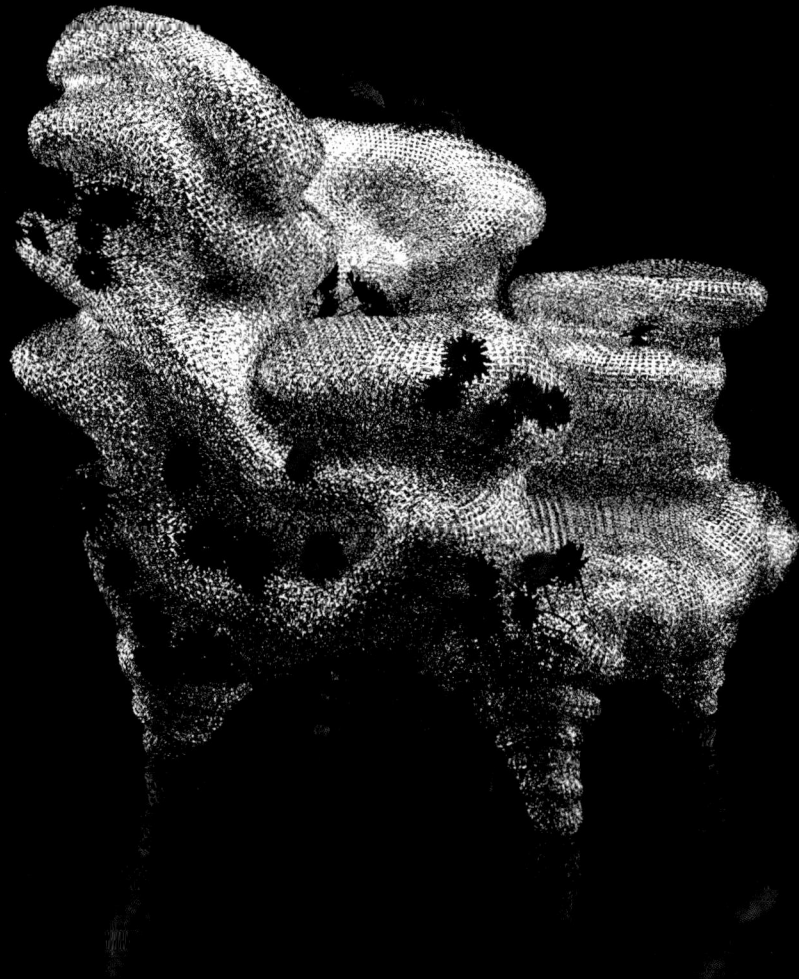

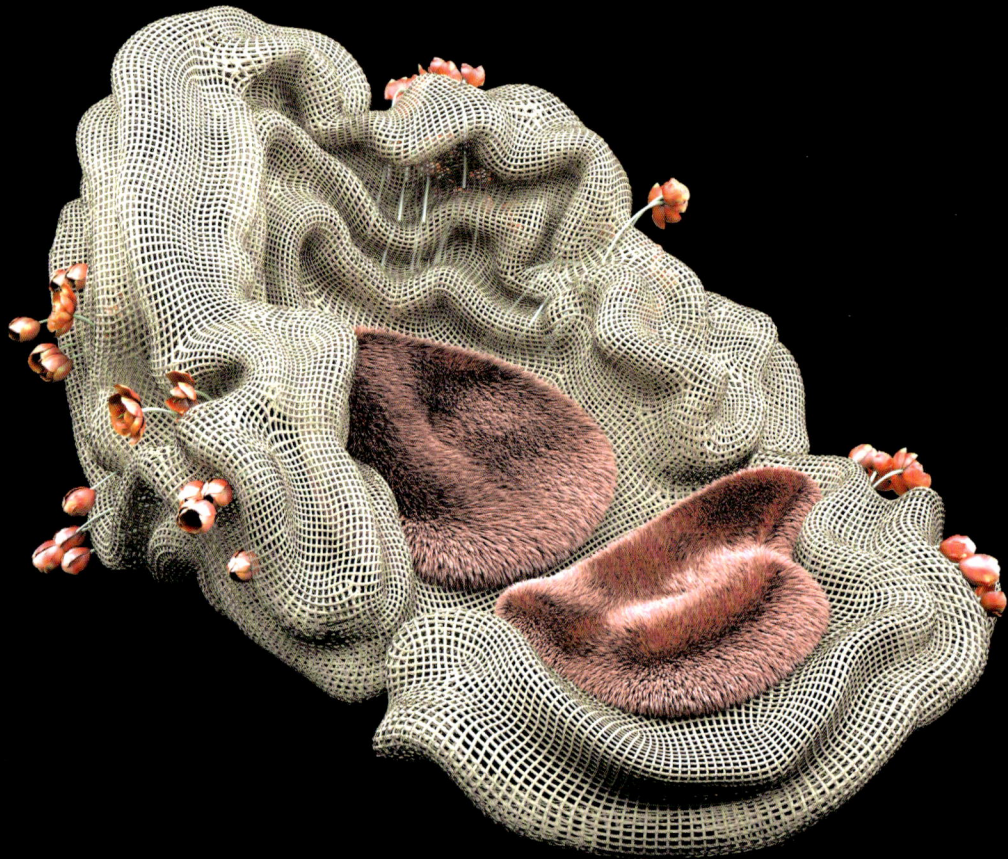

Augmented Fashion

To the degree that both body architecture
and architecture can be interpreted as
cumulative mutations from environmental
interactions across time, we may choose to
shift from a discussion of type to one about
species. Species are malleable, constantly
metamorphosing and adapting. From there,
we can imagine the augmentation of
human forms and sensing organs and
their interactions with the environment
as the new frontier for architecture. The
speed of the fashion industry, divided into
seasons and constantly being rendered
obsolete, acknowledges and embraces its
transient nature, while the slow pace of
built architecture calcifies form and resists
adaptation. Body augmentation could free
the human form from the rigidity of its built
surroundings.

Date: 2018
Programme: Product design

Related projects
Shar-Pei Chairs, 2018 (p. 354)
Necklace, 2018 (p. 380)

DR: Tell me about your current interest in fashion.

HDA: I find fashion fascinating, possibly the most influential and creative field in the world today. I am probably opening myself up to a lot of criticism by saying that, because architecture has always been predicated on the idea of immortality and durability, and fashion is precisely the opposite. But I think that architecture could learn from fashion – move faster and become more comfortable with obsolescence, for example, because no building lasts forever. Very few last more than twenty years; a building like the Pantheon is exceptionally rare. One out of perhaps a million buildings gets preserved, and that might be generous.

DR: Rather than thinking of architecture as contaminating fashion, it seems as if fashion is polluting your architecture.

HDA: In either case, one thing is polluting another. It is never 'interdisciplinary', which I think is a truly stupid concept. It sounds to me like an idea of how disciplines cancel each other out, and you end up with nothing. I am interested in contaminated disciplines, but disciplines nonetheless. In that sense, I am a bit of a classicist and believe in aspects of the discipline that have been around since the Renaissance.

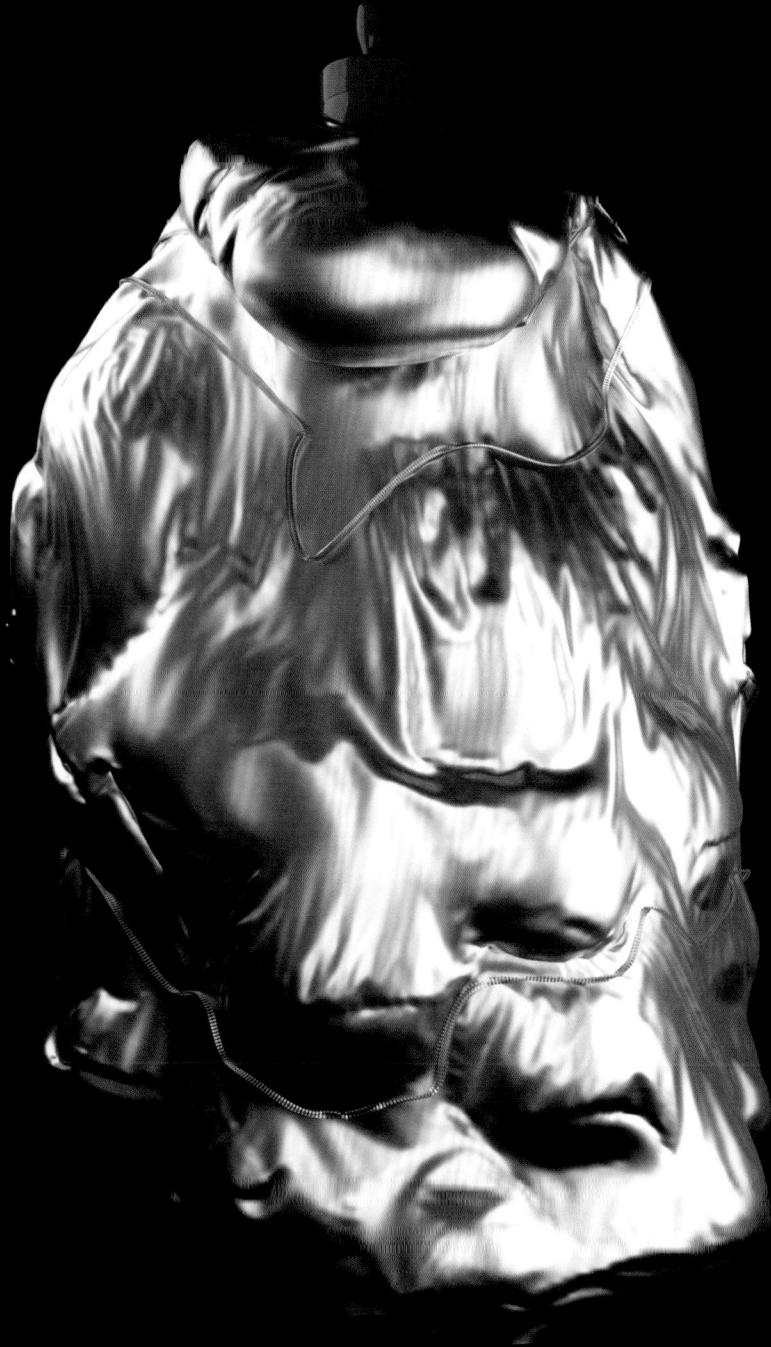

Rain jacket

DR: Tell me more about what you mean when you say: 'I like to keep my relationship to nature professional.'.

HDA: Well, I like nature when it's on a postcard. I like to look at it, but I don't like being in it. Nature freaks me out. You will never see me camping. That may be one of the reasons why I like architecture so much. I'm a city rat. I am exaggerating a bit, though – I have a profound appreciation of nature, but I care more about how nature looks. I don't really care that much about ecological ideas.

DR: Are you a picturesque architect?

HDA: I think my work has some picturesque qualities, but I wouldn't call myself a picturesque architect. I don't design to get a particular view. I care more about the overall form – even if those forms might be unusual. I always look for formal consistency and integrity. I like some of the concepts of naturalization – decay, for example – but I'm not really interested in the actual decay of natural materials. I'm more interested in how I might be able to formalize decay through a computer-model simulation.

In Spanish, there is a clear distinction between *belleza*, which means 'beauty', and *bonito*, which is more difficult to translate into English.

It is a lesser form of beauty, so it could perhaps be translated as 'cute' or 'pretty'. It's a more pedestrian form of beauty – more temporary, and of the moment. Something that is *bonito* today may not be *bonito* tomorrow.

DR: There's no truth in *bonito*.

HDA: Yes, I always liked this distinction in the Spanish language. *Bonito* is somewhere between beautiful and cute, but is neither. The idea of beauty that I'm interested in is one that keeps evolving. Maybe what I'm really after is sophistication, rather than beauty. This is what I love about Alexander McQueen's fashion designs. People didn't know how to respond to it initially, because it was such a new aesthetic language. 'Beautiful' was not the first thing that would come to most people's minds, but everyone understood that it was something very sophisticated. I would say the same thing about Francis Bacon's paintings. I'm pretty sure that when Bacon was painting, his contemporaries didn't think his art was beautiful. It's the same with jazz.

DR: So you like nature when it is *bonito*, but not when it is *belleza*.

HDA: Yes. I would also add that experiencing *belleza* can be a bit passive, whereas *bonito* can be seductive and active.

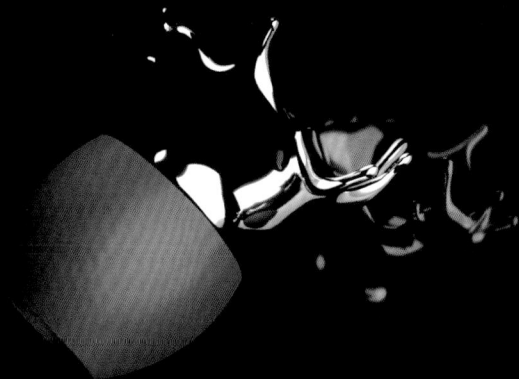

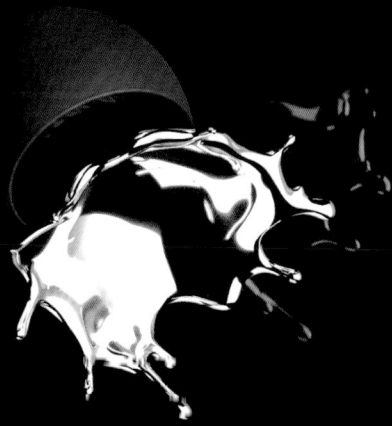

Ear buds – black and pink

DR: Critical theorists might say that all of this interest in aesthetics plays right into the hands of commodifying forces, that you're just producing capitalist spectacles.

HDA: Perhaps, but so what? What is the alternative? What is the alternative to exploring the possibilities of aesthetic pleasures when you're a designer? Not examining the possibility of form, or the possibility of beauty because we are afraid that it will be commodified, is silly and a waste of our energies.

DR: I think the critical theorists respond by saying the alternative is that the artist must critique and demystify power. But I agree with you that a never-ending project of demystification leaves us with a thoroughly disenchanted and joyless world. I appreciate the fact that there are dedicated academics that demystify power and disenchant fascistic images, but shouldn't it be the job of designers to re-enchant the world?

HDA: I'm entirely in agreement with you. Let's re-enchant the world. But also …

DR: … we take no pleasure in it. There's nothing left, right?

HDA: People will become commodified one way or another, by rejection or acceptance, so it is a profoundly religious argument that comes from an ancient idea about the rule of things, because it is always predicated under the idea that there is such a thing as a pure form of anything. I don't think that's possible in this world – and this comes from someone who is the closest thing to 'pure' that you will find in architecture, seeing as I'm probably one of the less successful practitioners you will find. Nothing that I've done has been codified by capitalism, or codified by academia, which is a form of capitalism, but not a form of capitalism. So I have always been somebody who rejects as much as possible the notion of the commodity.

I would be happy to be part of a commodity if they let me do it on my own terms. But even I was able to do my own work, I have to accept that it will be commodified. And if my job is done for me, my work has been commodified by rejection, by the market saying there is no place for it, and so it has been commodified anyway. Even when you're trying to be critical, if people notice that you have been critical, you're being commodified. This is a kind of an illusional form of puritanical religiosity, the idea that it is some kind of pure form or altruism, and I don't think it is possible anymore.

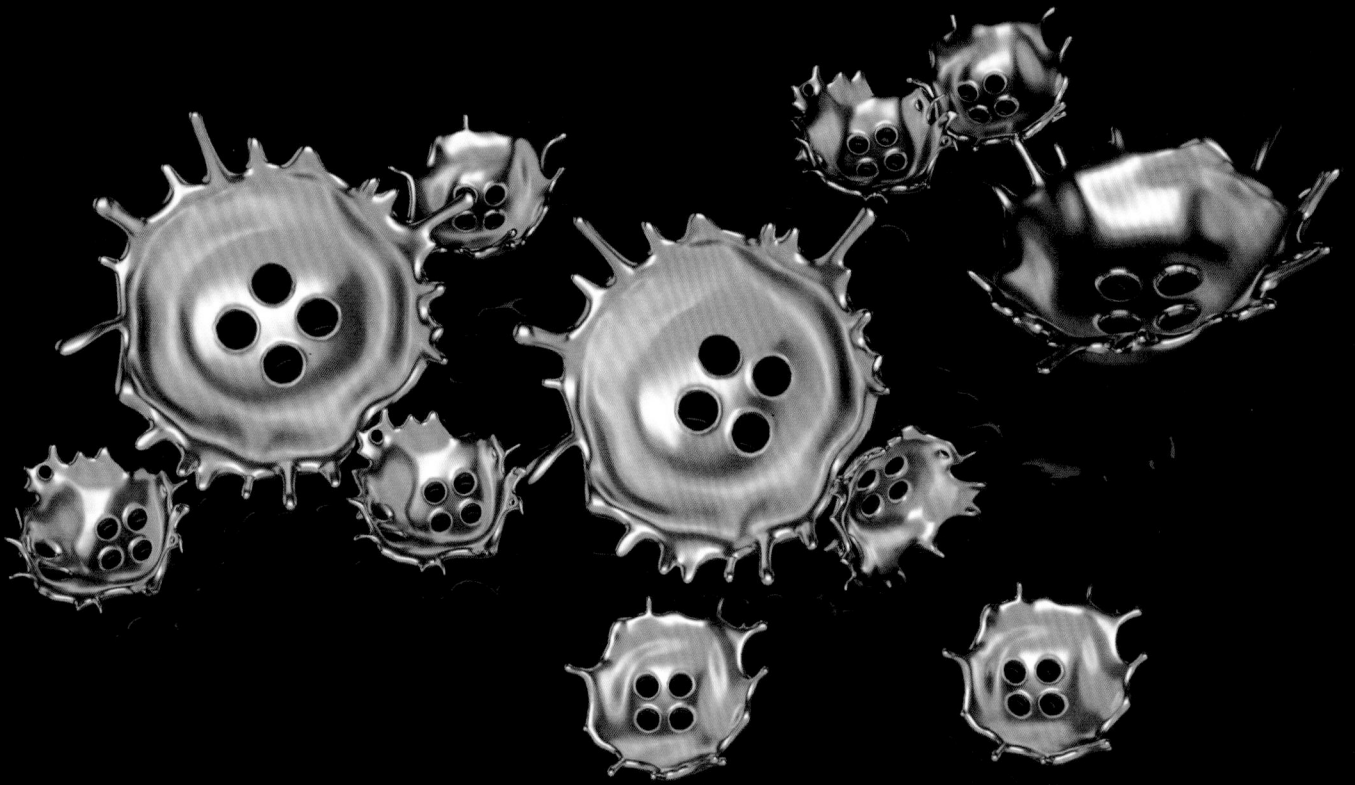

Splash button suit set

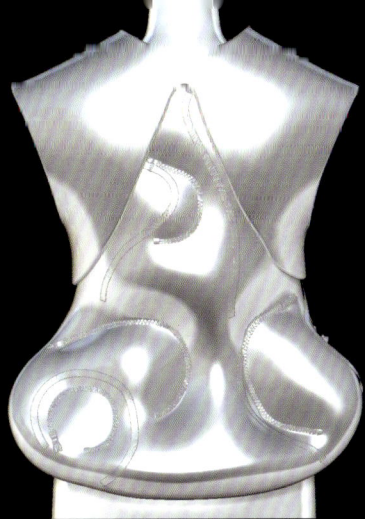

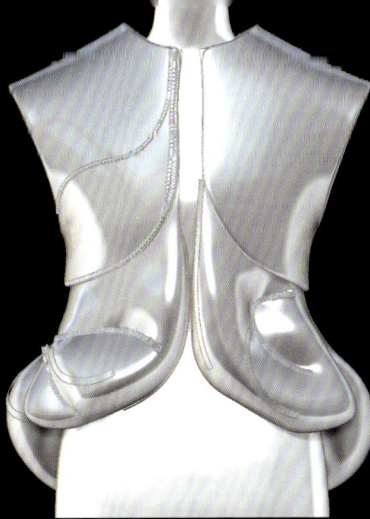

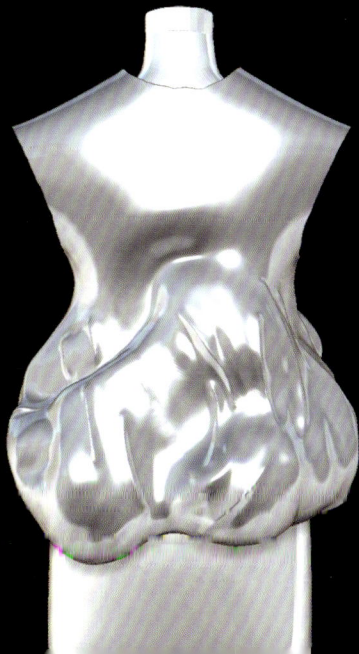

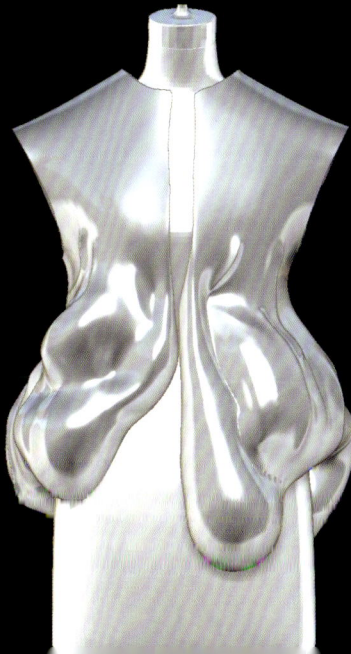

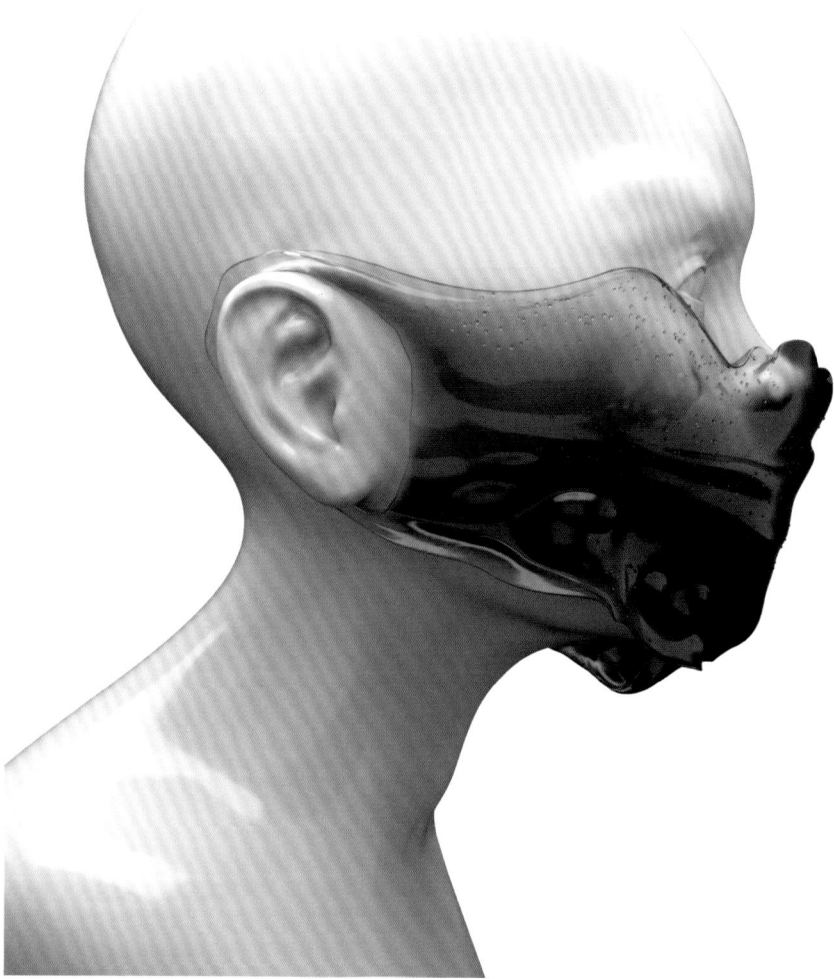

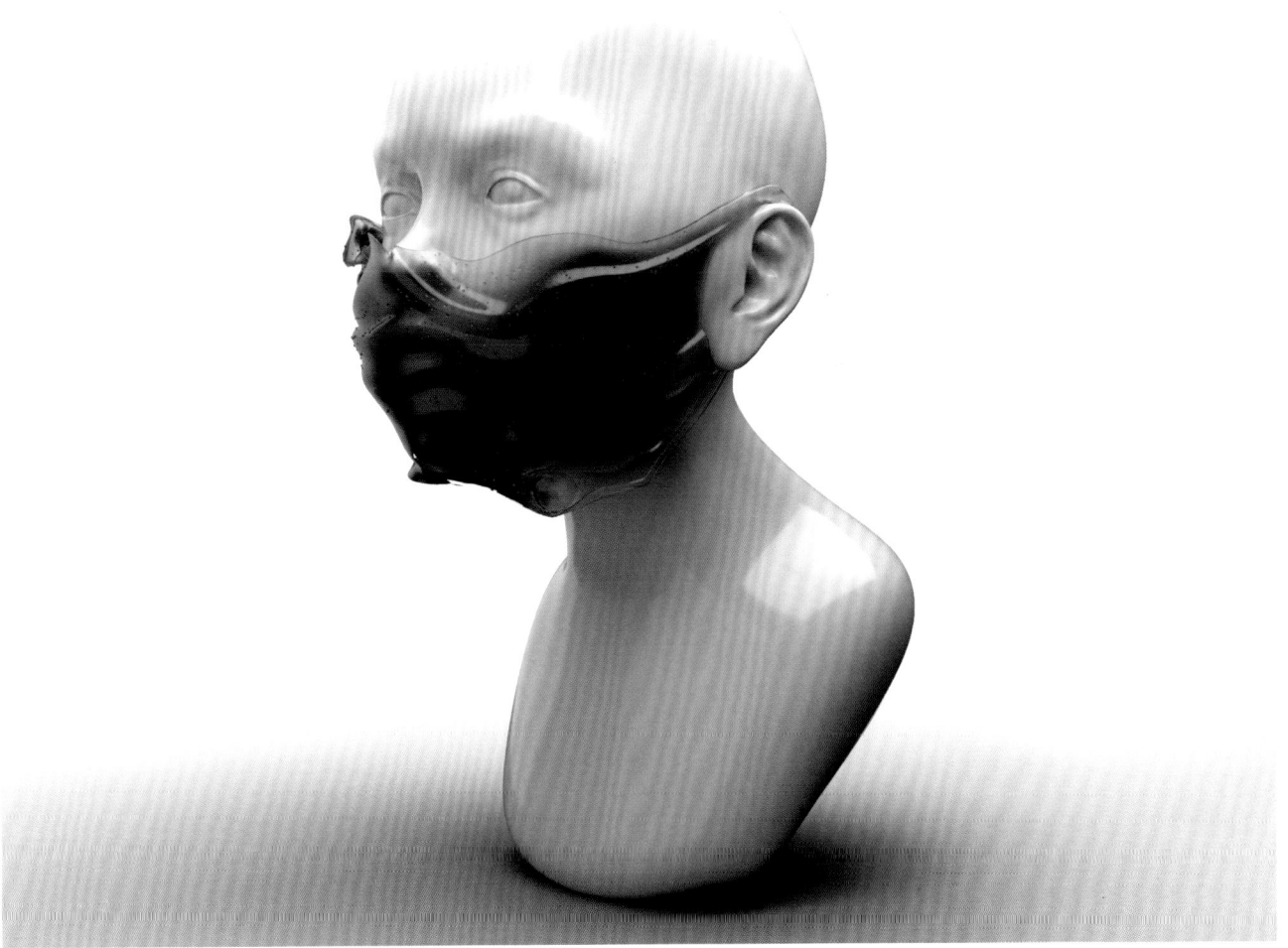

Face mask 1.0

Face mask 2.0

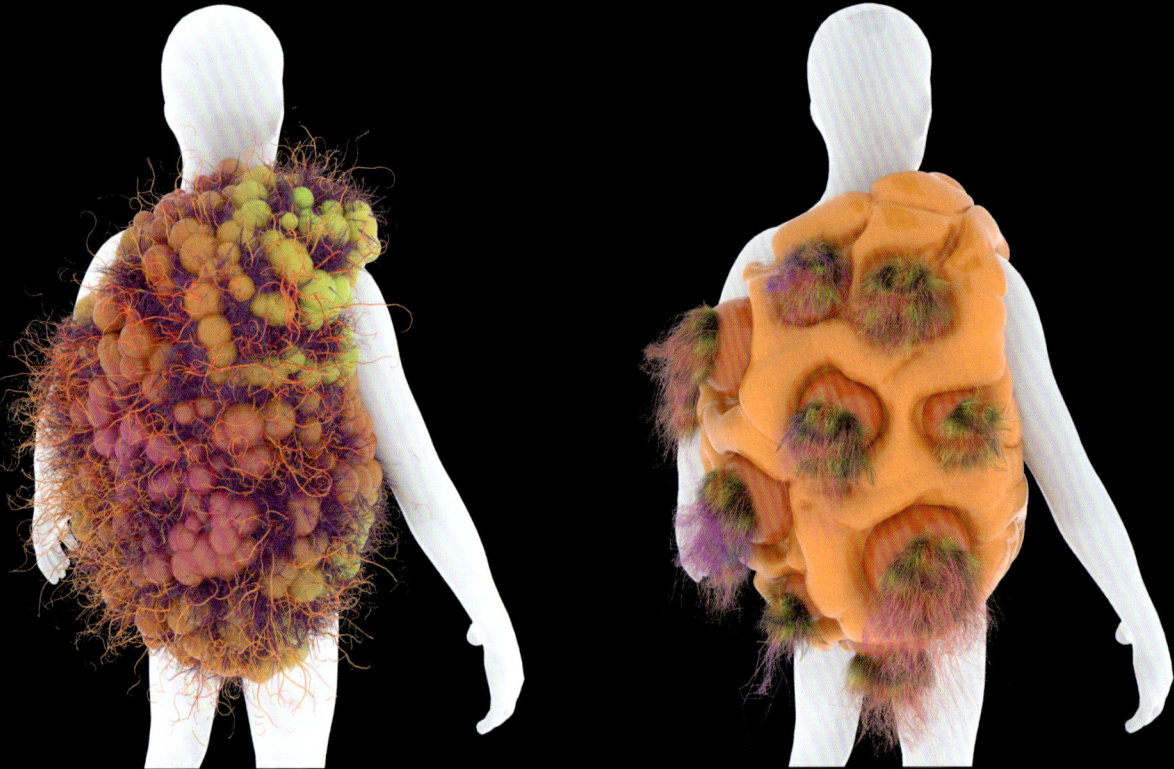

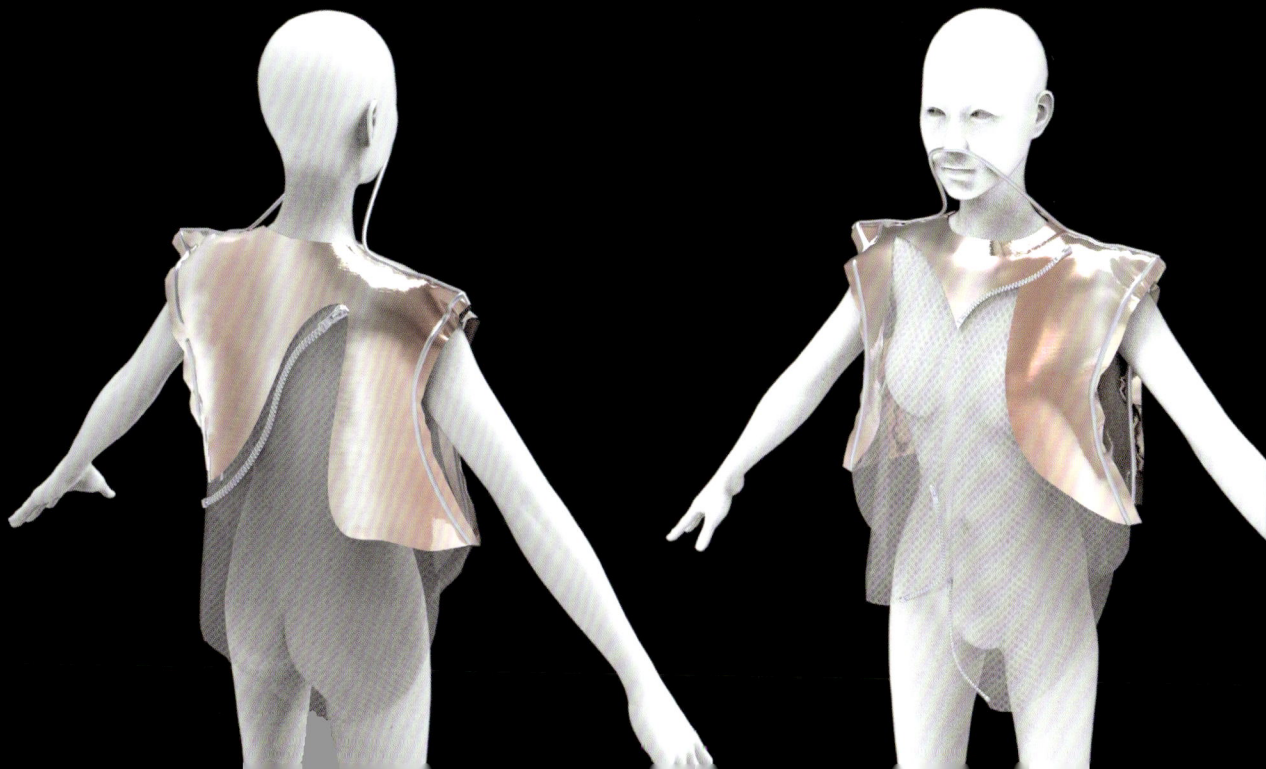

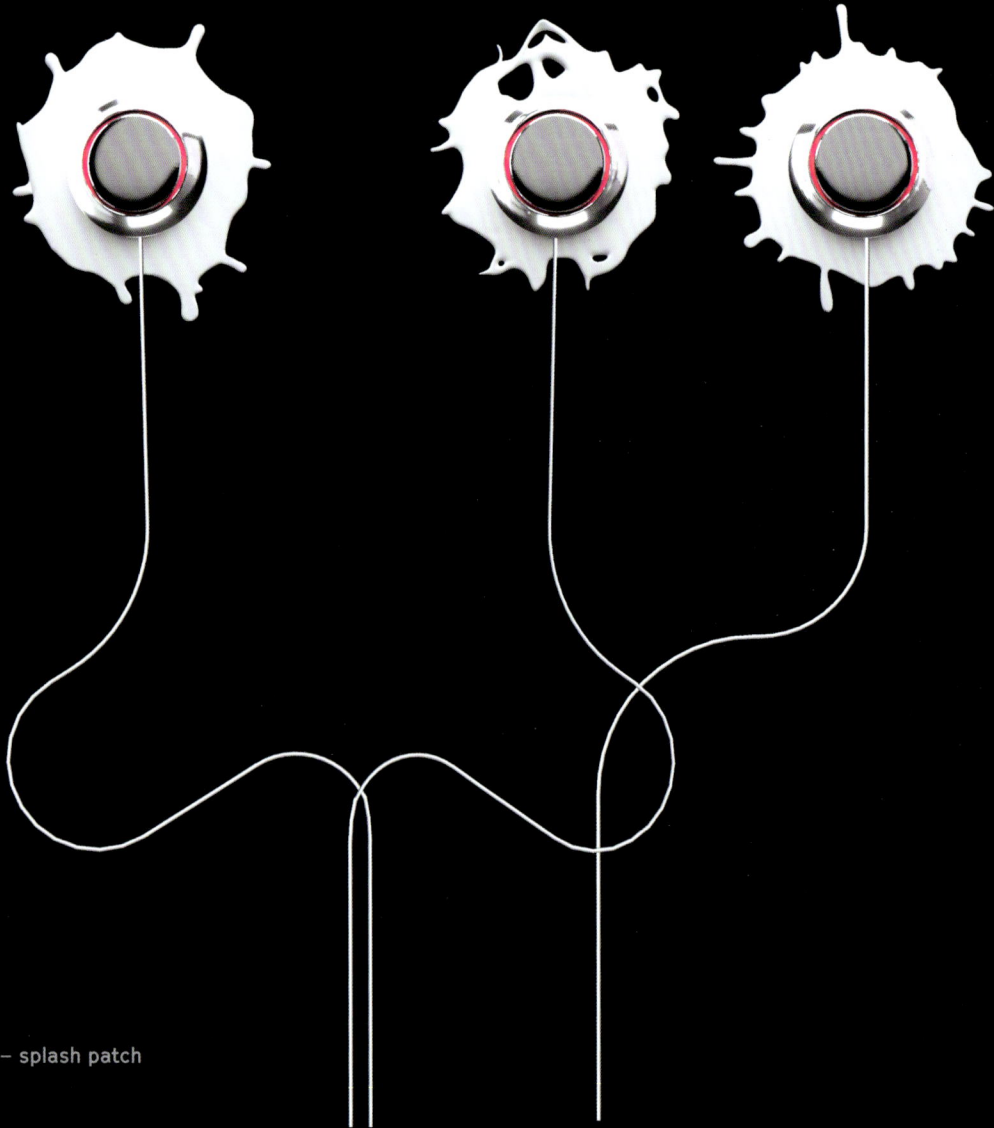

Health monitor – splash patch

DR: I find 'formalism' to be one of the most confusing words in architectural discourse today. I don't think anybody has a clear idea of what it means anymore, but perhaps we can understand it better by talking a little bit about the alternatives. Certainly, being a formalist is different from being a conceptualist. It is definitely different from being a phenomenologist, and it is also very different from being a functionalist.

Formalism

What does formalism mean to you? You have consistently, as long as I have known you, self-identified as a formalist. How do you know that you are a formalist?

HDA: This isn't an easy question, so let me try to unravel it a bit. First, on a simple level, the work that I love has been classified as formalist. So, guilty by association! But as somebody who was educated in the Modernist maxim of 'form follows function', I have to admit that it took me awhile to fully understand what that meant. I eventually realized that I have no interest whatsoever in form following function – which is probably why it took me so long to understand the concept. It is very contrary to the intuitive way that I work. For me, form doesn't follow anything, it isn't a

constraint to any problem outside of form itself. 'Form follows other forms' is perhaps a better way of saying it.

Perhaps surprisingly, I don't think that architectural form is autonomous. I don't really subscribe to the theory of architectural form. I think it should be promiscuous, and capable of appropriating any form, from anywhere. Functions change, and so do interpretations of what a form might mean, but the form endures. So I wonder why we would think that these more transient motivations are somehow more important than form?

When I was a student, I came across the catalogue of the *Deconstructivist Architecture* exhibition at MoMA, curated by Philip Johnson and Mark Wigley. It was a moment of revelation for me, because it was when I saw something that I understood to be the pure investigation of architectural form. I didn't see plans or sections or contexts. It was just architectural form, and nothing else. I was utterly fascinated by it. To a large degree, I still feel its influence. So I am formalist, because I care about form and, really, not much else.

DR: I that why you often say that you're
a believer in uselessness?

HDA: Yes, but, not uselessness in a banal,
negative sense – useless in the sense that
great music is useless. When music is functional,
I don't think we would place that much value on
it. Like mood music, elevator music or the music
playing in the background of a spa – when it is
functional, it is banal. We would never think of it
as a masterpiece of musical history. It is a little
harder for architecture to be useless than it is
for music, but when architecture is great, it is
not because the air conditioning and the lifts
are functioning well.

DR: Instead of saying 'form follows other
forms', wouldn't you rather say that form
follows nothing? Isn't the idea of form following
anything something that you are against,
because it would mean that there is something
more important than the form itself? Form
follows function, so function is more important
than form, or form follows finance, so money
is more important than form? Or form follows
meaning or narrative? So, form following nothing
– isn't that the position that any hardcore
formalist ought to have?

HDA: I'm OK with that.

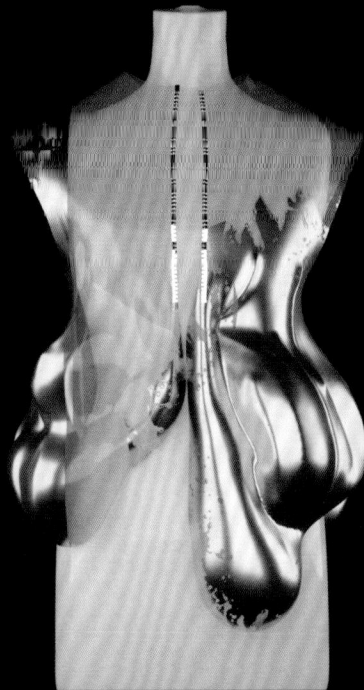
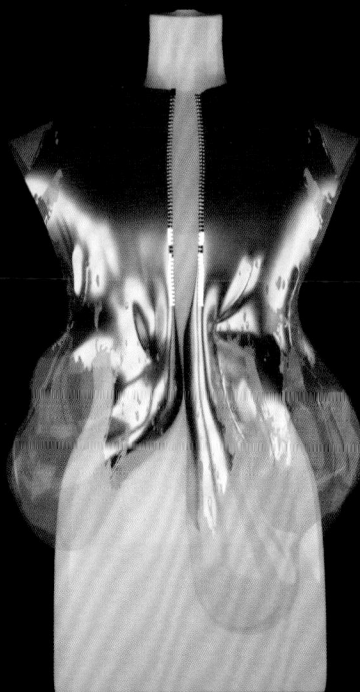
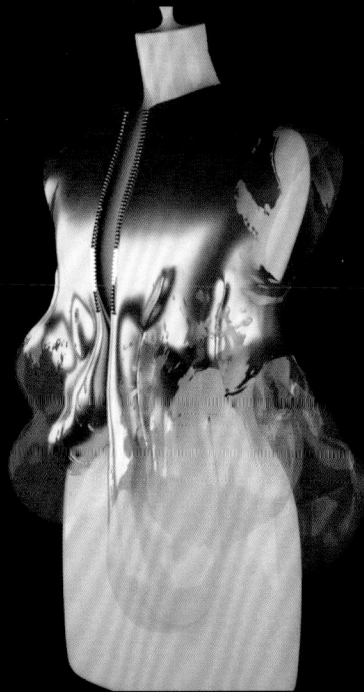

Necklace

This design is a mutation out of a series of product design and formal studies, which mixes the literal with flowers and broken edges.

Date: 2018
Programme: Product design

Related projects
Shar-Pei Chairs, 2018 (p. 354)
Augmented Fashion, 2018 (p. 360)

Project index

Queens Museum of Art, New York, 2001

U2 Tower, Dublin, 2002

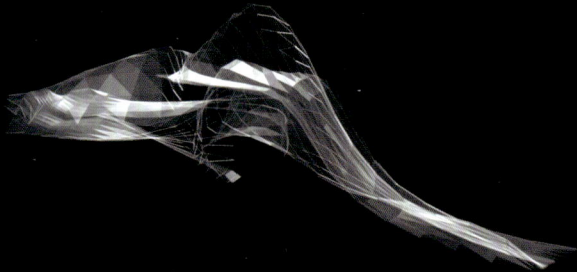

Bus Shelter, 2002

Tomhiro Museum, Japan, 2002

Grand Egyptian Museum, Cairo, 2002

Emotional Rescue, Los Angeles, 2002

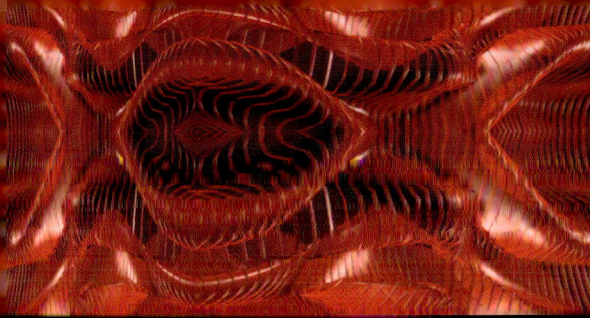
Mutant Manners, 2002

WTC, New York, 2002

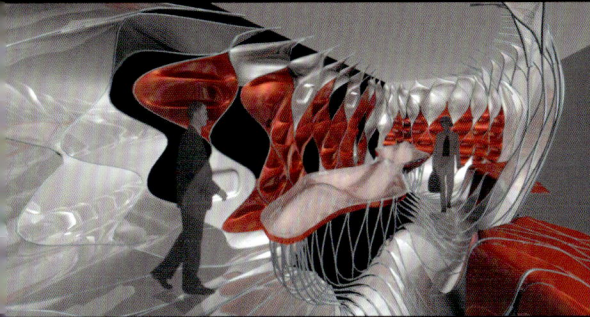
Newsstand, Los Angeles, 2003

Lexington Park, Kentucky, 2004

Jumping Jack Flash Watch Design, 2004

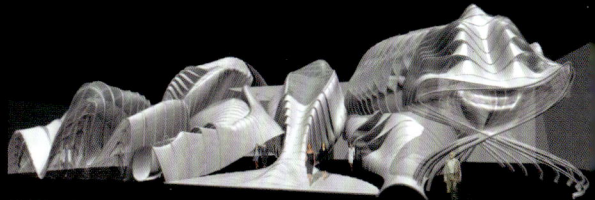
San Jose University Art Museum, California, 2004

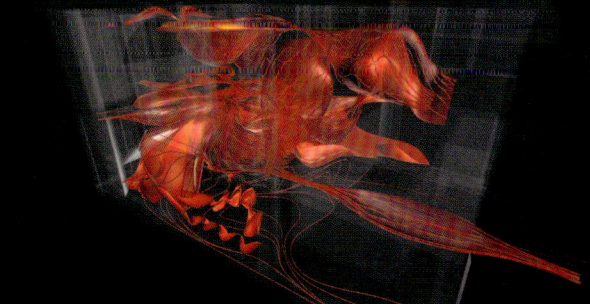
SCI-Arc Café, Los Angeles, 2004

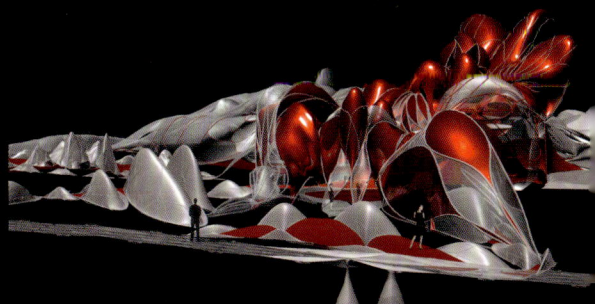
Busan Metropolitan City, South Korea, 2004

Be Boop, Costa Rica, 2004

PS1 MoMA, New York, 2005 (p. 28)

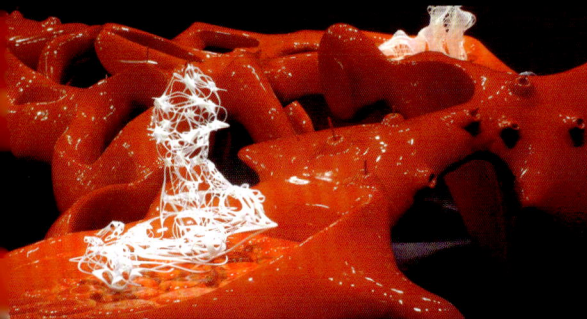

Sangre, San Francisco, 2006 (p. 34)

Asplund Public Library, Stockholm, 2006

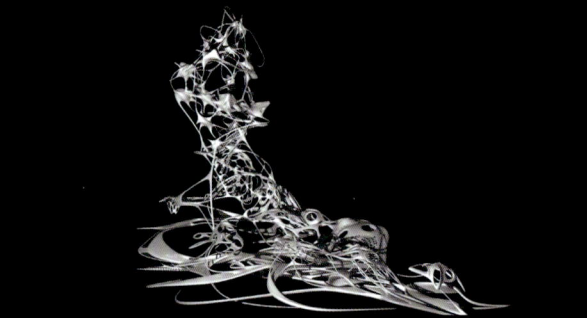

Art Hotel, Playa Grande, 2006

Cell Phone Prototype Concepts, 2006

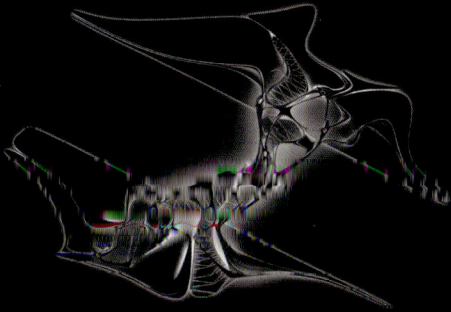
Fideos Brillantes, San Juan, 2007

City of the Future, Los Angeles, 2007

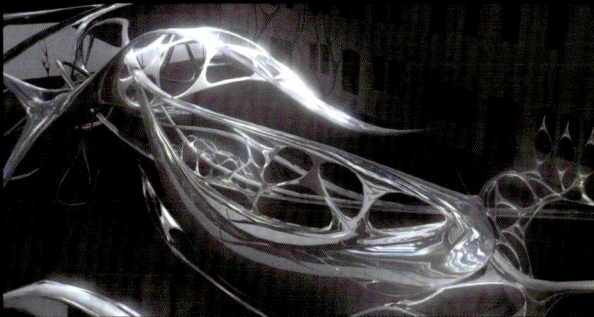
BCA Competition, Boston, 2007

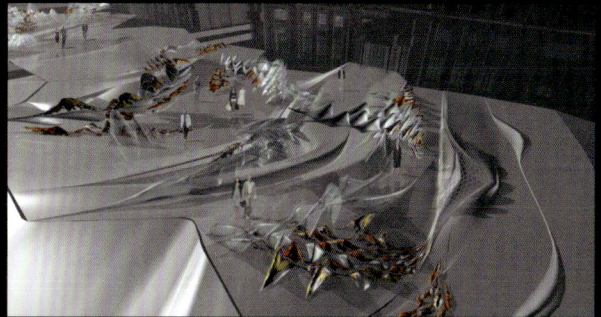
Lexington Memorial, 2007

X-Plosion, 2008 (p. 60)

Tabakalera, San Sebastián, 2008 (p. 140)

Pitch Black, Vienna/Shanghai, 2008/2016 (p. 164)

Lautner Redux, Los Angeles, 2008 (p. 188)

Sundsvall Art Centre, Sweden, 2008

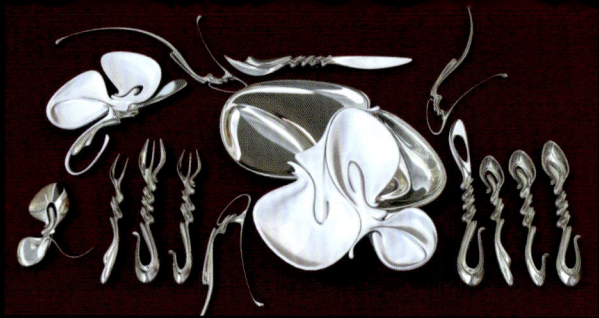
Instruments of Manner, 2009 (p. 106)

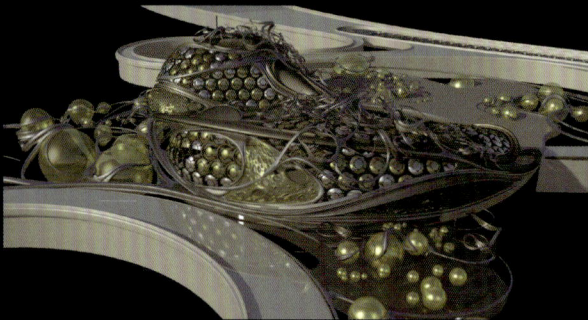
Korea Pavilion, 2009

Taipei Pop Music Centre, Taiwan, 2009

Warsaw National Museum of History, Poland, 2009

Mexican Funeral, 2010 (p. 54)

Rose Chair, 2010 (p. 50)

Seroussi Bench, 2010 (p. 226)

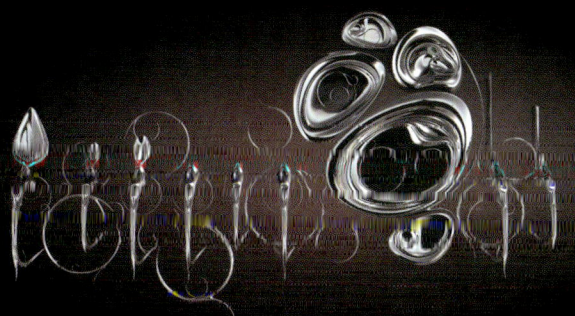
Instruments of Manner, 2010 (p. 108)

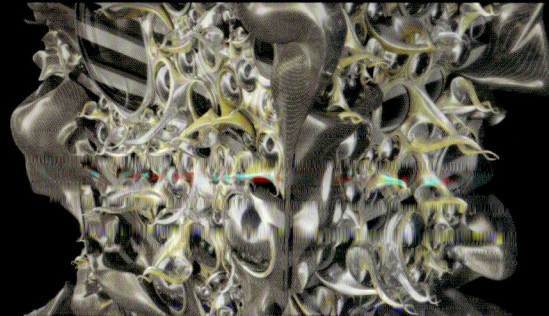
Piraeus Tower, 2010

Dubai Tower, 2010

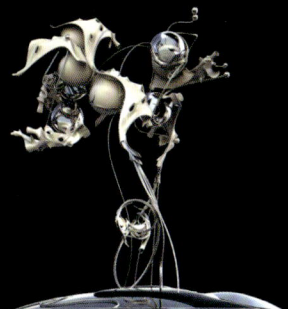
Miami Ritz Sculpture 1.0, 2011 (p. 66)

Taiwan Tower, 2010

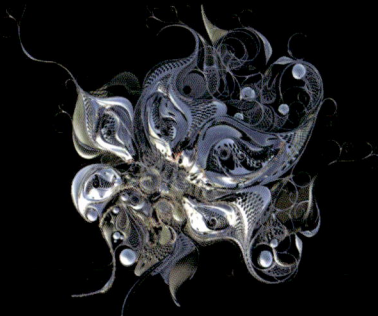
TBA 21_1.0, 2011 (p. 234)

TBA 21_2.0, 2011 (p. 240)

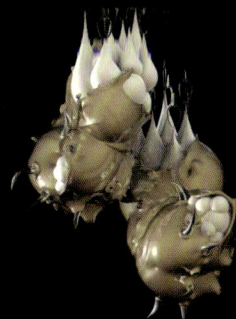
Monster, Monstrosity, Monstrous, 2011 (p. 298)

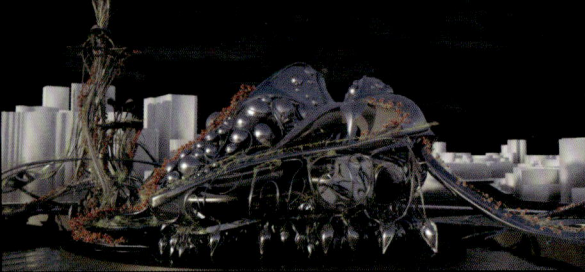

Kaohsiung Cultural Centre, Taiwan, 2011

Espresso Cup, 2011 (p. 300)

Helsinki Library, Finland, 2012 (p. 70)

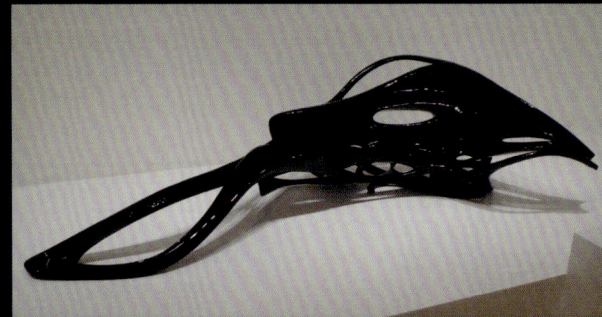

La Chaise Grotesque, 2012 (p. 42)

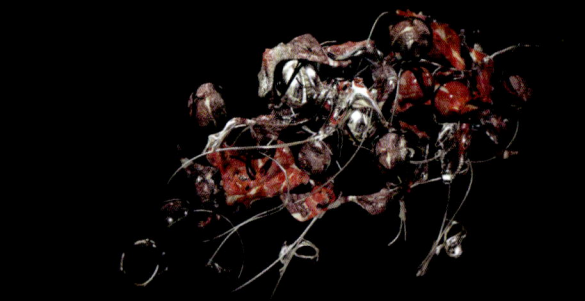

Still Flesh, 2012 (p. 304)

Instruments of Manner, 2012 (p. 124)

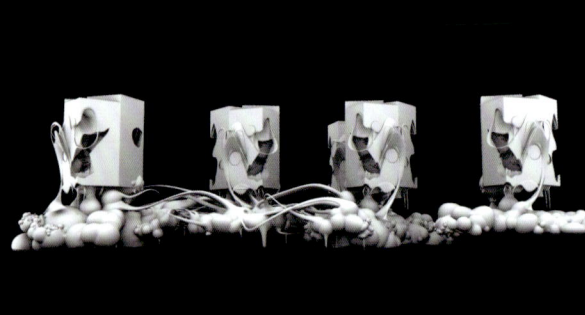

Keelung Harbour, Taiwan, 2012

Maribor, 2012

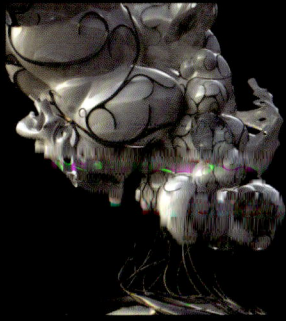
Miami Ritz Sculpture 2.0, 2012

JP Morgan Chase Remote, Los Angeles, 2013 (p. 126)

Taichung Cultural Centre, Taiwan, 2013 (p. 90)

Edison Lamp, 2013 (p. 308)

Teatro Colon, Bogotá, 2013 (p. 282)

Guggenheim Helsinki, Finland, 2014 (p. 98)

Lips Chair, 2013 (p. 310)

Budapest Museum, Hungary, 2014 (p. 270)

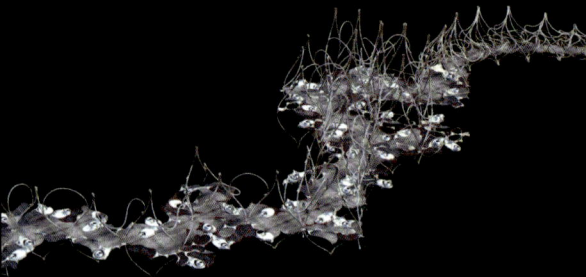
Sant Adrià de Besòs, Spain, 2014 (p. 154)

Barcelona Park, Spain, 2014 (p. 194)

Rusuupuisto, Finland, 2015 (p. 246)

Conexion Barcelona, Spain, 2015 (p. 204)

Chair Proto, 2015 (p. 314)

X-hibit, 2015 (p. 312)

Kuwait House, Kuwait, 2015

Shenzhen Library & Museum, China, 2015 (p. 322)

Emergency House, Mexico, 2016 (p. 348)

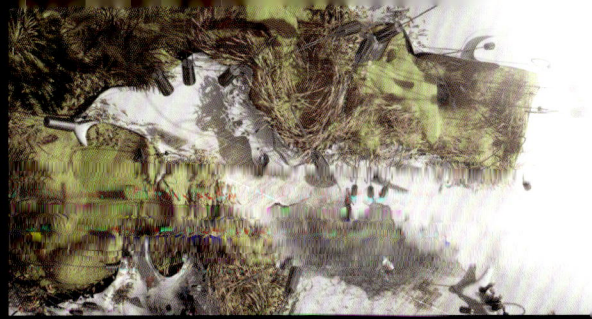

Office Park Waterfront, Shanghai, 2016 (p. 342)

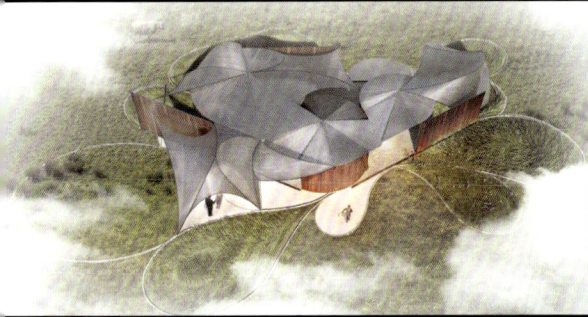

nfonavit House, Mexico, 2016

Flower Towers, Hanking, 2016

Lima Art Museum, Peru, 2016

National Museum of World Writing, 2017 (p. 332)

Augmented Fashion, 2018 (p. 360)

Necklace, 2018 (p. 380)

Mexicali Parks, Mexico, 2018

Art Centre China, 2018

Lead designers:
Ivan Bernal, Brian De Luna, Bryan Flaig, Edward Kim, Nick Kinney, Steven Ma, Rachael McCall, Joshua Taron, Michael Young

Collaborators:
Varouzhan Adamian, Polina Alexeeva, Chris Arntzen, Alex Belciano, Kara Block, Robert Bracket, Rebekah Bukhbinder, Erick Carcamo, Robert Cha, Nefeli Chatzimina, Ben Cheng, Eric Cheong, Andrew Cheu, Varun Chillara, Andrew Chittenden, Debbie Chiu, Scott Chung, Adrian Cortez, Théo Dattola, Alayna Davidson, Ana Derby, Henry Dominguez, Jennifer Dunlop, David Eskenazi, Thanasis Farangas, Jee Hee Farris, Laura Fehlberg, Marcus Friesl, Evan Geisler, Terry Gibbs, Junjie Guo, Jeff Halstead, Brian Kirk Henry, Keyla Hernandez, Asako Hiraoka, Brendan Ho, Chikara Inamura, Irem Iscan, James Jiang, Patricia Joseph, Jordan Kanter, Daniel Karas, Hunter Knight, Louis Koehl, Ryan Kukuraitis, Randal Larsen, Sophie Launault, Cunhao Lee, Bingyi Li, Koho Lin, Jackson Lukas, Langaojie Ma, Zane Mechem, Yash Mehta, Robert Mezquiti, Makoto Mizutani, Mads Moeller, Mirai Morita, Mark Nagis, Borna Nassab, Wing Lam Fiona Ng, Nicolay Nicolayson, Lily Nourmansouri, Hyoseon Park, Stefano Passeri, Nicholas Pisca, Nicholas Poulos, Thorne Ransom, Timothy Rives Rash, Michael Casey Rehm, Caleb Roberts, Austin Samson, Garrett Santo, Mohammad Soleimanifeijani, Kevin Sperry, Amanda Stjernstrom, Jeremy Stoddart, Atsushi Sugiuchi, Simon Story, Sanjay Sukie, Josh Taron, Tony Thrim, Ben Toam, Evan Tribus, Chen Ho Tsa, Nicolas Turchi, Chikara Unamura, William Virgil, Feiran Wang, Yuchen Wang, Sandy Watts, Jeremy Whitener, Doug Wiganowske, Dan Wolfe, Diego Wu-Law, Zheng Xu, Mengyu Yu, Gabriela Zappi, Homayoun Zaryouni, Yunyu Zhang, Huijin Zheng, Yibo Zhong

Hernan Díaz Alonso became director of SCI-Arc in 2015, where he had been a faculty member since 2001, serving in several leadership roles, including coordinator of the graduate thesis program from 2007–10, and graduate programmes chair from 2010–15. He is widely credited with spearheading SCI-Arc's transition to digital technologies, and played a key role in shaping the school's graduate curriculum over the last decade.

In parallel to his role at SCI-Arc, Díaz Alonso is principal of the Los Angeles-based multidisciplinary practice HDA-X (formerly Xefirotarch), which has been praised for its work at the intersection of design, animation, interactive environments and radical architectural explorations. Over the course of his career as an architect and educator, Díaz Alonso has earned accolades for his leadership and innovation, as well as his ability to build partnerships among varied constituencies. In 2005 he was the winner of MoMA PS1's Young Architects Program, and in 2012 received the AIA Educator of the Year award. In 2013 he won the AR+D Award for Emerging Architecture and a Progressive Architecture Award for his design of the Thyssen-Bornemisza Pavilion/Museum in Patagonia, Argentina.

Díaz Alonso's architectural designs have been featured in exhibitions at the Venice Biennale, the London Architecture Biennale and ArchiLab in Orleans, France, as well as solo exhibitions at SFMOMA, the Art Institute of Chicago and MAK Centre, Vienna. His work has been widely published in books and journals, including *Xefirotarch: Excessive* (2008), and is in the permanent collections of the FRAC Centre, SFMOMA, MoMA, the Thyssen-Bornemisza, MAK Vienna and the Art Institute of Chicago.

Diaz Alonso graduated from the Faculty of Architecture Planning and Design, National University of Rosario, and received a Master's degree with honours in Advanced Architectural Design from Columbia's Graduate School of Architecture, Planning and Preservation.

A gifted educator, Diaz Alonso has been recognized with appointments as Yale University's Louis I. Kahn Visiting Assistant Professor of Architectural Design (2010) and Eero Saarinen Professor of Architectural Design (2015); Visiting Design Studio Faculty at the Graduate School of Architecture, Planning and Preservation, Columbia University (2004–10); Architectural Design Professor in the Urban Strategies Postgraduate Programme at the University of Applied Arts Vienna (ongoing); and Distinguished Faculty Member at SCI-Arc. In 2018 DesignIntelligence named Díaz Alonso one of the 25 Most Admired Educators in the US, and in 2019 Diaz Alonso was the recipient of the American Academy of Arts and Letters Architecture Award.

Benjamin H. Bratton

Benjamin H. Bratton is Associate Professor of Visual Arts and Director of the Center for Design and Geopolitics at the University of California, San Diego, and Professor of Digital Design at the European Graduate School in Saas-Fee, Switzerland. He has been a visiting lecturer and critic at Columbia, Princeton, UCLA, University of Applied Arts Vienna, BauhausUniversity and Moscow State University, among others, and is the author of *The Stack: On Software and Sovereignty* (2016).

Joe Day

Designer and architectural theorist Joe Day heads Deegan-Day Design and serves on the design and history/theory faculty at SCI-Arc. In 2012 he was Louis I. Kahn Visiting Chair at Yale School of Architecture. Day is the author of *Corrections and Collections: Architectures for Art and Crime* (2013), and contributed to the 2009 edition of Reyner Banham's *Los Angeles: Architecture of the Four Ecologies*. He is on the Board of Trustees at SCI-Arc, and is a director at the W.M. Keck Foundation.

Marcelyn Gow

Marcelyn Gow is principal of Servo Los Angeles, and teaches design studios and critical theory at SCI-Arc. She received degrees from the Architectural Association, Columbia and ETH Zurich, and is co-editor of *Material Beyond Materials* (2012) and *Onramp No. 4* (2013). She received a Graham Foundation Award and a City of Los Angeles Individual Artist Fellowship, and has exhibited work around the world.

John Hoke, III

John Hoke, III is Chief Design Officer at Nike, and is a permanent design fellow at Pennsylvania State University, a member of the board of directors at Herman Miller, advisor to Maggio Fast Forward and a trustee at Pacific Northwest College of Art. He has also served as a trustee of the Cooper Hewitt and was a designer at Michael Graves Architecture & Design in Princeton, New Jersey.

Rachael McCall

Rachael McCall has been Lead Designer at HDA-X since 2016, as well as on the design and visual studies faculty at SCI-Arc. She holds degrees from the University of Queensland, and her graduate thesis *Frayed and Polished* won SCI-Arc's Gehry Prize in 2015. Her work has been exhibited in the US, Australia, Greece, Sweden, the Netherlands and Japan, and published in the US, UK, Italy and Australia.

Florencia Pita

Florencia Pita is founder of design and research collaborative Florencia Pita & Co in Los Angeles. She studied at Columbia and the National University of Rosario, and was a recipient of the 2000 Fulbright/Fondo Nacional de las Artes scholarship. She has worked in the offices of Greg Lynn FORM, Eisenman Architects and Asymptote Architecture, and her work is in the collections of MoMA, MAK Vienna and the Art Institute of Chicago. She teaches design studios and visual studies and is Graduate Thesis Coordinator at SCI-Arc.

David Ruy

Architect and theorist David Ruy received his BA from St John's College, where he studied philosophy and mathematics, and his M.Arch degree from Columbia University. He is director of the New York-based architectural studio Ruy Klein, whose work has been widely published and exhibited, and is represented in the permanent collections of MoMA and the FRAC Centre.

Acknowledgments

Since 2000, the work of our office has being driven and elevated by a phenomenally talented group of people. The projects in this book would not exist without them, and for this – and for so many other things – I am grateful. In particular, I would like to thank Drura Parrish, Josh Taron, Steven Ma, Ed Kim, Nick Kinney, Ivan Bernal and Rachael McCall.

Thank you also to the students, faculty and staff of SCI-Arc, for their inspiration, challenges, energy and, most of all, infinite amounts of fun. Being part of this school has been my proudest professional achievement.

Thank you to the Graduate School of Architecture, Planning and Preservation, Columbia University; Institute of Architecture, University of Applied Arts Vienna; and Yale School of Architecture.

My thanks to all my road-warrior colleagues, family and friends, for hours of conversations, reviews, trips and debates: Guillermo Banchini, Benjamin H. Bratton, Jose Lopez Cervantes, Joe Day, Neil Denari, Winka Dubbeldam, John Enright, David Erdman, Axel Fridman, Ming Fung, Mark Gage, Marcelyn Gow, Georgina Huljich, Ferda Kolatan, Elena Manferdini, Jerry Neuman, Francisco Pardo, Florencia Pita, Ali Rahim, Alexis Rochas, Joseph Rosa, David Ruy, Marcelo Spina, Peter Trummer, Tom Wiscombe and Reiner Zettl.

Among so many individuals that I love, admire and respect, I would like to thank Sir Peter Cook, Peter Eisenman, Frank Gehry, Zaha Hadid, Jeff Kipnis, Sylvia Lavin, Greg Lynn, Thom Mayne, Enric Miralles, Wolf D. Prix, Michael Speaks, Brett Steele, Mark Wigley and Eric Owen Moss for their mentoring, teaching, friendship and inspiration.

Photo credits

All images, unless otherwise noted, are by Hernán Díaz Alonso
Dental X-rays courtesy of Juan Figgoni: 12–13, 130–31, 266–67
Argentinian BBQ photography by Juan Figgoni: 6–7, 14–15, 254–55, 294
Photos by Rachael McCall: 26–27, 48–49, 68–69, 138–39, 224–25, 268–69, 320–21
Photos courtesy of Robert Mezquiti / PS1 MoMA: 29–33
Photos courtesy of Michael Erdman / SFMoMA: 35–41
Photos courtesy of Reiner Zettl / MAK Vienna: 166–71
Photos courtesy of Steven Ma: 165, 172–73
Photo by Jay L. Clendenin, © 2019 *Los Angeles Times*: 394

This book is dedicated to Maite, Charo and Flor,
whose love is everything.

On the cover: *Front* TBA 21_1.0 (2011); *back* Still Flesh (2012)
© Hernán Díaz Alonso

First published in the United Kingdom in 2019
by Thames & Hudson Ltd, 181A High Holborn,
London WC1V 7QX

Graphic design concept: David Espluga & Associates

The Surreal Visions of Hernán Díaz Alonso/HDA-X
© 2019 Hernán Díaz Alonso

British Library Cataloguing-in-Publication Data
A catalogue record for this book is available from
the British Library

ISBN 978-0-500-34350-0

Printed and bound in China by C&C Offset Printing Co. Ltd

To find out about all our publications, please visit
www.thamesandhudson.com. There you can subscribe
to our e-newsletter, browse or download our current catalogue,
and buy any titles that are in print.